JERRY ROBINSON

BANKRUPTCY

★★★ OF OUR NATION ★★★

REVISED and EXPANDED

YOUR FINANCIAL SURVIVAL GUIDE

21 income streams, inflation-proof strategies, and more!

First printing: March 2009
Second printing: April 2009
Revised and expanded edition: July 2012

New Leaf Press, P.O. Box 726, Green Forest, AR 72638
New Leaf Press is a division of the New Leaf Publishing Group, Inc.

ISBN: 978-0-89221-713-7
Library of Congress Number: 2009923747

Cover by Thinkpen Design

Unless otherwise noted, Scripture quotations are from the New King James Version of the Bible.

Please consider requesting that a copy of this volume be purchased by your local library system.

Printed in the United States of America

Please visit our website for other great titles:
www.masterbooks.net

For information regarding author interviews,
please contact the publicity department at (870) 438-5288

New Leaf Press
A Division of New Leaf Publishing Group
www.newleafpress.net

Others are saying . . .

Jerry Robinson's conclusions about the state of the American Empire are spot on in *Bankruptcy of Our Nation*. Not only is Jerry a modern-day Copernicus when it comes to economic issues, but he has the moral fortitude to tell the truth in these challenging times — which you will never get from the mainstream media.

Barry James Dyke
President of Castle Asset Management, LLC of Hampton, NH
Best-selling author, *The Pirates of Manhattan I & II*

Mr. Robinson has written a good history of the development of modern money systems with valuable specific practical recommendations based on the trajectory of that history. This is understandable history and practical investment advice in one volume. It will provide a valuable guide and positive investment returns to those who follow his well thought out advice.

Bud Conrad, chief economist, Casey Research
Author of *Profiting from the World's Political Crisis*

In his book, *Bankruptcy of Our Nation*, Jerry Robinson does an excellent job of explaining the "Petrodollar" system, which is the 1971 agreement between OPEC and the United States that, in return for military protection by the U.S., Middle Eastern oil-producing countries would accept only U.S. dollars for their oil and invest their profits in U.S. bonds. The present unraveling of this agreement will have a profound impact on the destruction of the U.S. dollar as the world's reserve currency and that, in turn, will put the U.S. into bankruptcy. This book explains exactly how this will come about, but equally important is the comprehensive section on what you can do to protect yourself.

G. Edward Griffin, author, researcher, and filmmaker

Bankruptcy of Our Nation is a must read for anyone with any money in the stock market. Whether it's in a brokerage account, 401K, IRA, Roth, wherever it is . . . this is the one book that needs to be on your reading list! As a financial advisor for the past 17 years, I have come to trust Jerry Robinson's timely advice and mission to educate the public about the hidden dangers in the U.S. and global economies.

Jerry, whom I have the honor and privilege of calling a friend, has put together a survival guide that will help steer you through what I believe will be a very tough road over the next several years. But in these hard times will come tremendous opportunity for those who are aware and ready to seize the moment. This is where Jerry delivers big time in *Bankruptcy of Our Nation*! He helps readers create an action plan to thrive in the days ahead. He covers ground that the mainstream media won't touch and when they do it will be far too late. Now is the time to start planning ahead for a tumultuous fallout from the reckless actions of the Fed. Don't waste another second, do yourself and your family a favor and read this book today.

Jay Peroni, CFP® Chief Investment Officer,
Faith-Based Investor, http://www.faithbasedinvestor.com
Author of *The Faith-Based Millionaire* and *The Faith-Based Investor*

A provocative and mind-opening analysis of what went wrong with our economy and a bold strategy for coping with the future.

John Perkins, *New York Times* best-selling author
*Hoodwinked, Confessions of an Economic Hit Man, The Secret
History of the American Empire, Shapeshifting, The World Is As
You Dream It, Psychonavigation, The Stress-Free Habit
Spirit of the Shuar*

I just finished reading Jerry Robinson's excellent book *Bankruptcy of Our Nation*. Not only does he get the entire picture, he makes it all easy to understand!

Charles Goyette, *New York Times* best-selling author of
Red and Blue and Broke All Over and *The Dollar Meltdown*

Jerry Robinson puts forth a thorough yet digestible study on the economically unsustainable financial system Americans have been bound to and some sound methods and practices the individual can take to break the chains and truly be individual.

Gerald Celente
http://trendsresearch.com

Contents

Acknowledgments

To my sweet Jennifer Dyan, the love of my life and my business partner. I cannot imagine life without you.

Also, special thanks to Brenda and Cris for their many hours of proofreading and editing. Finally, a big thank you to our growing online community at FTMDaily.com. I thank each of you for your loyal readership and your continued support.

Introduction

According to the laws of physics, an apple thrown upward into the air will be pulled downward by the invisible force of gravity. And while history does not necessarily subscribe to a set of predictable laws, it can teach us great lessons. These lessons can even be forceful at times. *It has been said that while history may never truly repeat, it does at least rhyme.* And unfortunately, in the case of the inevitable American economic decline, we have a wide array of historical precedents, which we will examine throughout this book.

The Excesses of Empire

The painful truth expressed in these pages is that the end of the American experiment will, more than likely, come sooner rather than later. America's ascendance into the heady realms of economic empire began in the post-World War II Bretton Woods era when it was the world's greatest creditor nation. Today, around 70 years later, America stands as the greatest debtor nation in world history. Decades of financial excess, coupled with an entitlement mentality, have left America financially bankrupt.

America clearly represents a reluctant economic empire in decline. And like all empires that have gone before it, its days are numbered. The death of an empire can be quick and painless; however, that is rarely the case. Instead, empires tend to die slow, painful, and humiliating deaths, and their demise is usually accompanied by at least two themes: an overextension of the empire's military and extreme economic overindulgence and depravity. America exhibits excesses in both of these categories.

Over the last few decades, several economic trends have pointed toward an eventual day of reckoning for the U.S. economy.

The Selling of America: Our nation's overconsumption, coupled with U.S. military adventurism since the Vietnam War era, has been largely financed by foreign creditors. With massive trade deficits and an exploding national debt, America is now in a highly vulnerable position as we move into an uncertain future. America's shameful lack of sound fiscal stewardship has created the largest national debt in human history: a colossal $16 trillion . . . and it is growing by the billions every single day with interest. Foreign countries own more pieces of America than ever before. Not only do foreigners own a large amount of America's real wealth (real estate, corporations, etc.), they also hold vast amounts of our government bonds. The repercussions of this large foreign ownership of American interests will be discussed in upcoming chapters.

Low Personal Savings Rate: Since the 1930s, the savings rate for the average American household has stood at around 10 percent. (From 1943 to 1945, the average savings rate was well over 25 percent.) However, as our nation began consuming more than it produced, the personal savings rate dropped dramatically — even turning negative in 2005 for the first time in our history.[1] More recently, and in the wake of the 2008 credit crisis, consumers have boosted their savings with the average rate now at about 5 percent, still well below the saving rate of previous generations.[2]

An Overreliance Upon Credit: U.S. consumer debt has reached all-time highs. This year, more Americans will declare bankruptcy than will divorce, graduate from college, or get cancer; 43 percent of American households spend more than they earn every month. Clearly, this lack of fiscal discipline must eventually end. Today, the U.S. credit industry has trumped the manufacturing industry in total revenues. This as the consumer-crazed nation purchases everything in sight through the use of high-interest credit in an effort to feed the hungry credit beast that they have created.

The Outsourcing of American Jobs: Over the last several years the United States has outsourced the majority of its domestic manufacturing to foreign countries, like China and India. Americans have opted instead to specialize in consumption.

The Breakdown of Social Security and Medicare: The federal government's utter mismanagement of the money that has been entrusted to them through the Social Security and Medicare programs is an absolute disaster. Millions of hard-working Americans are rightly concerned that the money that they were promised by their government will not be there when they reach their golden years. In the upcoming chapters, I will confront this topic and even provide you with unique strategies for preparing for the potential breakdown of these government programs.

A Systematic Destruction of the U.S. Dollar: U.S. "prosperity" is denominated in a debt-based and debt-backed currency, the U.S. dollar. But this illusion of prosperity in America is hardly recognized or highlighted by the financial elite or the nation's media. Since 1913, the Federal Reserve's excessive printing of the nation's currency has led to a 95 percent decrease in the dollar's value. Thanks to the Federal Reserve's noxious mix of quantitative easing programs (money-printing) and extended periods of artificially low interest rates, the financial markets have been completely distorted. These negative monetary policies have systematically devalued the U.S. dollar. In the upcoming chapters, I will provide creative financial solutions for preparing your family and finances for the inevitable hyperinflation that will arise from the Fed's destructive monetary policies.

No Accountability Over the Federal Reserve Bank: Since it was established as America's central bank in 1913, the Federal Reserve has operated without any meaningful congressional oversight. At the height of the 2008 economic crisis, the Fed has admitted that 90 percent of its emergency loans were issued to *foreign* banks. As long as the Fed is allowed to conduct its operations in secret, America's economy will remain hostage to the elite foreign banking interests.

The Abolishment of the Gold Standard: In 1933, the U.S. dollar lost its national gold backing. And later, in 1971, President Richard M. Nixon closed the international gold window. Put simply, in 1971, the United States led the entire global economy into a 100 percent paper money environment for the first time in world history. Today, thanks to our nation's paper currency system, it now takes one dollar to purchase what five cents could purchase in 1945.

America's Debt-Based Monetary System: After the gold standard was abolished, America's monetary system moved from being "gold-backed" to "debt-based." This book will explain America's current debt-based system in stark detail. You will learn how money itself is nothing more than debt. To understand this concept, we will examine the Federal Reserve System and the mind-blowing money creation process they employ.

U.S. Military Overextension: America's military-industrial complex has been growing uncontrollably since the day that President Eisenhower warned U.S. citizens of its lust for power. Our country's nation-building efforts have drained troop morale and drastically increased our debts. Presently, America has over 700 military bases in more than 120 nations — over half of the world's nations! The American obsession with maintaining global hegemonic power through military force is justified in the name of protecting the important causes of freedom, democracy, and justice worldwide. Or as former President William McKinley put it, "The American flag has not been planted in foreign soil to acquire more territory but for humanity's sake."[3] However, acting as the ever-vigilant and omnipresent global policeman requires an annual budget of over $550 billion.[4]

- That is five times larger than China's $92 billion annual military budget[5]
- Nine times larger than Russia's $63 billion[6]
- And 55 times larger than Iran's $11 billion[7]

In fact, funding the American military machine costs almost as much as the rest of the world's military expenses — *combined*. And while these exorbitant costs spent to maintain militaristic dominance are typical of an empire, they are clearly unsustainable.

Wars Conducted without Constitutional Authority: The U.S. Constitution requires a declaration of war to be made by Congress prior to a military action. However, the last war that was officially declared by Congress was World War II. This dereliction of duty by our national leaders is shameful and it demonstrates the clear disregard that both political parties have for our nation's own guiding principles and ideals.

Wars Conducted Without an Appeal to National Sacrifice: America's modern wars are fought without an appeal to national sacrifice. Instead, massive capital inflows from foreign creditors help fund America's military machine. Put simply, America could not afford its current lifestyle of overconsumption and conquest without the kindness (and money) of strangers.

America's Borders Are Not Secure: As U.S. taxpayers are forced to spend hundreds of billions of dollars to protect national borders halfway around the world, our own borders remain porous and insecure. Our national priorities are clearly backward.

Excessive Foreign Aid Dollars Extracted from America's Middle Class: Every year, Washington takes money from the working poor and middle class in order to give it away to leaders of corrupt countries in the form of foreign aid. This practice enriches the ruling class at the expense of average working Americans.

The Coming Breakdown of the Petrodollar System: In this book, you will come face to face with the system that will lead to the collapse of the U.S. dollar. It is known as the petrodollar system. The shocking details of how this system works will be revealed in an upcoming chapter.

Dependence upon Foreign Oil Supplies: U.S. and global demand for energy resources are increasing at a rapid rate. Unfortunately, projected global energy production will not be able to keep pace with global demand. A growing depletion of cheap energy resources, coupled with a threatened petrodollar system, will more than likely force America into becoming militarily aggressive in future resource wars with other growing nations (i.e., China, India, etc.).

Lack of a Sound Energy Policy: No country can maintain its position in the global economy without developing a sustainable strategy for meeting its own energy needs. Sadly, instead of allowing the free markets to dictate our energy supplies, the federal government has intervened with massive subsidies, taxes, and burdensome regulations that create distortions in the market price of energy. Federal drilling restrictions serve as roadblocks to domestic energy exploration. Unless true leadership can emerge to give our nation a sound energy policy, we face increasing danger to our economy in the months and years ahead.

As the hard facts above demonstrate, the American economy represents nothing more than a feeble house of cards completely vulnerable to the inevitable external forces that await every declining empire.

The Life Cycle of Democracies

Consider how the Scottish historian Alexander Tyler documented the typical life cycle of a democracy:

> A democracy cannot exist as a permanent form of government. It can only exist until the voters discover that they can vote themselves money from the public treasure. From that moment on the majority always votes for the candidates promising the most money from the public treasury, with the result that a democracy always collapses over loose fiscal policy followed by a dictatorship.

Tyler continues with this amazing statement:

> The average age of the world's great civilizations has been two hundred years. These nations have progressed through the following sequence: from bondage to spiritual faith, from spiritual faith to great courage, from courage to liberty, from liberty to abundance, from abundance to selfishness, from selfishness to complacency, from complacency to apathy, from apathy to dependency, from dependency back to bondage.[8]

Does this sequence sound familiar? In which stage of the life cycle do you believe America is currently?

In summary:

- The purchasing power of our U.S. dollar is declining in value.
- The U.S. government continues to print more money.
- We are engaged in an expensive and endless global war on terror.
- American jobs are being exported to foreign nations.
- Americans are spending too much and saving too little.

- We have requested little, if any, economic "sacrifice" on the part of our citizenry.
- Our trade deficit and budgetary deficits are at all-time highs.
- Our national debt is at an all-time high and growing exponentially.
- We are completely dependent upon foreign nations to fund our overconsumption through the sale of our debts.

As long as foreign countries continue to finance our way of life, perhaps we can extend this madness. But what happens if foreign countries begin to decrease their funding of our debts?

The truth is, the American public is living in massive monetary deception. The direction that the American economy is heading is extremely difficult to swallow. However, if our aim is truth, then we will willingly embrace the facts and take the necessary steps needed to shelter ourselves, our families, and our finances. While it may be hard to believe right now, the message of this book is one of great hope. Our hope is in knowing which direction the trends are taking us. It is in this knowledge that you will be able to protect and shelter whatever wealth you have already accumulated, and in addition profit from the greatest financial crisis that the world has ever witnessed. As you read the following chapters of this book, be of good cheer. Despite man's best efforts, God is still in control. And with God, the end is only the beginning.

Warning: Spiritual Discernment Used in this Book

In the interest of full disclosure, I should tell you up front that I am a follower of Christ. However, allow me to quickly add that I have not reached the ranks of the "spiritually arrogant." I view my faith as the most humbling aspect of my existence. And I can think of nothing that turns me off more than spiritual smugness and self-righteousness. The world would be a better place without the crusaders who become obsessed about the speck of dust in someone else's eye while ignoring the enormous log in their own eye. So, expect no fiery pronouncements to be issued from my pen. I have made my share of mistakes and do not view my role to be as a judge of others and their shortcomings. The reason for my upfront candidness on this matter is because I believe that you, as the reader, have a right to know that your author's worldview has been colored by his faith.

As a believer and follower of Jesus Christ, it is my earnest belief that hope is never completely lost, because God's sovereign plan of the ages will forever prevail — no matter how desperate things may appear on the surface. But if my brief time on this earth, and my understanding of history, have taught me anything, it is that only fools place their trust in man's ability to rule himself. In fact, if history is a guide to anything, it is a guide to the consistent knuckleheaded acts of mankind throughout the ages. From a spiritual perspective, I believe that mankind's current predicament stems from the fact that man was not designed nor was he ever meant to rule himself. According to an orthodox view of the Christian faith, human suffering is rooted in man's rejection of the omnipotent rule of his Creator. When given a choice, man opted for self-rule. This ancient act of rebellion, in the Garden of Eden, explains humanity's pain and suffering over the last 6,000 years. And if we choose to believe the Bible when it explains that mankind's rebellion will become worse with time, it would also explain why the 20th century has been noted as the "bloodiest century" on record.[9] (Ironically, the 20th century has also been labeled the "American Century.")

In many ways, America represents the culmination of all that man has ever aspired to: life, liberty, and the pursuit of happiness. And yet despite the amazing personal freedoms, rights, and liberties that the "American experiment" graced upon the Western hemisphere, man's inability to lead himself has continually bubbled to the surface. Unable to personally rid himself of his true sin nature, man has attempted in vain to cloak his inherent deficiencies at self-rule. As a result, America is following the same path as every economic empire before it. And lest we confuse ourselves, American Christians must quickly grasp this point: America is not the light of the world. The sun shone before America was here, and it will continue to shine long after our nation's self-inflicted demise. So let us not proceed in shock or surprise at the complex political and economic webs that have been woven in America. Despite what the Western-centric thinker may suggest, the ancient writings of the Bible are clear. They confirm that the biblical prophecies concerning the "last days" are Israel-centric and Middle Eastern-centric. They are anything but America-centric. In other words, I believe that the Bible clearly suggests that the global political and economic spotlight will be firmly transferred to this volatile region in the coming years.[10]

Put simply, America's fall is historically identifiable, though unfortunate. And it is all but certain.

Endnotes

1. Laura Smitherman, "Personal Savings Rate Dips to Zero for First Time Since Great Depression," *The Baltimore Sun*, January 31, 2006.
2. For the most up-to-date personal U.S. savings rate, see the report on Personal Income and Outlays from the Bureau of Economic Analysis, http://www.bea.gov/national/index.htm#personal.

3. From a 1900 campaign poster for the Republican party, July 12, 1900.
4. Paul Eckert, "Analysis: Pinched U.S. Seen Holding onto Big Pacific Presence," Reuters, http://www.reuters.com/article/2011/08/12/us-usa-defense-asia-idUS-TRE77B0K020110812, August 12, 2011.
5. Ibid.
6. Ibid.
7. "Russia confirms 2011 defense spending hike," UPI, http://www.upi.com/Business_News/Security-Industry/2010/11/10/Russia-confirms-2011-defense-spending-hike/UPI-91241289393180/, November 10, 2010.
8. David L. Wood, *Why Worry About the Gradual Loss of Our Liberties?* (Oakland, OR: Elderberry Press, 2003), p. 36.
9. Numerous biblical references point to the increase of wickedness as mankind nears what the Apostle Paul called "the last days" (2 Timothy 3:1–5). See also Matthew 24:12. For documentation on the 20th century being termed the "bloodiest century," see Niall Ferguson's book, *The War of the World: Twentieth-Century Conflict and the Descent of the West* (New York: Penguin Press, 2006).
10. The writings of the biblical prophets Daniel, Ezekiel, Zechariah, and the Apostle John, envision a time when the Middle East, and Israel, in particular, play the dominant role in the fulfillment of biblical prophecy. See Daniel 2 and 7, Ezekiel 38 and 39, Zechariah 12, and the Book of Revelation. See also the Olivet discourse, which provides an overview of the "last days" as delivered by Jesus Christ himself in Matthew 24, Mark 13, and Luke 21.

Chapter 1

What Is Money . . . Really?

Permit me to issue and control the money of a nation, and I
care not who makes its laws.[1]
— Mayer Anselm Rothschild of the Rothschild banking family

All the perplexities, confusion, and distress in America arise,
not from defects in their Constitution or Confederation, not
from want of honor or virtue, so much as from the downright
ignorance of the nature of coin, credit, and circulation.[2]
— John Adams

*OVERVIEW: Money has taken many different forms throughout history:
shells, feathers, salt, gold, silver, and paper currency. This chapter lays the
groundwork for understanding the current crisis confronting the U.S.
dollar by examining the underlying concepts of money. What exactly is
money? How is it measured? What gives it value? In addition to answering
these questions, this chapter will also explain the three types of money that
have been used throughout history: commodity money, receipt money, and
fiat money.*

There is an old joke about money that goes something like this:
"Money may not buy happiness, it sure does buy everything
else." Benjamin Franklin referred to man's obsession with money this
way: "He that is of the opinion money will do everything may well be

suspected of doing everything for money."[3] Regardless of our own view of money, one thing is certain: *Money is a necessity for life in this world.*

Before attempting to answer the essential question of what money really is, let us first consider how the American culture, and our own upbringing, has affected our view of money. From my own research, I have discovered that an individual's view of money is determined by at least three fundamental factors.

Economic System. The first and perhaps most influential factor that affects a person's view or conception of money is the economic system into which the person is born. For example, a person born and raised in the United States is introduced to a capitalistic economic system from birth. The virtues espoused under capitalism include the right to private property, the division of labor, and individual rights.

In contrast, those who are born in China are taught to view money through the lens of a communistic economic system. Under communism, individuals have fewer rights and the government plays a much greater role in every aspect of life.[4]

Family Financial Philosophy. The second factor that shapes a person's view of money is the financial philosophy espoused by his family. Whether they realize it or not, parents are teaching their children by their words, and more importantly by their actions, about what is important in life. For example, a mother who spends excessive amounts of money teaches a different set of financial values to her children than a mother who is an avid saver or astute investor. The spendthrift mother is silently teaching her children that overconsumption is a desirable and perhaps even a virtuous act. Meanwhile, the mother who gains joy from saving and investing is teaching her children that preserving and growing money is far more important than spending it.

To use another example, a father who exemplifies a strong work ethic to his children is teaching them that money is best earned through hard labor. In contrast, a father who runs his own successful business is silently teaching his children that money is best earned through a combination of personal hard work and by employing the efforts of others.

Finally, some families treat the topic of money as taboo and rarely discuss it around their children. Inevitably, these families are teaching their children that silence about financial matters is preferable to openly discussing the topic.

Spiritual Values. The third factor that ultimately determines a person's view on money is rooted in their religious and moral understanding of life itself. For example, it is common for a person who has had a strict religious upbringing to view money as inherently evil.

To illustrate this point, allow me to tell you about a Christian woman I once counseled named "Margaret." Like many Christians, Margaret was taught from a young age that that money was unspiritual and dirty. Once, during a conversation with her, I asked her why she considered money to be evil. Apparently, this question was appalling to Margaret. She quickly retorted, "You are a minister! Don't you read your Bible? The Bible clearly states that money is the root of all evil."

Margaret was feisty, to say the least. I decided to respond with a question of my own. (I'll admit that I am a bit Socratic in my discussions on Christianity. By Socratic, I mean that when someone asks me a question, I will often reply with a question of my own. This is a method that Jesus used quite extensively. And if it was good enough for Him, it is good enough for me.)

I politely replied, "Well, I feel rather embarrassed. I was not aware that the Bible said such a thing. Here, Margaret, here's a Bible. Would you please show me where it says this so I can help others understand this, too?"

"I do not know. But *it is* in there," she replied with a tone of disgust.

Knowing exactly the verse that she was taking out of context, I quickly turned my Bible to 1 Timothy 6:10 and read it aloud: "For the love of money is a root of all kinds of evil, for which some have strayed from the faith in their greediness, and pierced themselves through with many sorrows."

With her face aglow with a deep pride, she quickly chimed in, "That's it. That's the verse that I was talking about. Haven't you ever read that before?"

My Socratic tendencies would not allow me to give her a straight answer yet. It was too important for her to clearly see the folly of her logic. I responded, "Margaret, if this is true, do you realize how this changes everything that I have ever known and taught about money? In fact, I am thinking of another verse right now that I feel we should read, too. Can I read it to you?"

With a smug assurance, Margaret nodded.

I continued, "Well, if money is evil, then we better pay extremely close attention to this next verse. It is found in 1 Thessalonians 5:22. It says, 'Abstain from every form of evil.' Margaret, if this is true, and if money really *is* evil, then this means that you and I need to get rid of all of our money as quickly as possible!"

Margaret laughed nervously and asked what I meant.

With a more compassionate tone, I re-read 1 Timothy 6:10 to her and said, "Margaret, the Bible never says that *money* is evil. What this verse is saying is that *the love of money* is the root of all evil. If money itself was evil, then we would both be in violation of God's Word simply by possessing it. Do you understand why this is an important difference?"

Margaret took the Bible and read the verse again, as if for the first time. Then, the moment that I had been hoping for occurred as she gently said: "My father always told me that money was evil and those who had lots of money were not godly. But this verse does not say that, does it?" As she asked this question, her tone became much more accepting and friendly.

"That's right, Margaret. The Bible is extremely balanced in its view on money. In fact, the Bible never says that money is good or evil. You see, money is just an object. It is we humans who take money and perform good or evil works with it," I said with even more compassion.

Due to Margaret's religiously dogmatic views on money, she had spent her entire life downplaying its importance in her life. She even avoided the topic out of perhaps an irrational fear that it was displeasing to God. This is just one example of how a person's view of money can be shaped and influenced by their spiritual values. I believe money to be completely amoral. Money is not capable of being moral or immoral. It is merely an object. Instead, money can be used for good purposes or for bad purposes. Those who are searching for the morality of money do well to consider the intentions of its possessor, not the money itself.

To summarize, everyone's view of money has been shaped by a combination of the three factors stated above. Why is understanding this important? Because our particular view of money greatly influences our financial decisions. Often, the influences upon our own view of money become so powerful that they can create false ideas and ultimately destructive mindsets, as in the case of Margaret.

The fact that you are holding this book is proof that you have a desire to improve your own understanding of money. It is also likely that you are deeply concerned about America's uncertain economy and how you can protect your family and yourself. If so, then this book is exactly what you have been looking for.

In order to understand the true impact of the global financial crisis, and how you can prepare yourself and even profit from it, we will now confront several foundational questions that deserve to be answered. These questions include:

- What is money?
- How is money measured?
- What gives money its value?
- And finally, if money can be printed to prevent a financial crisis, why not just print more?

In this chapter, I will answer each of these important questions. My goal, however, is not to bore you with tedious details and lots of financial jargon. Instead, my desire is to inspire you over the next few chapters by helping you gain a basic understanding of the current monetary and banking systems and why this knowledge is vital to your financial security. While these questions may seem completely irrelevant to you right now, I hope to demonstrate in the chapters ahead how understanding the answers will empower you with the financial knowledge you will need to profit in the uncertain days ahead. Believe it or not, your ability to protect yourself and your family financially is greatly connected to your understanding of the four basic questions above. I believe that the answers will surprise you.

Now that I have your attention, let us proceed.

So . . . What Is Money?

That is a great question — what exactly is money?

If asked to give a definition of money to someone, how would you define it?

If you answered that money is the paycheck that you receive at the end of every week from your employer, you would be only partially correct. Economists have grappled with this question and have come up with three basic answers. The three definitions of money are as follows:

- Money is . . . a *medium of exchange*
- Money is . . . a *store of value*
- Money is . . . a *unit of account*

Let's briefly define each of these.

Money is a . . . Medium of Exchange

One way to define money is to say that it is something universally accepted as payment for goods and services or for the repayment of debts. In America, for example, a U.S. dollar is recognized by everyone as money. Therefore, it is acceptable as payment for any and all goods and services within the nation's borders. U.S. businesses who sell a good or a service do not accept U.S. dollars because they like the way the dollar looks or how they smell. That would be ridiculous! Instead, the reason that a merchant is willing to accept payment in U.S. dollars is because they know that the dollar is an acceptable means of payment for their needs. Put simply, they will accept dollars for payment *because they know they can immediately turn around and use those same dollars to purchase something for themselves.* However, if you walked into a store and attempted to pay with a handful of bananas instead of dollars, then you would be out of luck. Why? It is nothing personal against bananas. It is only because bananas are not currently a recognizable and universal means of payment for goods and services. So for something to be considered money, it must serve as a *medium of exchange.*

Money Is a . . . Store of Value

Economists also define money as a *store of value.* By this, they mean that money must be able to be stored away and used later. For example, if the U.S. dollar was perishable, or had an expiration date, then it could not serve as an effective store of value. This can be applied to our earlier example of bananas. Within a week or less, a banana can rot. Bananas would not make a very stable form of money as they would lose their value very quickly. Money should be nonperishable and must hold its value for future needs and wants over time.

Money is a . . . Unit of Account

Finally, money must be a *unit of account.* What does that mean? It means that the prices within an economy should be expressed in a universally accepted monetary unit. For example, without a single universally accepted form of money, how could storeowners price their items? The prices of goods and services would be very difficult to determine without a unit of account. What if you wanted to pay for your goods with your bananas and another customer wanted to pay with pineapples? How could the store owner possibly know how to price his goods under such a complex system? Today's economic environment has become far too complex and interdependent to rely upon such an antiquated system of barter. People no longer have to produce everything they consume. Instead, they can simply trade money for the goods or services that they do not, or cannot, produce. Our modern economy requires a cohesive and universal monetary system that can serve as a unit of account.

The Brief Evolution of Money

The history and evolution of money is a story that spans thousands of years. And while money and trade have become more sophisticated over time, we have evidence that several early civilizations had forms of advanced monetary systems. One of the first civilizations to develop a system of trade with a form of money was ancient Sumer. The Sumerians were highly advanced in many areas, including their system of economy and trade.

From the days of ancient Sumer to our present day, money and trade have taken many different forms. The most primitive type, and earliest form, of money is *commodity money*. Commodity money is a unique form of money that serves a dual purpose. It can be used for trade or it can be consumed by the owner. Early civilizations, for example, used common items as commodity money, including spearheads, shells, feathers, and salt. In ancient times, for example, salt could be used for trading purposes. But the owner always had the option of consuming the salt himself. Salt could also be used for antiseptic purposes and for preserving food, among other uses. This is unlike our current paper money system that serves only one purpose, that is, trade. Paper money has no other use if it is not backed by a commodity. Because commodity money has a dual purpose, it is said to have an *intrinsic value*.

Over time, the portability and durability of money became important to merchants and traders as societies became more interconnected.

As the old saying goes, "Necessity is the mother of invention." This need for more versatility in financial transactions led to the rise of gold and silver as money. Unlike crops, gold and silver were scarce, durable, and non-perishable. In addition, gold and silver were far superior to livestock in that they 1) were much easier to transport, 2) required little maintenance costs, and 3) had the unique capability of being divided for exact payment. Soon, gold and silver were made into the form of coins with their values stamped on them. This simple but revolutionary act made financial transactions more convenient and represented man's first real attempts at coined currency.

It did not take long, however, for those in search of dishonest gain to exploit the gold and silver monetary system. How? Those who wanted to cheat the system did so *by placing gold or silver plating over cheaper metal discs* to imitate the appearance of solid gold and silver coins. Local governments would often step into the "money-making business" to prevent such counterfeiting efforts. Despite these efforts, counterfeiting remained a constant challenge to most forms of money. This is true even to this day.

The superior aspects of gold and silver meant that they soon became the money of choice for many people. But as people began to accumulate large sums of gold or silver coins in their homes, concerns over keeping them safe from theft or loss became a major concern. This demand for safety led to the creation of one of the earliest forms of modern banking, known as *goldsmith banking*.

Under the *goldsmith banking system,* which became popular in 17th-century England, a person would simply deposit his gold with his local goldsmith. Much like modern banking, the goldsmith would provide the depositor with a paper receipt stating the amount of gold on deposit. If the person wanted to redeem his gold, he simply returned his paper receipt to the goldsmith. (In exchange for this convenience of keeping the gold in a safe place, the town's goldsmith would charge a small monthly maintenance fee.) Because these paper receipts were viewed as "good as gold" they became extremely valuable. As communities grew and trade activity increased, these paper receipts began to be accepted as payment for simple financial transactions.

Eventually, traders and merchants in need of capital began seeking out loans from the goldsmiths. Most goldsmiths embraced the new income opportunity and were willing lenders. Despite the novelty of this financial system, the lending process was fairly simple. The goldsmith created and issued a paper receipt to the borrower which gave the appearance that the borrower had gold in the goldsmith's vaults. But in reality, no new gold reserves were backing this loaned paper receipt. The goldsmith knew that the only way this scheme would be discovered was if many of his depositors were to demand all of their gold at the same time. Because the goldsmith considered this highly unlikely, he could continue to profit from his newfound lending power with little fear of a default risk. (This idea of lending money not currently on deposit has become a highly profitable venture for bankers. It is known as *fractional-reserve banking* and is discussed at length in chapter 7, "Modern Money Mechanics: What the Banksters Do Not Want You to Know.")

As the Industrial Revolution began, the demand for loans grew dramatically. The large profit potential through this new sleight-of-hand lending process led to a rise in competition. Small regional banks began issuing their own forms of paper currency, similar to the paper receipts created by goldsmiths, in order to compete. As nations grew in population and in commercial activity, the various forms of issued currency became overwhelming, often stifling the flow of commerce. When nations faced such pressures, the largest banks would seek a monopoly on national lending by recommending a unified paper currency system to the governing authorities. These new paper currency systems were often backed by some form of commodity, usually gold or silver. Of course, implementing and regulating a national paper currency system was a monumental task requiring vigilant oversight. Western governments, in particular, often capitulated to the banking interests by permitting the creation of one national *central bank*. The central bank's role often included issuing the national currency of choice (almost exclusively paper money), regulating the money supply, and controlling interest rates. In addition, the central bank would often be responsible for monitoring the nation's banking activity, and serving as the lender of last resort, due to its unique capability of creating the national currency.

Despite the sophistication of the new central banking arrangement, discrepancies between the government's fiscal policies and the central bank's monetary policies often led to economic upheaval. The result of these conflicting policies, coupled with the unpredictable economic growth patterns of an emerging nation, often led to financial imbalances. These imbalances proved extremely difficult for central banks. Maintaining a commodity backing for every piece of paper money in circulation soon became a laborious process and served to limit the growth potential of the economy. After all, if the government required the nation's money supply to be restricted to the available amount of a particular commodity, such as gold, then economic growth would suffer.

The initial solution to these early liquidity crises required a strong trade policy and often a mighty military. Governments knew that to maintain the growth of their gold-backed currencies required a growing supply of gold. For example, 16th-century England had few, if any, gold mines. And yet the British Empire boasted one of the world's largest gold reserves. How was that possible? Through conquest. While trade restrictions, such as banning gold exports and export subsidies, were also common in this age of *mercantilism,* clever trade policies were rarely enough for the largest of nations. Military conquest of other nations in search of gold was virtually required to maintain a growing empire. Colonization efforts, often implemented under the auspices of Christian missionary activity, served at least two purposes: 1) to provide a fresh source of gold for the colonizing nation and 2) to create a new market for export purposes.

Empires, however, are notorious for having voracious spending appetites. Despite multiple conquests, the monetary constraints would soon become severe enough to force a new solution. The temptation for spendthrift governments was obvious: cut the commodity backing of currency and turn on the printing presses. (History is replete with warnings for those nations who dared to remove the commodity backing from their currency. For a history of national economies that have been severely damaged or completely destroyed through the overproduction of paper money, see chapter 3.)

Throughout history, all governments have come to the same conclusion: remove the commodity backing from its own national currency, thereby creating more flexibility. When a nation detaches its paper currency system from any and all commodity backing, its currency is then considered by economists to be a *fiat currency*. When a currency is issued by fiat, it is backed only by government guarantees, not a commodity. Fiat money has no intrinsic value. Its value is derived strictly by government law, and unlike the first two types of money (commodity and receipt) there is no natural limit to the quantity of fiat money that can be produced. The benefits of such a system to a government should be obvious. Without the economic constraints imposed by gold, the money creation process available to governments with fiat currencies is virtually unlimited.

How Is Money Measured?

Regardless of the type of money a nation uses, one important quality that it must possess is an ability to be measured. This is especially true in the case of fiat currency. In response to our modern fiat dollar system, U.S. economists have devised four categories to measure the nation's money supply. These four measurements are known simply as M0, M1, M2, and M3.

M0 Money Supply: This measurement includes all coin and paper currency in circulation, as well as accounts at the central bank that can be exchanged for physical currency. This is the narrowest measure of the U.S. money supply and only measures the amount of liquid money in the hands of the public and certain deposits with the Federal Reserve.

M1 Money Supply: This measurement includes everything in M0 as well as currency held in demand deposits (such as checking accounts and NOW accounts) and traveler's checks (which can be liquidated into physical currency.)

M2 Money Supply: This category includes everything in M1, plus all of the currency held in saving accounts, money market accounts, and certificates of deposit with balances of $100,000 or less.

M3 Money Supply: As the broadest measure of the U.S. money supply, this category combines all of M2 (which includes M1) plus all currency held in certificates of deposit with balances over $100,000, institutional money market funds, short-term repurchase agreements, and eurodollars (U.S. dollars held in foreign bank accounts).

What Gives Fiat Money Its Value?

If you have a U.S. dollar bill nearby, pick it up. Examine it closely. Notice its many symbols and its colors.

Now ask yourself: What exactly is it that gives the U.S. dollar its value? And why are so many people willing to exchange their valuable goods and services, or work long hours at jobs they may or may not enjoy, for these small pieces of green paper?

Answer: *Faith in the scarcity of the dollar.*

Allow me to elaborate on this answer.

Since fiat currencies are not physically backed up by a particular commodity such as gold, they have no *intrinsic value.* (By intrinsic value, I am referring to the actual value of the physical piece of paper itself.) Using this definition, fiat currencies are technically worthless. Governments and central banks are fully aware of this and some even understand the inherent danger of fiat monetary systems. To overcome the potential hurdles faced by an intrinsically worthless currency, the U.S. government required acceptance of the U.S. dollar in nearly all domestic financial transactions through the passage of legal tender laws. Due to this legal binding, Americans willingly accept the fiat U.S. dollar because they *believe* it has value. It is true that the dollar has value, but this value is not of an intrinsic nature. Instead, the dollar's "value" is derived from a carefully managed perception by the nation's monetary authorities. This belief, *or faith*, in the dollar's value, despite having no real intrinsic value, is a common trait shared by all fiat currencies. Interestingly, if the public were ever to lose faith in the value of the currency, the entire house of cards would fall.

Through the use of constitutional contortion, the United States has created a national demand for a fiat currency. Maintaining the illusion of

Understanding Intrinsic Value

Many different commodities have been used as money throughout history. Take silver, for example. In addition to being used as money for centuries, the shiny metal also has many industrial uses such as photography, dentistry, jewelry, mirrors, optics, and medicine. With so many varied uses, it is no wonder that silver was widely adopted as money throughout history. Silver, and other similar types of commodity money, has intrinsic value. That is, it has value outside of its role as money.

Compare this to the U.S. dollar. How many uses does a dollar have? Paper money is different from commodity money in that it has no intrinsic value, although some have argued that in enough quantities, the dollar bill could be used as firewood, thereby giving it some intrinsic value. In fact, that is exactly what happened to paper money in Germany during the 1920s! You can read more about that monetary nightmare in chapter 3.

the dollar's value requires that the monetary authorities avoid a reckless increase of the U.S. money supply. Historically speaking, such increases have had disastrous effects upon the purchasing power of the underlying currency. Avoiding a dollar collapse requires a perpetual faith among the American public in the Fed's willingness and ability to keep the currency in a limited supply.

Conclusion

Today, all global currencies are issued by fiat and are controlled by an arrangement between governments and their central banks. For the first time in history, no currency on the planet is backed up by a physical commodity. And why have individuals been willing to accept these fiat paper currencies in exchange for goods produced and services rendered? Ironically, the answer is rooted in the public's faith and trust in their respective government. The reason that the American public, or any society for that matter, is willing to accept a fiat currency in exchange for goods produced and services rendered is due to the belief that the government will maintain the currency's value by keeping it in limited supply.

At this point, some readers may wonder why governments should strive to keep their fiat currency in limited supply. After all, couldn't we eradicate global poverty by printing excessive amounts of currency and giving it to the world's poorest citizens? *If it were only that easy!*

While some readers may understand why this is impossible, it is nevertheless a very important question because we have several examples of economically ignorant leaders throughout recent history who have attempted this very thing. Other leaders have attempted to grow their economies out of tough situations by printing excessive amounts of currency.

What happens when a government decides to unleash the printing presses and overproduce its fiat currency? Does everyone suddenly become wildly rich due to all of the newly printed currency? Does printing fiat currency solve problems or just create more problems? In our next chapter I will answer these questions with a historical examination of fiat currencies. Sadly, fiat currencies, like the U.S. dollar, have led *every* nation that has abused them to the brink of economic disaster.

Quick Summary

✓ Our own personal view of money is shaped and influenced by three factors: 1) the economic system we are born into, 2) our family's financial philosophy, and 3) our instilled spiritual and moral values.

✓ Money is morally neutral. It can be used for positive or negative reasons. Financial morality is found in the intentions of the user, not in the money itself.

✓ Three forms of money have been used throughout history: 1) commodity money, 2) receipt money, 3) fiat money

✓ Commodity money took the form of exchangeable commodities often with intrinsic value such as salt, livestock, and crops.

✓ Along with the advance of civilizations came the need for a form of money that was relatively scarce, portable, easily divisible, and durable.

✓ Precious metals, such as gold and silver, fit all of these requirements, making them the obvious choice.

✓ Over time, goldsmith banking allowed individuals a safe place to store their gold in exchange for a paper receipt that was considered as "good as gold."

✓ These paper receipts, or receipt money, were extremely popular due to their ease of use.

✓ The governing authorities eventually saw a need to monopolize the money creation process in order to ensure economic stability.

✓ This government intervention led to the rise of central banks and fiat monetary systems that have ultimately proven to be disastrous, as we shall see in upcoming chapters.

✓ Fiat money has no intrinsic value. Instead, its value is derived from legal tender laws and a public perception that the monetary authorities will keep it in a limited supply.

✓ Today, every currency on the planet is considered to be fiat.

Endnotes

1. Dallas D. Johnson, *Consume! The Monetary Radical's Defense of Capitalism* (New York: Dynamic American Press, 1940), p. 89.
2. Charles Francis Adams, *The Works of John Adams, Second President of the United States* (New York: Little, Brown & Co., 1853), p. 447.
3. Nathan G. Goodman, editor, *A Benjamin Franklin Reader* (New York: Thomas Y. Crowell Co., 1945), p. 288.
4. More in-depth explanations of the various types of political and economic systems can be found outside of this book. My purpose here is simply to point out that a person's view on money is often directly tied to how his government teaches him to view money.

Chapter 2

A Short History of Fiat Currencies

There is no subtler, no surer means of overturning the existing basis of society than to debauch the currency. The process engages all the hidden forces of economic law on the side of destruction, and does it in a manner which not one man in a million is able to diagnose.[1]

— Sir John Maynard Keynes

With the exception only of the period of the gold standard, practically all governments of history have used their exclusive power to issue money to defraud and plunder the people.[2]

— Friedrich A. Hayek, Nobel prizewinner, economist

OVERVIEW: In our last chapter, the topic of fiat currencies was introduced. In this chapter, a brief history of fiat currencies will be provided. A fiat currency, like the U.S. dollar, is a currency that is not backed by any type of commodity. Since an underlying commodity does not give value to the fiat currency, only one thing can determine its value: scarcity. Governments and their central banks, however, have a terrible track record of keeping fiat currencies in scarce supply. No fiat currency has ever succeeded in the long run. Ever. This chapter analyzes some of history's fiat currencies. Will America follow the same historical pattern?

"O Ye of Little Fiat . . ."

Fiat currencies are faith-based currencies. Individuals who live, work, and transact in a fiat currency system are a people of great faith. Faith, you say? What exactly does *faith* have to do with a *fiat currency system*? Faith has everything to do with a fiat currency. As we have already learned, a fiat currency system is one determined by the governing authorities with no backing of any physical commodity. Because fiat currencies do not derive their value from anything tangible, their value is determined by their scarcity. Fiat currency systems, like that of the U.S. dollar, demand an enormous amount of trust from the public in the monetary competency of their governments. Why? Because the future value of a fiat currency is entirely dependent upon the financial wisdom and vigilant oversight of the nation's monetary authorities in keeping the currency in a limited and strictly measured supply. Those who use and transact in a fiat currency system demonstrate great faith in their government's ability to make sound monetary decisions.

If the authorities choose to adopt unsound monetary policies, such as massively inflating the amount of currency in circulation, the public will suffer as each fiat dollar becomes worth less, if not *worthless*! Under such an irresponsible monetary system, the citizenry will seek to preserve their purchasing power by reducing their holdings in the fiat currency as it declines in value. However, the fiat currency is not always the only casualty in such situations, as the public often loses trust in the entire system, including the current political leaders, the central bank, and even the national banking system.

Therefore, it is not a misnomer to call fiat currencies what they truly are: *faith-based currencies*. The faith expressed by the public is not rooted within the currency itself, but instead, within the ability of the nation's monetary authorities to properly steward the value of the fiat currency.

Question: Is the U.S. dollar the first fiat (faith-based) currency in existence? And if it is not, what kind of historical track record do fiat currencies have? Are fiat currencies more likely to succeed or to fail?

Answer: The U.S. dollar is not the first fiat currency in history. In fact, the first known fiat currency system was originated under the Song Dynasty in China during the 11th century.[3] Since the dawn of fiat creation, governments who have chosen to adopt fiat currency systems have had one unfortunate thing in common: they have abused their money-printing privileges through the overproduction of their national currency until it becomes completely worthless. Interestingly, a cursory examination of the rationale behind many of these periods of currency collapse began with reasonable objectives. In other words, it is difficult to find a historical example of a fiat currency collapse that was initiated with sinister motives to destroy the currency. Instead, history demonstrates that the varied periods of currency overproduction occurred when a government became seduced by the suggestion that their economic misfortunes could be solved through the production of just "a little more" money. But printing money "out of thin air," as the fiat currency system so easily allows, always comes at an enormous cost. History is clear. Every fiat currency devised throughout history has faced the same embarrassing and miserable death: utter collapse by overproduction. The fact that so many currency collapses throughout history were initiated under the auspices of "good intentions" should be a cause for concern to all who distrust the true motives of the monetary authorities in our modern era.

A comprehensive historical review of fiat currencies also reveals another interesting phenomenon. Often, just prior to the demise of a fiat currency, the nation's economy appears to be experiencing widespread prosperity.[4] Of course, this "prosperity" is simply an illusion. In reality, as more of the fiat currency is produced and circulated throughout the national economy, the average standard of living experiences a temporary increase which creates an illusion of growing wealth in the nation. While this illusion appears real, the "prosperity" that is encountered by the masses of people is of artificial origin, manufactured and fueled by the government's overproduction of the currency. After a nation experiences this inflation-fueled illusion of prosperity, the death of the currency is not far behind. The irony is cruel.

Economics 101: What They Didn't Teach You in School

Before we begin our brief excursion through history concerning fiat currencies, consider this brief illustration regarding currency overproduction. Imagine for a moment that two brothers — we will call them Bill and Joe — wake up to find themselves stranded on a deserted

There Is Nothing New Under the Sun

According to the Bible, King Solomon was the wisest man who ever lived (1 Kings 4:31). As one of the greatest kings of ancient Israel, Solomon lived a life of luxury and comfort in the upper echelons of his society. History tells us that his riches were immense (1 Kings 3:13; 2 Chronicles 1:12). As a king, he was denied no request. His popularity and fame as a successful ruler were spread throughout the entire region. And based upon his biblical writings, it is obvious that the man was filled with great knowledge, common sense, and wisdom.

But upon a deeper inspection of Solomon's writings, another striking theme emerges: a profound sense of despair. Despite his vast wealth, wisdom, and fame, the great king discovered that a life lived apart from the Creator was futile and that humanity's quest for meaning outside of God would always be fruitless. His observations were summed up best when he said, "All is vanity" (Eccles. 1:2, 12:8). Solomon's sobering realization gives new meaning to the oft-said phrase, "Ignorance is bliss."

Another one of Solomon's famous quotes is found in the Book of Ecclesiastes: "Generations come and generations go, but the earth never changes. The sun rises and the sun sets, then hurries around to rise again. The wind blows south, and then turns north. Around and around it goes, blowing in circles. Rivers run into the sea, but the sea is never full. Then the water returns again to the rivers and flows out again to the sea. Everything is wearisome beyond description. No matter how much we see, we are never satisfied. No matter how much we hear, we are not content. History merely repeats itself. It has all been done before. Nothing under the sun is truly new. Sometimes people say, 'Here is something new!' But actually it is old; nothing is ever truly new. We don't remember what happened in the past, and in future generations, no one will remember what we are doing now" (Eccles. 1:4–11; NLT).

Norman Cousins would later paraphrase King Solomon in his famous quip, "History is a vast early warning system."[5] But perhaps George Santayana said it best when he wrote, "Those who do not know history are doomed to repeat it."[6] Does this mean that history always represents destiny? No. However, we must admit that while history may not always repeat, it certainly rhymes. And the rhyming of history is what this chapter is about. While each historical case of fiat currency collapse is unique, it is all rooted in the same basic problem: human greed.

island. After several desperate attempts to be rescued, the two brothers soon realize that the tropic island may have become their new home.

They soon begin surveying the island in search of food, water, and shelter. Bill soon discovers a fruit tree and immediately lays claim to it.

Joe, who is literally starving, begs his brother Bill for a piece of fruit. Under normal circumstances, Bill would accept money as payment for his newfound treasure trove. But what good is paper currency on this island?

After he realizes that no amount of begging will work on his stingy brother, Joe devises a plan. In his pocket, Joe has eight golf balls. He approaches Bill with the idea of using the eight golf balls as the island's new official currency. Bill agrees and under their new "currency" system, both men receive four golf balls with which to trade for things that the other man may find.

Finally, Joe, who is famished and desperate for food, offers Bill one of his golf balls for a piece of fruit from Bill's tree. Bill considers it a fair trade. Suddenly, as the two men are finalizing their transaction, a very loud noise, like something striking the ground, is heard just a few hundred feet away. Eager to see what has caused the noise, Joe and Bill run to investigate. What they discover shocks them both. Right there on the white sandy beach in front of them lays a very large wooden crate attached to a parachute. The outside of the box reads: "Golf Balls — 100,000 count."

Now considering what we have learned so far, what effect do you think this new box containing 100,000 golf balls is going to have upon the price of the piece of fruit that Joe wants to buy?

Answer: The price of Bill's fruit will go up dramatically. And the price increase happens instantaneously as the available money supply on the island (golf balls) has suddenly increased from 8 to just over 100,000 in a few brief moments! Given this dramatic increase in the money supply, do you think that Bill is still willing to accept just 1 golf ball for his precious fruit? Why not 50 or 100? Or even 1,000?

Interestingly, Bill could not ask for more than 8 golf balls for his fruit prior to the discovery of the 100,000 golf balls. And yet, just moments after the discovery of the golf balls, his price could rise immediately.

This above illustration provides a classic example of the effects that changes in the money supply have on prices within an economy. This is the definition of inflation: an increase in the money supply. Inflation is basically a hidden tax on consumers and will be discussed in further detail in our next chapter. Of course, the government and their paid economists prefer to define inflation as an increase in the prices within the economy. However, *price increases are only a symptom* of the increasing money supply. The reason why governments prefer to define inflation as an increase in prices and not in the money supply is simple. If inflation is simply an increase in prices, then how can anyone blame the government? Instead, we should blame those greedy capitalists and businesses who are always trying to raise prices. Don't be fooled. Inflation is an increase in the money supply. The only one to blame is the government and their central banking scheme.

At its most rudimentary level, our current monetary system shares many similarities with our golf ball illustration. In essence, the more scarce the money supply, the lower the price of the goods and services denominated in that currency. The opposite is also true. The more abundant the money supply, the higher the prices will be for the same goods and services. This is because the amount of money within any economy is directly related to, and has a direct effect upon, the prices within that economic system.

Is milk more expensive? If so, either the dairy business is passing on its higher costs to consumers, or more currency has been pumped into the economy.

Has bread become more expensive than it used to be? Either the costs of making bread have gone up, or the government is allowing more currency to be injected into the economy.

Therefore, if the price of everything seems to be going up within a particular economy, ask this question: Is the government increasing the supply of money within the system? In our modern era, the answer is almost always yes, regardless of where you live.

When an increase in a nation's money supply, or inflation, becomes uncontrollable, it is called *hyperinflation*. Hyperinflation is one of the most dangerous economic problems that can confront a nation as it causes dramatic price increases which eventually cripple the underlying economy. Unfortunately, hyperinflation has been at the root of nearly every fiat currency system collapse in history.

A Brief History of Fiat Currencies

Let us now examine several nations that have resorted to the use of fiat currencies throughout history. While all of these experiments with paper currency ended in disaster, let them serve as a testimony and reminder to mankind's tendency toward greed, coupled with his embarrassing inability to rule himself.

Ancient Rome

Our brief journey through the history of fiat money begins in the time of ancient Rome. The story of the rise and fall of the Roman Empire offers a wealth of insights. And while the empire's rise was due to a variety of interesting factors, the reasons for its fall are rather predictable and historically identifiable: significant government overspending, financial greed, an entitlement mentality, and military overextension.

Obviously, the colossal costs of financing the empire's perpetual state of war, plus its numerous public works projects and entitlement programs, required ever-increasing tax revenues. Over time, many could not bear the increasing tax burden and sought relief through tax evasion. As many sought financial relief by opting to evade their taxes, the empire's revenues consistently fell short. Instead of making draconian spending cuts, the empire moved to create a stealth tax that no one could hide from: inflation. (As history will demonstrate, a shortfall in government revenue rarely leads to meaningful cuts in public spending.)

While Rome did not use paper money, the empire still provides one of the first pure examples of currency debasement in history. The official currency of the Roman Empire was the denarius, a metal coin composed of *100 percent pure silver*. The pure silver content of the Roman denarius remained intact until Emperor Nero came to power. In A.D. 64, Rome suffered a great fire, which required a massive urban rebuilding effort. The immense rebuilding costs required more money than the Roman treasury held in reserves. In order to raise adequate funding for the reconstruction, Nero exacted higher tax revenues from Rome's provinces.

But Nero did not stop there. In an effort to raise even more money, the maniacal emperor intimidated coin makers at the mint to *dilute the silver content* in the denarius. To accomplish this, the silver content of the empire's silver coins was melted down and replaced partially with iron or copper. Similarly, the empire's gold coins were diluted and partially replaced with copper. Because the dilution of the silver and gold coin content was done in limited amounts, few citizens noticed the new hybrid coins.

As the empire's financial needs grew, cheaper metals like copper and tin began to replace the gold and silver coins that had once been the empire's currency. Using these cheaper metals meant that more currency could be produced and the money supply could be artificially expanded. The inflationary pressures caused by the increased supply of currency naturally led to higher prices within the Empire.

In A.D. 301, Emperor Diocletian sought to end the increasing prices through price controls. By issuing the Edict of Prices, Diocletian threatened any and all merchants with the death penalty if their prices went above Rome's acceptable range.

Through the debasement of the Empire's currency, the government leaders were able to raise large sums of new money for their pet projects. However, Rome's flirtation with currency debasement became an obsession. By the end of the Roman Empire, a denarius coin was approximately .02 percent silver and 99.98 percent iron! As the Roman currency continued declining in value, merchants and laborers alike shunned its use.[7] The Empire's failed economic policies, coupled with its widespread currency debasement, eventually led to massive hyperinflation and the fall of the Roman Empire.[8]

China

Today, China is an economic powerhouse that has gained the attention of savvy investors from around the world. But relatively few know that this Far East nation was the first to develop paper money. The paper notes, known as the Jiaozi, were originated and issued under the Song Dynasty in the 10th century A.D. Ironically, the purpose for introducing the paper currency was to combat inflationary pressures created by an overproduction of iron coins. To counter the declining value of the iron coins, a bank in the Szechuan province began issuing the paper currency in exchange for the devalued coins. Initially, the new paper money system seemed to be successful. However, it did not take long before the monetary authorities began overproducing the paper currency, causing it to decline in value. The currency was eventually abandoned.[9]

Shortly thereafter, under the Yuan Dynasty, the Chinese attempted another form of paper currency. The Chao, as it was known, lasted for a short time. Its demise came after an extreme overproduction of the currency led to massive hyperinflation.

By the mid-15th century, the Ming Dynasty, apparently unimpressed with the enormous failures caused by their novel monetary experiments, decided this time to completely abandon the use of paper money within the country, choosing instead to return to silver coinage.

France

In 1720, France got a taste of paper money gone awry, thanks in part to Scottish economist John Law and his Mississippi Bubble scheme.

Confronted with massive deficits left to him by his great grandfather (King Louis XIV), King Louis XV was eager to find a way to balance the government's budget. With the nation teetering on the edge of insolvency, John Law convinced King Louis XV to adopt a paper currency and enforce its usage among the public by making it the only acceptable form of payment for taxes. Soon, the paper money became very popular with the French people. After a few wrong turns economically, including an investment scheme in the Louisiana swamplands, France resorted to overprinting the currency. Within four years of the introduction of paper money into the system, France and its citizens went from being impoverished to being fantastically wealthy (on paper), and then back into poverty again. The paper money experiment conducted by Law and King Louis XV completely destroyed the French economy.

But just one generation later, during the French Revolution, France had apparently forgotten the lessons of the past. In 1791, the nation made yet another attempt at issuing a paper currency called the Assignat. By 1795, just four short years later, as the national inflation rate raged at an alarming 13,000 percent, the Assignat became completely worthless. The French Revolution was eventually brought to an end under the strong leadership of Napoleon Bonaparte. Napoleon re-established a gold-backed monetary system in France to replace its failed paper money system, which led the country into an era of prosperity.

Later, in 1936, France nationalized the Bank of France and removed the gold backing from the French currency. The new fiat paper currency that was introduced became completely worthless just over a decade later.

Weimar Republic (Pre-Hitler Germany)

Our next lesson in the dangers of paper money takes us back to a pre-Hitler Germany. Hyperinflation struck the Weimar Republic of Germany in the post-World War I era of the 1920s. At the Treaty of Versailles, Germany accepted its defeat and was forced to pay war reparations to France. War-torn and humiliated, Germany and its frail economy had little hope of being able to repay its enormous war debts. As Germany's reparation payments became increasingly inconsistent, France grew impatient.

Determined to make Germany pay, France led a military invasion into the debt-ridden country in January 1923. French and Belgian troops stormed a German industrial area, known as the Ruhr, where Germany was known to hold much of its wealth. Once the Ruhr had been successfully occupied, the German economy faced even further calamity. The German leaders reacted by printing even more of their increasingly worthless paper money, known as the mark, in order to satiate their French overlords. But as the German government continued to print millions of marks to remain solvent, Germany's citizens began noticing a dramatic increase in their wages. This increase was due to the excess currency that was being created within the system. There are pictures from Germany showing workers being paid with wheelbarrows full of currency. The problem, however, was that the prices of goods and services was growing at a faster rate than wages. For example, in 1922 a loaf of bread cost an average of 160 marks. But by the fall of 1923, the same loaf of bread cost 1,500,000 marks!

As was the case with most nations before them, Germany believed that it could overcome the rising prices by printing even more money. The results, of course, were completely disastrous. Not only did the overproduction of the German mark wipe out much of the German population's life savings, it also caused prices to rise dramatically on life's most basic necessities, like food and clothing. Mass hunger in the nation led to starvation in the poorest communities. Soon, poverty spread to the more affluent communities as the prices of goods and services skyrocketed, with no end in sight. As the German currency became completely worthless, many families found that it made more economic sense to burn the stacks of their marks than to use them to purchase firewood. Others used the marks as decorative wallpaper. And while Germany's bout with hyperinflation was extreme, it provides us with the startling possibilities that can occur when a nation ignores fundamental economic and monetary laws.

In 1924, after their spectacular monetary failure, Germany replaced the mark with a new and improved currency, the "Rentenmark." In addition, France learned that if it sought to regain Germany as a viable economic partner, it must become more reasonable in its debt repayment schedule. These new arrangements provided some much-needed relief to the German government and its people. The good times would not last for long, however. Later, in the wake of the U.S. stock market collapse of 1929, Germany fell into another deep economic depression. This financial meltdown led to another round of social chaos which would ultimately provide the perfect breeding ground for the rise of another one of history's maniacal dictators: Adolf Hitler.

Recent Fiat Failures

It has been demonstrated that history is replete with examples of the failure of fiat currency systems. However, let us now turn to the currency collapses that have occurred in more recent years.

Austria, 1922: Poor monetary policies from 1914 to 1923 led to massive inflation in the post-World War I era of Austria. The Austrian government kept the printing presses running day and night to deal with their growing fiscal crisis. Between January 1921 and August 1922, Austria's currency, known as the crown, suffered a 10,000 percent inflation rate. Eventually, the public's faith in the crown was shattered. By 1924, the Austrian government introduced a new currency to replace the crown, called the shilling. Austria's citizens received one new shilling for every 10,000 crowns that it turned in to the monetary authorities.[10]

Greece, 1944: In 1944, Greece suffered its worst inflation ever. The inflation reached 8.5 billion percent per month! During this period of inflation, prices doubled every 28 hours.

Hungary, 1946: In 1946, Hungary's fiat currency suffered from 4.19 quintillion (4.19 x 1018) percent inflation. (Prices doubled every

15 hours.) Each morning, millions of Hungarians listened to a radio broadcast just to keep up with how much their money was worth that day. This is one of the worst cases of hyperinflation in history.

Israel, 1984: In 1984, after battling inflation for a decade, Israel suffered an inflation rate of 445 percent, which was later tamed by price controls.

Argentina, 1989: The 20th century was economically unkind to the Argentinian people. Despite their immense wealth of natural resources, the country consistently faced massive budget deficits throughout much of the 1980s. Faced with insurmountable debt to foreigners and to Argentina's citizens, the political solution was clear: inflate the currency to pay off the debts. The inflation rate reached levels of over 5,000 percent and soon the country adopted a new currency to replace the old worthless one.

Peru, 1990: In 1990, Peru faced a monthly inflation rate of 397 percent, due to its poor monetary policies.

Norway, 1992: In 1992, Norway, Italy, and Finland experienced major currency problems with their fiat currencies.

Yugoslavia, 1994: From 1993 to 1994, Yugoslavia experienced one of the worst bouts of hyperinflation in history. Mathematical equations are required to measure the height of inflation that struck Yugoslavia during this time. The inflation rate during this period: 5×1015 percent!

Ukraine, 1995: From 1993 to 1995, the country of Ukraine suffered from hyperinflationary pressures. At one point, their inflation rate reached 1,400 percent per month!

Mexico, 1994: In 1994, the Mexican peso collapsed in what was known as "the Tequila Hangover."

Asian Crisis, 1997: In 1997, the Asian Currency Crisis began as Thailand's fiat currency, the baht, collapsed. The effects of the collapse spread to other Far East nations.

Russia, 1998: In 1998, the Russian ruble collapsed. Like Germany's Weimar Republic, Russian workers were paid in wheelbarrows full of rubles. While the situation was far from comical, some in the working class joked about the worthless currency: "We pretend to work and they pretend to pay us."

Turkey, 2001: Beginning in 2001, Turkey experienced major bouts with hyperinflation as its currency, the lira, became increasingly worthless. Currency reform came in 2005, when Turkey issued a new Turkish lira (1 was exchanged for 1,000,000 old lira).

Zimbabwe, 2007: In 2007, after several years of increasing inflation rates, the African nation of Zimbabwe was gripped by massive hyperinflation. By the summer of 2007, the inflation rate was 11,000 percent. One year later, the official monthly inflation figures were over 11,250,000 percent! At this rate of inflation, Zimbabwe residents had to spend their paychecks as soon as they received them just to keep the money from losing its worth.

The Failures of Fiat Money Ignored

While the landscape of world history is littered with failed fiat currencies, history is also replete with vigilant warnings from our ancestors regarding the inherent dangers of fiat currencies. Below I have compiled a list of warnings issued by some of the brightest men in world history regarding the failures of fiat-based money. You will notice some references to gold and silver as a wise backing to a nation's currency. I will explain those references momentarily.

Paper money eventually returns to its intrinsic value — zero. — Voltaire[11]

You have to choose [as a voter] between trusting to the natural stability of gold and the natural stability of the honesty and intelligence of the members of the Government. And, with due respect for these gentlemen, I advise you, as long as the Capitalist system lasts, to vote for gold. — George Bernard Shaw[12]

Sound money still means today what it meant in the nineteenth century: the gold standard. — Ludwig von Mises[13]

Paper money is like dram-drinking, it relieves for a moment by deceitful sensation, but gradually diminishes the natural heat, and leaves the body worse than it found it. Were not this the case, and could money be made of paper at pleasure, every sovereign in Europe would be as rich as he pleased.

But the truth is, that it is a bubble, and the attempt vanity. Nature has provided the proper materials for money: gold and silver, and any attempt of ours to rival her is ridiculous. — Thomas Paine[14]

If you increase the quantity of money, you bring about the lowering of the purchasing power of the monetary unit. — Ludwig von Mises[15]

We are in danger of being overwhelmed with irredeemable paper, mere paper, representing not gold nor silver; no sir, representing nothing but broken promises, bad faith, bankrupt corporations, cheated creditors, and a ruined people. — Daniel Webster[16]

The governments alone are responsible for the spread of the superstitious awe with which the common man looks upon every bit of paper upon which the treasury or agencies which it controls have printed the magical words legal tender. — Ludwig von Mises[17]

Of all the contrivances for cheating the laboring classes of mankind, none has been more effective than that which deludes them with paper money. — Daniel Webster[18]

Based upon the preceding quotes and all that is known from recorded history, it is hardly conceivable as to why our modern society would dare to build and hold the majority of its wealth in a fiat paper money system. Yet today, *every economy in the world uses a fiat currency!* Why would nations place their wealth near the precarious cliffs of a fiat currency system? If fiat currencies have a 100 percent chance of failure, then why do modern governments even consider them?

One obvious answer is human greed. Fiat currency systems allow governments, businesses, and consumers to spend more than they actually have. This is because modern fiat money is debt-based money. Today's monetary systems are based and rooted in debt. In fact, money itself is simply debt. While many financial commentators are quick to point out that you should "get out of debt," this book is going to explain that the money you hold in your pocket is debt itself. The current system is entirely flawed. How all of this is possible is completely exposed in chapter 7 ("Modern Money Mechanics: What the Banksters Do Not Want You to Know"). In that chapter, I will unveil another possible reason why nations have opted for fiat currencies over more sound and honest money. What we will discover in that chapter will be shocking, to say the least.

Insanity has been defined as doing the same thing over and over again but expecting a different result. Considering the consistent failures of fiat currency systems throughout history, you may find yourself asking why the world has not created a better monetary system by now. The answer is not easy to find, but it can be found. Solutions do not magically appear simply because a problem exists. Solutions are created only when enough people ask the question and demand an answer.

The Biblical View of Fiat Currencies

One of the tragedies of our modern day is found in the passivity of the population regarding its government's monetary policy. For the most part, economic literacy levels are at all-time lows around the world. Part of this is due to the increasing complexity of the global financial systems. But it is also due to a growing apathy among the citizenry of various nations. This apathy has allowed government to grow, both in size and in strength, virtually unchecked. The larger the government, the more severe the problems eventually become.

For people of faith the solution to our modern financial crisis is not found in political or economic activism, but rather in simple awareness. This awareness of the monetary system has traditionally been rejected by faith-based communities on the grounds that money is an unspiritual topic. For example, many evangelical Christians have completely shunned economic awareness in the name of spirituality. This is staggering, especially when one considers that the founder of Christianity, Jesus Christ, had more to say about money and possessions than any other topic, including faith, hope, heaven, and hell combined! In fact, over 2,350 verses of the Christian Bible contain a reference to money, wealth, and possessions. Obviously, financial matters are an important topic to the Christian faith.

Considering that the Bible has so much to say about the topic of money, is it possible that it has anything to say about fiat currencies? While this may seem like a strange question, you may be surprised to find that the Bible has a very strong opinion on the topic of fiat currencies. Of course, you will find no scriptural reference to the word "fiat." That is because this is a relatively modern word. Instead of denouncing fiat currencies, the Bible condemns what it calls "unjust weights and balances." Interestingly, this phrase is a *direct reference* to the concept used to manipulate fiat currencies in our modern era. Allow me to explain.

In ancient times, business and commerce were conducted through the use of scales and measures. For example, if a person needed a pound of grain, he would go to the local grain merchant with an acceptable form of payment. The merchant would then weigh out a pound of grain on his scale. When the Bible denounces "unjust weights and balances," it is referring to the unscrupulous merchants who swindle the average consumer through the use of inaccurate scales and balances. By readjusting their scales in their own favor, merchants could easily cheat and deceive their customers. The Bible obviously takes issue with this practice, equating it with thievery. Apparently, this was a pervasive problem in ancient times as the Bible condemns the practice on numerous occasions.

> Proverbs 11:1 — "Dishonest scales are an abomination to the LORD, but a just weight is His delight."

> Proverbs 20:10 — "Diverse weights and diverse measures, they are both alike, an abomination to the LORD."

In Leviticus 19:35–36, the Bible instructs the Israelites that all of their economic transactions (buying and selling) should be conducted with honest weights. "You shall do no wrong in judgment, in measurement of weight, or capacity. You shall have just balances, just weights . . ." (NASB).

Obviously, the Bible expressly forbids the unscrupulous practice of using "unjust weights" and "false balances." In our highly advanced modern economy, we may be tempted to think that unjust weights and balances are an irrelevant practice of the past that no longer applies to us. But is this true? And if not, what would an example of this practice in our modern world look like?

I would suggest to you that fiat currencies perfectly fit the biblical definition of an "unjust weight" and a "false balance." But before I explain how, let's consider some other modern examples that are easier to grasp, using automobiles.

One example of a "false balance" would be if an automotive mechanic were to charge you for installing a new part on your vehicle but secretly installed an old used part. That would be considered a "false balance" by biblical definition.

Here's another example: Imagine that an auto dealer secretly manipulated the odometers on their vehicles so that they would display fewer miles than the engine actually had in order to charge a higher price. This would clearly be an example of an unjust weight and balance.

Likewise, a "false balance" would include our current fiat-based monetary system where the currency is backed by nothing but debt and can be printed at will. In fact, each one of the cases of hyperinflation discussed in this chapter provides a classic example of a biblical "false balance." The governments of each of these countries violated biblical principles regarding just weights and balances when they began destroying the purchasing power and life savings of their citizens.

A fiat currency system, in which the currency is backed by nothing and its value can be manipulated at will, is by definition an unjust weight. And so therefore, by biblical definition, fiat currency systems are clearly unjust systems.

What a tragedy it is that Christianity de-emphasizes economic literacy among the faithful, thus allowing its billions of adherents to misunderstand one of the most basic of biblical principles. This economic ignorance on the part of Christians is even more pronounced when one realizes that they are the ones insisting that the absurd statement, "In God We Trust," remain upon the nation's fiat currency. Based upon a proper biblical understanding of fiat currencies, I would say that it is highly unlikely that the God of the Bible is interested in having His name plastered on such an "abomination" as the fiat U.S. dollar. How the faith-based community fails to comprehend this is beyond me.

To further understand America's currency system of "unjust weights and balances," consider these two very different dollar bills.

1923 One Dollar Bill
(Silver Certificate)

Notice what the 1923 U.S. dollar says at the top of the bill: Silver Certificate: This certifies that there has been deposited in the treasury of the United States of America.

Then notice toward the bottom of the bill it states: One silver dollar payable to the bearer on demand.

What does this mean? It simply means that the owner of this dollar bill could trade it in at any time for one dollar's worth of silver. This is because in 1923, the dollar was a form of receipt money which could be redeemed in a fixed rate for gold or silver.

Compare the above language to a modern U.S. dollar as seen below. Notice that the language on the front of this U.S. dollar bill has

Modern U.S. Dollar Bill (Federal Reserve Note)

Did You Know?

On April 2, 1792, the United States Congress passed the Coinage Act. This act established the United States Mint and regulated coinage of the United States. President George Washington and the Congress strongly detested paper currencies and therefore made special provisions within the act to ensure that anyone who attempted to debase the currency would be put to death. Ironically, today George Washington's face is plastered on the front of the fiat U.S. one dollar bill — the same kind of currency that would have brought the death penalty just two short centuries ago.

changed. At the top, it simply states: Federal Reserve Note. And at the bottom, the language has changed from One Silver Dollar payable to the bearer on demand to simply One Dollar.

The difference between these two dollar bills is a visual representation of America's shift from receipt money to fiat money. You should try taking these modern "Federal Reserve Notes" into your local bank and asking the bank teller for some silver in exchange. You will either be laughed out, or thrown out, of the bank.

In summary, today's U.S. dollar is a completely worthless piece of paper that derives its value through the faith of the public and the policies dictated in Washington. Isn't it amazing that after all of the fiat failures throughout history, here we are standing at the same cliff of disaster yet again?

Quick Summary

✓ Fiat currencies require an enormous amount of faith and trust in the monetary authorities by the public.

✓ Inflation is defined as an increase in a nation's money supply.

✓ Hyperinflation occurs when a nation's money supply becomes out of control.

✓ Every fiat currency devised throughout history has faced the same embarrassing and miserable death: *utter collapse by overproduction.*

✓ While the landscape of world history is littered with failed fiat currencies, history is also replete with warnings from our ancestors regarding the inherent dangers of fiat currencies.

✓ Biblically speaking, fiat currencies are modern versions of "unjust weights" and "false balances."

Endnotes

1. John Maynard Keynes, *The Economic Consequences of the Peace* (Charleston, SC: BiblioBazaar, LLC, 2008), p. 168.

2. Mark Watterson, *Don't Weep for Me, America: How Democracy in America Became the Prince* (Pittsburgh, PA: Dorrance Publishing, 2008), p. 68.

3. George Selgin, "Adaptive Learning and the Transition to Fiat Money," *The Economic Journal* 113 (484) (2002): 147–65.

4. *Scientific Market Analysis, The Nightmare German Inflation* (Princeton, NJ: Scientific Market Analysis, 1970).

5. *Saturday Review*, editorial, April 15, 1978.

6. Bob Davis, *Whatever Happened to High School History?* (Ontario: James Lorimer & Company, 1995).

7. "Roman Currency of the Principate," Tulane University, http://www.tulane.edu/~august/handouts/601cprin.htm.

8. Addison Wiggin, *The Demise of the Dollar — And Why It's Even Better for Your Investments*, Chuck Butler, contributor (England: John Wiley and Sons, 2008), p. 59.

9. Dave Ramsden, "A Very Short History of Chinese Paper Money," June 17, 2004, http://www.financialsense.com/fsu/editorials/ramsden/2004/0617.html.

10. Richard M. Ebeling, *The Great Austrian Inflation*, http://www.fee.org/pdf/the-freeman/0604RMEbeling.pdf.

11. Moriah Saul, *Plantation Earth: The Cross of Iron and the Chains of Debt* (Canada: Trafford Publishing, 2003), p. 24.

12. Herbert G. Grubel, *World Monetary Reform: Plans and Issues* (Stanford, CA: Stanford University Press, 1963), p. 333.

13. Ludwig von Mises, Percy L. Greaves, trans., *On the Manipulation of Money and Credit* (Dobbs Ferry, NY: Free Market Books, 1978), p. 279.

14. Michael Foot and Isaac Kramnick, editors, *Thomas Paine Reader* (New York: Penguin Classics, 1987), p. 197.

15. Ludwig von Mises, *Economic Policy: Thoughts for Today and Tomorrow* (Auburn, AL: Ludwig von Mises Institute, 2006), p. 66.

16. *The Works of Daniel Webster* (Boston, MA: Little, Brown, 1890), p. 413.

17. Ludwig von Mises, *Human Action: A Treatise on Economics* (Chicago, IL: Contemporary Books, 1949), p. 448.

18. Forrest Capie, *Major Inflations in History* (Brookfield, VT: E. Elgar Pub., 1991), p. 304.

Chapter 3

The Rise and Fall of the Golden Permission Slip

Gold still represents the ultimate form of payment in the world.

— Alan Greenspan, Testimony before U.S.
House Banking Committee, May 1999

"The silver is Mine, and the gold is Mine,"
says the LORD of hosts.

— Haggai 2:8

OVERVIEW: The entire global economic order was shattered after the devastation of World War II. Re-establishing economic stability was of vital concern to global leaders. A plan for restoring order to the international economic community came at a historic conference held in July 1944 in the state of New Hampshire. More commonly known as the Bretton Woods conference, the meeting created a new global fixed exchange rate regime with a gold-backed U.S. dollar playing a central role. This is the story of the rise and fall of this "dollars for gold" system.

The "Economic" D-Day of 1944

When historians write about the year 1944, it is often dominated with references to the tragedies and triumphs of World War II. And while 1944 was truly a pivotal year in one of history's most devastating conflicts of all time, it was also a significant year for the international economic system. With Europe in shambles, and Britain on the proverbial "ropes," global leaders resolved to restore confidence and order to the financial markets. Creating viable solutions to fix the global economic instability would require international cooperation.

In July 1944, the United Nations Monetary and Financial Conference (more commonly known as the Bretton Woods conference) was held at the Mount Washington hotel in Bretton Woods, New Hampshire, with 730 delegates from 44 Allied nations attending. The express purpose of the historic gathering was to regulate the war-torn international economic system. Among other things, this would require determining a replacement of the British currency for the purposes of settling international transactions. Due to the sizeable gold reserves held by the United States, the attendees were keenly aware that the dollar was the only currency that could potentially replace the role of the now weakened British pound. The participants agreed to a new currency arrangement, known as a fixed exchange rate regime, with the U.S. dollar playing a central role. Under this new arrangement, which economists commonly refer to as the Bretton Woods system, the U.S. dollar would be linked to gold at a pre-determined fixed rate of $35 per ounce. In turn, all other currencies were then pegged to the dollar, as it was viewed as being as "good as gold." This immediate convertibility from U.S. dollars into a fixed amount of gold brought much-needed economic relief and helped to restore confidence in the global financial markets.

As the nation entrusted with the issuance the global reserve currency, the United States emerged as the lone economic victor in the

---

Quick Fact

In addition to establishing the U.S. dollar as the global reserve currency, this historic conference also initiated a number of new government institutions, including:
- The World Bank
- The International Monetary Fund (IMF)
- The World Trade Organization (originally called the General Agreement on Trades and Tariffs, or GATT)

The Bretton Woods Arrangement
(Can you say "Middleman"?)

Foreign Currency	U.S. Dollar	Gold

Source: ftmdaily.com

post–World War II era. In fact, one senior official at the Bank of England described the deal reached at Bretton Woods as "the greatest blow to Britain next to the war." Why? The Bretton Woods system provided immense power to the emerging American economic empire as global currency demand shifted from the British pound to the U.S. dollar.

Bretton Woods Conference

John Maynard Keynes (right) represented the UK at the conference, and Harry Dexter White represented the United States.

Bretton Woods — The Changing of the Guard

At the end of the 19th century, the city of London was the capital of a global superpower. Through its aggressive and systematic colonization efforts, the British Empire had been able to dominate and control more geography than any previous empire before it. At the height of its rule, it was accurately stated that "the sun never set" on the British Empire. Put simply, Great Britain was the largest economic empire the world had ever seen. Its financial and military prowess made the empire's official currency, the British Pound Sterling, the most sought-after currency on earth. But like most empires before it, military overextension and economic arrogance left Great Britain ripe for replacement by a leaner and more nimble competitor. By the end of World War II, Britain's excesses had nearly sealed its fate. Along with the rest of the European community, the British Empire was left economically devastated. The economic challenger that would rise to the occasion to fill the economic vacuum was none other than the United States of America.

At this point, an appropriate question to be asking is: "Why would Britain and all of these other nations be willing to allow the value of their currencies to be dependent upon the value of U.S. dollar?"

The answer is quite simple: they didn't really have a choice. These war-weary nations were broke. And there was literally no other currency, outside of the dollar, that was able to fill the growing demands of the global economic system. The fact that nations could convert their dollars into gold at a fixed rate of $35 per ounce helped alleviate concerns about the dollar's new global role. After all, the Bretton Woods system did provide nations with an escape hatch in the event they had buyer's remorse. If a particular nation no longer felt comfortable with the dollar, they could easily convert their dollar holdings into gold and sit on the economic sidelines. While this flexibility helped restore a much-needed stability in the global financial system, it also accomplished one other very important thing: the Bretton Woods agreement instantly created a strong global demand for U.S. dollars as the preferred medium of exchange for settling international transactions.

And along with this growing *demand* for U.S. dollars came the need for . . . a larger *supply* of dollars.

Now that I have explained how the U.S. dollar was crowned as the global reserve currency in 1944, let us turn to the benefits of such an arrangement.

The Golden "Permission Slip"

To fully appreciate the economic benefits that the United States derives from its enviable role as the holder of the world's reserve currency requires an understanding of why a global demand for dollars is beneficial.

To illustrate, imagine that right now I have listed a beautiful beachfront home for sale at a price of $2 million. Now also imagine that we could instantly decrease the total money supply within the U.S. economy to a mere $1 million dollars. What would happen to the value of my home for sale? It would drop dramatically! Why? Is my home suddenly become less valuable? No. Instead, the decline in my home's value was directly caused by the sudden decrease in the overall money supply within the economy. It would be impossible for me to ask for $2 million for my home because, in our imaginary economy, there is now only $1 million in existence.

More Dollars, Higher Prices

In an economy with a total of $1 million dollars in circulation, a house could never be worth $2 million dollars.

But, in an economy with a total of $1 trillion dollars in circulation, you could have thousands of homes worth $2 million dollars.

And as we have already explained, printing more dollars leads to an increase of asset prices. In essence, more dollars leads to higher prices within the economy. So, if an increase in the overall money supply causes asset prices to rise, then what effect does an increasing global demand for dollars have on an economy? In essence, it gives the U.S. government a "permission slip" to print more dollars. After all, we can't let our global friends down, can we? If they "need" dollars, then let's print some more dollars for them.

Is it a coincidence that printing dollars is the U.S. government's preferred method of dealing with our nation's economic problems today? The U.S. government only has four basic ways to solve its economic problems:

1. Increase income by *raising taxes* on the citizens
2. *Cut government spending* by reducing public benefits
3. *Borrow money* through the issuance of government bonds
4. *Print money*

It should be obvious that raising taxes and reducing spending can be political suicide. Borrowing money is a politically convenient option, but the government can only borrow so much. So that leaves the government with the final option of printing money. Printing money is a unique, albeit temporary, solution that requires no immediate economic sacrifice and no spending cuts. Therefore, it is the perfect solution for a country run by morally weak leaders who desperately want to avoid making any sacrifices. But as we explained in a previous section, a monetary policy that relies upon the continued printing of money places the nation at great risk of huge inflation.

Q: So how has the United States been able to avoid suffering from massive inflation despite their continued reliance upon reckless money-printing campaigns?

A: Through the "permission slip" to print excessive amounts of dollars it was given as a result of the Bretton Woods system.

The only reason that the United States can print so much money without experiencing huge inflation is because the Bretton Woods system created a global demand for dollars. Understanding this "permission slip" concept, and how the United States has abused it will be very important as we continue.

Have you ever asked yourself why the U.S. dollar is called a Federal Reserve *note*? Once again, the answer is simple. The U.S. Dollar is *issued and loaned* to the United States government by the Federal Reserve Bank. Because our dollars are *loaned* to our government by the Federal Reserve, which is a private central banking cartel that I will explain in much more detail later in this book, the dollars must be *paid back*. And not only must the dollars be paid back to the Federal Reserve; they must be paid back *with interest*!

And who sets the interest rate targets on the loaned dollars? *The Federal Reserve.*

Reader Question

Q: Who benefits from this continual global demand for dollars? (Ron T., Sacramento, CA)

A: Ron, there are several. The U.S. government benefits from the ability to create money out of thin air. Politicians benefit as global dollar demand gives them a convenient way to finance their excessive spending. U.S. citizens benefit from rising asset prices, although these are tempered by the creeping amounts of inflation created through such money printing.

However, by far the largest beneficiary of global dollar demand is America's central bank, the Federal Reserve. If this does not make immediate sense, then pull out a dollar bill from your wallet or purse and notice whose name is plastered right on the top of it.

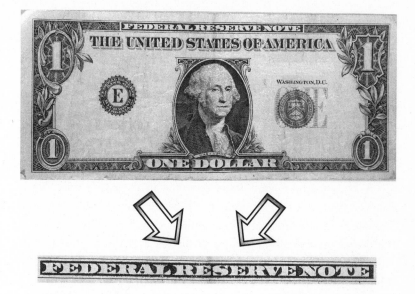

Clearly, the Federal Reserve, or the "Fed," as it is so affectionately called, has a vested interest in maintaining a stable and growing global demand for dollars. After all, they create the dollars, loan the dollars at interest to the U.S. government, and then set their own interest rates! What a wonderfully profitable venture the Federal Reserve has created for itself. It should be obvious why the Fed has consistently despised any congressional oversight and has blocked any and all attempts to have its records audited by any outside parties.

The Bretton Woods Breakdown

$$\frac{\text{The Vietnam War} + \text{The Great Society}}{\text{Massive Deficit Spending}}$$

In summary, the American consumer, the federal government, and the Federal Reserve all benefit from a global demand for U.S. dollars.

There is an old saying that goes, "He who holds the gold makes the rules." This statement has never been more true than in the case of America in the post–World War II era. By the end of the war, nearly 80 percent of the world's gold was sitting in U.S. vaults. And thanks to the Bretton Woods agreement, the U.S. dollar had officially become the world's undisputed reserve currency and was considered by most nations to be "as good as gold."

A study of the United States economy in the post-World War II era demonstrates an era of dramatic economic growth and expansion. The monetary and political leverage gained through the Bretton Woods agreement catapulted the United States to a position of economic supremacy on the global stage. The late 1940s through the early 1960s, commonly known as the Baby Boom generation for its explosive birth rate, gave rise to the one of the most prosperous eras in America's history.

Did You Know?

Until 1965, the only way to earn a living from the United States government was to be elderly or disabled. But under the Great Society program, dependency by American citizens upon government "assistance" reached new heights.

By the mid-1960s, however, the U.S. economy came under growing economic pressure as Washington began abusing its global reserve currency status through their adoption of a "warfare and welfare" mentality. Under the heavy-handed presidency of Lyndon B. Johnson, a new federal government spending spree began, known as the Great Society program. This big government agenda, promoted to Congress by Johnson in January 1965, sought to provide new federal funding for public education, a so-called war on poverty, urban renewal, conservation, and crime prevention.

In addition to confronting a whole host of social issues, Johnson created two new government-run systems: Medicare and Medicaid. Medicare provided government-subsidized health insurance for the elderly while Medicaid gave lower income households access to government-sponsored healthcare. With the creation of these two entitlement programs, American citizens could now, for the first time, earn a living from their government.

While the United States was busy creating a large amount of handouts for its citizens, it was simultaneously waging an undeclared war in Vietnam, at an estimated $5.1 billion per month. By the late 1960s and early 1970s, America had suffered large numbers of casualties. According to most estimates, the Vietnam War had a price tag in excess of $200 billion, which placed a severe strain upon the national economy.

So how did the United States pay for its growing warfare and welfare state? It simply borrowed the money, also known as deficit spending. As Washington's deficit spending spiraled out of control, inflationary pressures became a growing threat and the United States was confronted with its first trade deficit of the 20th century.

An expensive and unpopular war in Vietnam and record government handouts to the American public, funded by outrageous levels of deficit spending, led some nations to rightfully question the economic competence of America. After all, the Bretton Woods system had made the entire global economic order dependent upon a fiscally sound U.S. economy.

As the economic and political turmoil took its toll on America during the late 1960s, nations who had willingly placed their hopes on a stable U.S. dollar began losing confidence in America's financial stewardship. This declining faith in America's willingness to get its fiscal house in order led to massive pressure on the "gold for dollars" system that had been established at Bretton Woods.

By 1971, as America's trade deficits increased and domestic spending soared, a growing number of nations who believed that the United States was abusing its leadership role within the global economy began publicly challenging the United States by demanding gold in exchange for their dollar holdings.

Did You Know?

Throughout history, gold has been, and will likely remain, the beneficiary of poor fiscal and monetary policies. The death of the Bretton Woods system in 1971 was no different.

And while America's growing fiscal recklessness concerned the international economic community, what alarmed them most was the growing imbalance of U.S. gold reserves to its debt levels. Clearly, America had never intended to be the globe's gold warehouse. Instead, the convertibility of the dollar into gold was meant to generate a global trust in U.S. paper money. Simply knowing that the U.S. dollar could be converted into gold if necessary was good enough for some — but not for everyone. The nations who began to doubt America's ability to manage their own finances decided to opt for the recognized safety of gold.

As 1971 progressed, so did foreign demand for U.S. gold. Foreign central banks began cashing in their excess dollars in exchange for gold. As America's gold reserves declined, dollars came flooding back into the U.S. economy. By the summer of 1971, the U.S. was bleeding gold. Washington realized that the game was over.

Reader Question

Q: Could the United States have prevented the breakdown of the Bretton Woods arrangement if it had wanted to? If so, how? (Tom D., Las Vegas, NV)

A: Good question, Tom. You would think that the large and growing demand by foreign nations for gold instead of dollars would have been a strong indicator to the United States to clean up its act and get its fiscal house in order. Instead, America did exactly the opposite. As Washington continued racking up enormous debts to fund its imperial pursuits and its overconsumption, foreign nations sped up their demand for more U.S. gold and fewer U.S. dollars. Washington was caught in its own trap and was required to supply real money (gold) in return for the inflows of their fake paper money (U.S. dollar). They had been hamstrung by their own imperialistic policies. Washington knew that the system was no longer viable, and certainly not sustainable. But what could they do to stem the crisis? Did they have any options? Yes, but there were really only two options.

The first option required that Washington immediately reduce its massive spending and dramatically reduce its existing debts. This option could possibly restore confidence in the long-term viability of the U.S. economy. The second option would be to increase the dollar price of gold to accurately reflect the new economic realities. But there was an inherent flaw in both of these options that made them unacceptable to the United States at the time — they both required fiscal restraint and economic responsibility. Then, as now, there was very little appetite for reducing consumption in the name of "sacrifice" or "responsibility."

The Shock Heard Around the World

The Bretton Woods system of 1944 created an international gold standard with the U.S. dollar as the ultimate beneficiary. But in an ironic twist of fate, the agreement that was designed to bring stability to a war-torn global economy was the very system that threatened to plunge the world back into financial chaos by the early 1970s. The "dollars for gold" standard of Bretton Woods simply could not bear the financial excesses, coupled with the imperialistic pursuits, of the American economic empire.

By 1971, Washington insiders knew that "dollars for gold" was no longer sustainable. In the first six months of that year, over $20 billion of assets had left the country as foreign nations expressed their deep distrust in Washington's financial stewardship. In May, West Germany completely abandoned the Bretton Woods system, which led to an immediate rise in the value of its currency over the U.S. dollar. In July, Switzerland converted nearly $50 million back into gold. France was particularly aggressive and demanded nearly $200 million in gold.

On August 15, 1971, under the leadership of President Richard M. Nixon, Washington chose to maintain its reckless consumption and debt patterns by detaching the U.S. dollar from its convertibility into gold. By "closing the gold window," Nixon destroyed the final vestiges of the international gold standard. Nixon's decision effectively ended the practice of exchanging dollars for gold, as directed under the Bretton Woods agreement. It was in this year, 1971, that the U.S. dollar officially abandoned the gold standard and was declared a purely fiat currency.

Did You Know?

Since August 15, 1971, all global currencies (with the temporary exception of the Swiss franc) have been issued by fiat with no real commodity backing of any kind.

Goodbye, Yellow Brick Road

As all other fiat empires before it, Washington eventually came to view gold as a constraint to its colossal spending urges. A gold standard, like the one provided by the Bretton Woods system, required

The Nixon Shock

Want to watch an excerpt of the actual televised speech delivered by President Nixon on August 15, 1971, in which he ended the U.S. dollar's convertibility into gold? Go online to http://www.ftmdaily.com/nixonshock.

America to publicly demonstrate fiscal restraint by maintaining holistic economic balance.

By "closing the gold window," Washington had affected not only American economic policy — it also affected global economic policy. Under the international gold standard of Bretton Woods, all currencies derived their value from the dollar. And the dollar derived its value from the fixed price of its gold reserves. But when the dollar's value was detached from gold in 1971, it became what economists call a "floating" currency. (By "floating," it is meant that a currency is not attached, nor does it derive its value, from anything externally.) Put simply, a "floating" currency is a currency that is not fixed in value.

Like any commodity, the dollar could be affected by the market forces of supply and demand. When the dollar became a "floating" currency in 1971, the rest of the world's currencies, which had been previously fixed to the dollar, suddenly became "floating" currencies as well.

In this new era of floating currencies, the U.S. Federal Reserve, America's central bank, had finally freed itself from the constraint of a gold standard. Now, the U.S. dollar could be printed at will — without the fear of having enough gold reserves to back up new currency production. And while this newfound monetary freedom would alleviate pressure on America's gold reserves, Washington was quick to recognize that this seismic shift in economic policy could eventually lead to a declining global demand for the U.S. dollar. After all, the primary reason that the world had so readily held dollars in reserve was due to its international convertibility into gold. With the dollar no longer convertible into gold, how long would it be before global dollar demand declined?

Did You Know?

Floating currencies, with floating exchange rates, attract manipulation by speculators and hedge funds. Currency speculation is, and remains, a threat to floating currencies. Proponents of a single global currency point to the ongoing manipulation of currencies to promote their agenda.

Strong global demand for a nation's currency can help a nation grow from a small economy to a vast empire. This global demand for dollars, which had fueled America's prosperity and had allowed it to continue its warfare and welfare policies, was now seriously threatened.

Another concern facing Washington had to do with America's extravagant spending habits. Under the international gold standard of Bretton Woods, foreign nations willingly held U.S. debt securities because they were denominated in gold-backed U.S. dollars. Would foreign nations still be eager to hold America's debts despite the fact that these debts were denominated in a fiat debt-based currency that was backed by nothing?

The elites in Washington were not interested in learning the answers. Instead, they took swift action to ensure global demand for the dollar would not be permanently affected by its new "fiat" and "non-convertible" status.

Enter the *petrodollar system.*

Quick Summary

✓ The devastation of the global economic order in the wake of World War II led world leaders to form a conference to create solutions. This conference, known as Bretton Woods, led to the creation of a new global fixed exchange rate regime with the U.S. dollar playing a central role.

✓ Under the Bretton Woods system, an ounce of gold could be purchased at a fixed international rate of $35 per ounce. Because this fixed rate was regulated, the U.S. dollar was considered "as good as gold."

✓ This new international "dollars for gold" system created under Bretton Woods restored global economic stability to war-weary economies. As a result, foreign nations pegged their currencies to the dollar with the ability to convert their dollar holdings to gold at any time.

✓ In the late 1960s, the Bretton Woods system broke down as foreign nations cashed in their dollars for gold. This was largely due to global concern over Washington's reliance upon deficit spending to fund its warfare and welfare policies.

✓ On August 15, 1971, President Richard Nixon closed the international gold window, which ended the Bretton Woods system and the dollar's convertibility to gold. It was on this day that virtually every global currency became fiat, with no commodity backing.

Chapter 4

The Petrodollar System: Same Game with a New Name

I hereby find that the defense of Saudi Arabia
is vital to the defense of the United States.[1]
— Franklin D. Roosevelt, U.S. president 1933–1945

There is nothing new in the world except the history
you do not know.[2]
— President Harry Truman

OVERVIEW: In 1971, the Bretton Woods system collapsed after Washington severed the link between the dollar and the international gold standard. The United States was acutely aware that the failure of the "dollars for gold" arrangement could potentially strike a major blow to global dollar demand. In response to these concerns, and with the protection of global demand for the dollar as their highest priority, Washington soon unleashed its craftiest ploy yet: the petrodollar system. With global demand for oil increasing, the Nixon administration held a series of high-level talks with Saudi Arabia and other oil-producing nations, with the goal of requiring every global oil sale to be priced in dollars. In exchange, Washington offered military assistance and protection for the region's vast oil fields. In this chapter lies the origin of our modern global economy. It is a story that few Americans have heard.

"Dollars for Oil" Replaces "Dollars for Gold"

In the early 1970s, the final vestiges of the international gold-backed dollar standard, known as the Bretton Woods system, had collapsed. Many foreign nations, who had previously agreed to a gold-backed dollar as the global reserve currency, were now having serious mixed feelings toward the arrangement. Nations like Britain, France, and Germany determined that a cash-strapped and debt-crazed United States was in no financial shape to be leading the global economy. They were just a few of the many nations who began demanding gold in exchange for their dollars.

Despite pressure from foreign nations to protect the dollar's value by reining in excessive government spending, Washington displayed little fiscal constraint and continued to live far beyond its means. It had become obvious to all that America lacked the basic fiscal discipline that could prevent a destruction of its own currency. Like previous governments before it, America had figured out how to "game" the global reserve currency system for its own benefit, leaving foreign nations in an economically vulnerable position.

It is unfair, however, to say that the Washington elites were blind to the deep economic issues confronting it in the late 1960s and early 1970s. Washington knew that the "dollars for gold" had become completely unsustainable. But instead of seeking solutions to the global economic imbalances that had been created by America's excessive deficits, Washington's primary concern was how to gain an even greater stranglehold on the global economy.

After America, and its citizens, had tasted the sweet fruit of excessive living at the expense of other nations, there was no turning back.

But in order to maintain global dollar demand, the Washington elites needed a plan. In order for this plan to succeed, it would require that the artificial dollar demand that had been lost in the wake of the Bretton Woods collapse be replaced through some other mechanism.

That plan came in the form of something known as *the petrodollar system*. To understand the petrodollar system, let us begin by defining what a petrodollar is: a *petrodollar* is a U.S. dollar that is received by an oil producer in exchange for selling oil and that is then deposited into Western banks.

Despite the seeming simplicity of this arrangement of "dollars for oil," the petrodollar system is actually highly complex and one with many moving parts. It is this complexity that prevents the petrodollar system from being properly understood by the American public.

If you have never heard of the petrodollar system, it would not surprise me. It is certainly not a topic that makes its way out of Washington circles too often. The mainstream media rarely, if ever, discusses the inner workings of the petrodollar system and how it has motivated, and even guided, America's foreign policy in the Middle East for the last several decades.

Allow me to provide a very basic overview regarding the history and the mechanics of the petrodollar system. It is my belief that once you understand this "dollars for oil" arrangement, you will gain a more accurate understanding of what motivates America's economic (and especially foreign) policy. So, let's take a closer look. . . .

The Rise of the Petrodollar System

The petrodollar system originated in the early 1970s in the wake of the Bretton Woods collapse.

President Richard M. Nixon and his globalist sidekick, Secretary of State Henry Kissinger, knew that their destruction of the international gold standard under the Bretton Woods arrangement would cause a decline in the artificial global demand of the U.S. dollar. Maintaining this *artificial dollar demand* was vital if the United States were to continue expanding its welfare and warfare spending.

U.S. Secretary of State Henry Kissinger worked his diplomatic "magic" in Saudi Arabia to create the petrodollar system.

In a series of meetings, the United States — represented by then U.S. Secretary of State Henry Kissinger — and the Saudi royal family made a unique agreement.[3]

According to the agreement, the United States would offer military protection for Saudi Arabia's oil fields. The United States also agreed to provide the Saudis with military assistance, weapons, and perhaps most importantly, protection from Israel's growing military arsenal.

The Saudi royal family knew a good deal when they saw one. They were more than happy to accept American military protection of their oil fields along with assurances of intervention between themselves and neighboring Israel.

Naturally, the Saudis wondered how much was all of this U.S. military muscle was going to cost. . . . What exactly did the United States want in exchange for their weapons and military protection? The Americans laid out their terms. They were simple, and two-fold.

> 1) The Saudis must agree to price *all* of their oil sales in U.S. dollars only. (In other words, the Saudis were to refuse all other currencies, except the U.S. dollar, as payment for their oil exports.)

> 2) The Saudis would be open to investing their surplus oil proceeds in U.S. debt securities.

You can almost hear one of the Saudi officials in a meeting saying: "Really? That's all? You don't want any of our money or direct ownership of our oil? You just want to tell us how to price our oil and then you will give us military support and protection from our enemies? You've got a deal!"

Oil producing nations get:
- Weapons
- Military protection

The United States gets:
- Oil priced in dollars
(creates artificial demand)
- Artificial demand for U.S. Treasuries

The Petrodollar System 101

Source: ftmdaily.com

However, the United States had done its homework. They knew that gaining economic favor with the Saudis would be a good start to maintaining their dollar hegemony.

Fast forward to 1974, and the petrodollar system was fully operational in Saudi Arabia. And as the United States had perhaps cleverly calculated, it did not take long before other oil-producing nations wanted in. By 1975, *all* of the oil-producing nations of OPEC had agreed to price their oil in dollars and to hold their surplus oil proceeds in U.S. government debt securities in exchange for the generous offers by the United States. Just dangle weapons, military aid, and protection from Israel in front of Third World, oil-rich, Middle East nations . . . and let the bidding begin.

Nixon and Kissinger had succeeded in bridging the gap between the failed Bretton Woods system and the new petrodollar system. The global artificial demand for U.S. dollars would not only remain intact, it would soar due to the increasing demand for oil around the world in the decades to come. And from the perspective of empire, this new "dollars for oil" system was much preferred to the former "dollars for gold" system because it had much less stringent economic requirements. Without the constraints imposed by a rigid gold standard, and with global oil transactions on the rise, the U.S. monetary base could be grown at exponential rates.

It should come as no surprise that the United States maintains a major military presence in much of the oil-rich Persian Gulf region to this day, including the following countries: Bahrain, Iraq, Kuwait, Oman, Qatar, Saudi Arabia, United Arab Emirates, Egypt, Israel, Jordan, and Yemen.

The truth is hard to find when you look to the corporate-controlled mainstream media. But it is simple when you follow the money. . . .

"I hereby find that the defense of Saudi Arabia is vital to the defense of the United States."
            —President Franklin D. Roosevelt

How the Petrodollar System Encourages Cheap Exports to the United States

While the U.S./Saudi agreement may have smelled of desperation at a time of decreasing global dollar demand, it can now be considered one of the most brilliant geopolitical and economic strategies in recent political memory.

Today, virtually all global oil transactions are settled in U.S. dollars. (There are a few exceptions and they will be highlighted in our next chapter, appropriately titled "Petrodollar Wars.") When a country does not have a surplus of U.S. dollars, it must create a strategy to obtain them in order to buy oil.

The easiest way to obtain U.S. dollars is through the foreign exchange markets. This is not, however, a viable long-term solution as it is cost-prohibitive.

The Petrodollar System
(How long can this system last?)

Foreign Currency　　　　　　U.S. Dollar　　　　　　　Oil
Source: ftmdaily.com

Many countries have opted instead to develop an export-led strategy with the United States to exchange their goods and services for the dollars they need to purchase oil in the global markets. (This should help explain much of East Asia's export-led strategy since the 1980s.) Japan, for example, is an island nation with very few natural resources. It must import large amounts of commodities, including oil, which requires U.S. dollars. So Japan manufactures a Honda and ships it to the United States and immediately receives payment in U.S. dollars. Problem solved . . . and export-led strategy explained.

The Amazing Petrodollar "Permission Slip"

As you can imagine, the petrodollar system has proven tremendously beneficial to the U.S. economy. In addition to creating a marketplace for affordable imported goods from countries needing dollars, the petrodollar system provides at least three other immediate benefits to the United States.

- It increases global demand for U.S. dollars
- It increases global demand for U.S. debt securities

• It gives the United States the ability to buy oil with a currency it can print at will

Let's briefly examine each one of these benefits.

The Petrodollar System Increases Global Dollar Demand

In our previous chapter, I explained how global demand for the dollar is important to maintaining a rising levels of prosperity. In many ways, currencies are just like any other commodity: the more demand that exists for the currency, the better it is for the producer. Allow me to develop and refine this thought even further with the following illustration.

Hamburgers, permission slips, and the petrodollar

Let's imagine that you decided to open a hamburger stand in a small town with a population of 50,000. Of course, not everyone likes hamburgers, so only a certain percentage of your town's population will actually ever be potential customers. And since you are obviously not the only hamburger stand in town, your competitors will all be attempting to market to the same segment of your town's population as you will.

Now, as an owner of a hamburger stand in a very small town, would you prefer to have demand for hamburgers from your own town only . . . or would you like to have hamburger demand from other nearby towns and communities, too? (My guess is that you would like to have more customers, as that potentially means more money in your pocket!)

Now, let's take it a step further with another question. Would you rather have demand for your burgers from your own town and nearby communities only . . . or would you prefer to have all of the hamburger demand in your entire state?

Once again, the answer should be obvious. Every good business owner understands that increasing customer demand is a positive thing for their company's bottom line.

To put it another way, if consumers all over your state are demanding your burgers, you have just been given a "permission slip" to hire more burger flippers so that you can produce more burgers. (This concept of a "permission slip" created by growing levels of demand is important. So keep it under your hat for a moment.)

Okay, now allow me to go even one ridiculous step further.Imagine that Oprah Winfrey is driving through your state and just so happens to stop in at your growing hamburger stand. (I know — this is getting ridiculous — just bear with me. I really do have a point here.) After Oprah tries your hamburger, she expresses utter amazement at your culinary skills. Oprah is now a raving fan of your burger joint and invites you onto her show to tell the whole world about your hamburgers. It doesn't take an economist to figure out what is going to happen to the demand for your burgers — it is going to skyrocket.

Your hamburger demand is now global. Congratulations!

As the demand for your hamburgers increases dramatically, so too the supply must increase. Your newfound global hamburger demand has given you a "permission slip" to buy even more frozen patties and hire new fry cooks.

The important concept here is that a growing demand "permits" the producer to increase his supply.

Now, let's conclude our hamburger illustration by imagining that an up-and-coming rival hamburger company becomes a major competitor with your hamburger restaurant chain. As many of your customers begin visiting your new competitor, the demand for your hamburgers begins to wane. As the demand for your burgers drops, you no longer have a "permission slip" to buy as many frozen patties as you had before. As demand for your burgers continues to fall, it makes little sense to hire more workers. Instead, to remain competitive, you must lay off workers and buy fewer frozen patties just to keep your company afloat. Furthermore, you may even need to sell your existing burgers at a discount before they spoil.

If you chose to ignore the warning signs and continue hiring new employees and buying more patties than were actually demanded by your customers, you would soon find your company nearing bankruptcy. At some point, logic would dictate that you must decrease your supply.

So how does this apply to our current discussion on the U.S. dollar?

Let us now apply the same economic logic that we used to explain the increasing and decreasing demand for your hamburgers to our discussion on the global demand for U.S. dollars.

If it is only Americans who "demand" U.S. dollars, then the supply of dollars that Washington and the Federal Reserve can "supply," or create, is limited to our own country's demand.

However, if Washington can somehow create a growing global demand for its paper dollars, then it has given itself a "permission slip" to continually increase the supply of dollars.

This is exactly the type of scenario that the petrodollar system created in the early 1970s. By creating direct incentives for all oil-exporting nations to denominate their oil sales in U.S. dollars, the Washington elites effectively assured an increasing global demand for their currency. And as the world became increasingly dependent on oil to run their economies, this system paid handsome dividends to the United States by creating a consistent global demand for dollars.

And, of course, the Federal Reserve's printing presses stood ready to meet this growing dollar demand with freshly printed U.S. dollars. After all, what kind of central bank would the Federal Reserve be if they were not ready to keep our dollar supply at a level consistent with the growing global demand?

FACT: The artificial dollar demand created by the petrodollar system returned to Washington the "permission slip" to supply the global economy with freshly printed dollars that it lost after the demise of the Bretton Woods system.

The artificial dollar demand created by the petrodollar system has "permitted" Washington to go on multiple spending sprees to further create their "welfare and warfare" state. And with so many dollars floating around the globe, America's asset prices (including houses, stocks, etc.) naturally rose. After all, as we have already demonstrated, asset prices are directly related to the available money supply.

With this in mind, it is easy to see why maintaining a global demand for dollars is vital to our national "illusion of prosperity" and our "national security." (The lengths to which America has already gone to protect the petrodollar system will be explained in our next chapter.)

When, not if, the petrodollar system collapses, America will lose its "permission slip" to print excessive amounts of U.S. dollars. Just like the hamburger stand owner who loses customers to a rival company, the United States will no longer be able to print dollars as the demand for them will have decreased. When this occurs, the amount of dollars in existence will far exceed the actual demand. This is the classical definition of hyperinflation. Since 2006, I have been teaching that America's bout with hyperinflation will be tied in some way with a breakdown of the petrodollar system and the artificial dollar demand that it has created.

When hyperinflation strikes America, it will be very difficult to stop without drastic measures. One possible measure will be a quick and massive reduction in the overall supply of U.S. dollars. However, with a reduction of the supply of dollars will come a massive reduction in the value of assets currently denominated in dollars. I will provide a potential scenario of a coming petrodollar collapse along with personal strategies that you can take.

The petrodollar system increases demand for U.S. debt securities.

In addition to creating an artificial demand for dollars, the petro-dollar system also provides Washington with instant buyers for its debt securities, providing America with a double loan from virtually every global oil transaction. Considered one of the more brilliant aspects of the petro-dollar system, oil consumers are first required to purchase oil in U.S. dollars. Second, the excess profits of the oil-producing nations are then placed into U.S. government debt securities held in Western banks.

This system would later become known as pet-rodollar recycling, as coined by Henry Kissinger. Through their exclusive use of dollars for oil transactions, and then depositing their excess profits into American debt securities, the petrodollar system is a "dream come true" for a spendthrift government like the United States.

Despite its obvious benefits, the petrodollar recycling process is both unusual and unsustainable. By distorting the real demand for government debt, it has "permitted" the U.S. government to maintain artificially low interest rates. Washington's dependence upon these artificially low interest rates allows large amounts of reckless spending to continue unchallenged. But unless the United States has discovered a novel way of defying history and the basic laws of economics, the massive economic distortions and imbalances generated by the petro-dollar system will eventually self-correct when the artificial dollar and U.S. debt demand is removed. That day is coming.

The petrodollar system allows the United States to buy oil with a currency it can print at will.

A third major benefit of the petrodollar system for the United States has to do with the actual purchase of oil itself. Like all modern developed economies, America has built most of its national infrastructure around the use of petroleum-based energy supplies. And like many nations, the United States consumes more oil each year than it has been able to produce on its own. Therefore, it has become dependent upon foreign nations to fill the supply gap. What makes America different, however, is that it can pay for 100 percent of its oil imports with its own currency . . . which it can print at will.

Again, it does not take much economic knowledge to figure out that this is a great deal.

To illustrate, consider another quick example: Imagine that you and I both live in an unusual city where the only method of payment for gasoline for our automobiles is carrots. Now, imagine that I own the exclusive rights to grow carrots in our town. This means that if you ever hope to fill up your tank with gasoline, you must first deal with me. You can come and attempt to barter with me, or you can just buy carrots from me outright. But regardless, it is an inconvenient fact of life for you. However, it is exactly the opposite for me. Since I can create carrots out of the ground, I just plant a seed, water the seed, and then exchange the carrot for gasoline. What a deal!

America has managed to create a similar place for itself in our modern oil-dependent global economy. With oil exclusively priced in dollars, our nation can literally print money to buy oil . . . and then have the oil producers hold the debt that was created by printing the money in the first place.

What other nation, besides America, can print money to buy oil and then have the oil producers hold the debt for the printed money?

Obviously, the creation of the petrodollar system was a brilliant political and economic move. Washington was acutely aware in the early 1970s that the demand curve for oil would increase dramatically with time. Therefore, they positioned the dollar as the primary medium of exchange for all global oil transactions through the petrodollar system. This single political move created a growing international demand for both the U.S. dollar and U.S. debt — all at the expense of oil-producing nations. (For a very simplistic explanation of the petrodollar system by the author, Jerry Robinson, watch his free online video at http://www.ftmdaily.com/petrodollarvideo.)

How the Petrodollar System Has Affected U.S. Relations with Israel

Before we conclude, there is one politically sensitive topic that needs to be addressed that will help further clarify the true effects of the petrodollar system — namely, how the petrodollar system has complicated America's relationship with Israel.

If Americans were asked today if the United States has been a close friend and ally of Israel, most would answer with a resounding yes. This is especially true of evangelical Christians who believe that America's foreign policy in the Middle East should be driven, and even dictated, by Israel. Evangelicals are often wooed by political candidates who promise to "look out for" Israel or to "stand up for" Israel.

But is there any solid evidence that America's foreign policy measures and actions in the Middle East have been guided by anything but upholding and protecting the petrodollar system? I would strongly suggest that the answer is no. Instead, I would suggest that the American population, and evangelicals in particular, have been hoodwinked with the "pro-Israel" chatter that proceeds from many politicians.

There is little doubt that many Americans, and even America itself, feels a deep spiritual connection to the land that gave birth to the Judeo-Christian heritage. This cannot be debated. However, the political and economic incentives that drive a nation's policies are rarely determined by morals as much as they are by money or power, which are often one and the same. To deny this would require a total revision of world history. Instead, history indicates that America has cleverly used its "relationship" with the Jewish state as a cover for its military adventurism in the Middle East. (In the next chapter, I will suggest that much of the military intervention America has undertaken in the Middle East has had more to do with protecting the petrodollar system and less to do with defending Israel.)

Nevertheless, many Americans, who have been programmed by the skillful rhetoric pumped out of Washington's political spin rooms and the corporate-controlled mainstream media, will argue just the opposite. But have you ever wondered why America, and other Western interests who benefit from continued good relations with oil-producing nations, urge Israel to restrain herself every time she seeks to use force to defend her interests or territory?

As you may recall, the agreement that the United States made under the petrodollar agreement states that the they would provide protection for Middle Eastern oil-producing nations from any and all outside threats, including the Jewish state.

Would a "true" friend belittle your autonomy and self-determination by denying your right to defend yourself, all because they have made backroom deals with your enemies for financial gain?

And consider the foreign aid money that is doled out to the region. When dispensing foreign aid dollars to the Middle East, does America give more money exclusively to Israel because she is a friend?

The answer is no. Instead, Israel's enemies within the region receive eight times more in foreign aid dollars from America than Israel does.

Would a "true" friend give your sworn enemies eight times more money and resources than he does to you?

As a fellow believer with a passion for Judeo Christian values, I would strongly suggest that now is the time for Americans to re-examine what American "support" for Israel really looks like.

The Jewish identity, as expressed in Zionism, is one that is deeply rooted in autonomy and self-determination. It is my belief that America's so-called "support" for Israel has served as a crafty cover for maintaining a military presence in the region . . . all to protect our national interests, which includes the petrodollar system.

America has attempted to play both sides of this Middle East game for far too long. And it has used the corporate-controlled media to shape and control the perceptions of the American public for decades. They have kept us ignorant of the truth. It is time that Americans wake up and follow the money. Keeping the Middle East inflamed and destabilized has been a stated goal of Western interests for decades. This is the name of the game when your goal is empire. And empires do not have friends . . . they have subjects.

Maintaining the petrodollar system is the American empire's primary goal. Everything else is secondary.

Quick Summary

- A petrodollar is a U.S. dollar that is received by an oil producer in exchange for selling oil and that is then deposited into Western banks.
- The artificial demand that had been created, and then lost, under the Bretton Woods system was restored to even higher levels under the petrodollar system.
- The petrodollar system was one of the most clever political strategies of the 20th century.
- Four primary benefits to America from the petrodollar system include: 1) an artificial demand for dollars, 2) an artificial demand for U.S. government debt, 3) the ability to print the currency in which oil must be purchased, and 4) an influx of cheap imported goods from foreign nations who need our dollars to purchase oil.
- When a country does not have a surplus of U.S. dollars, it must create a strategy to obtain them in order to buy oil. This helps to explain the adoption of export-led strategies by several resource-poor nations, particularly in the Far East.

Endnotes

Several authors have worked to compile data on the origins of the petrodollar system in addition to this volume, some exhaustively, including Richard Duncan, William R. Clark, David E. Spiro, Charles Goyette and F. William Engdahl.

1. U.S. Congress, Senate, Committee on Foreign Relations, Subcommittee on Multinational Corporations, "Multinational Oil Corporations and U.S. Foreign Policy" (Washington, DC: Government Printing Office, 1975), p. 37–39.
2. http://www.brainyquote.com/quotes/quotes/h/harrystru398848.html.
3. The U.S.- Saudi Arabian Joint Commission On Economic Cooperation. http://ftmdaily.com/wp-content/uploads/2012/03/US-Saudi-Arabian-Joint-Commission-on-Economic-Cooperation.pdf.

Chapter 5

Petrodollar Wars: Protecting Dollar Demand through the Barrel of a Gun

What is our oil doing under their sand?

— Seen on a bumper sticker

War is a racket. It always has been. It is possibly the oldest, easily
the most profitable, surely the most vicious.[1]

— Marine Corp General Smedley Butler

*OVERVIEW: The petrodollar system that was created in the 1970s has
served America well, both economically and politically. What began as a
strategic driver of dollar demand after the collapse of the Bretton Woods
system in 1971 has provided benefits that few Americans could have ever
imagined. Put simply, this "dollars for oil" system has greatly enriched
our nation. But this national prosperity has come at the expense of other
nations and their potential prosperity, especially in the oil-rich region of
the Middle East and Central Asia. This chapter documents how America
has handled the growing international challenges to the petrodollar system,
with a specific focus on the 2003 Iraq war. The consequences have been
nothing short of tragic.*

America — the Primary Guardian of the Petrodollar System

From the dawn of the petroleum age, developed nations have devised all sorts of creative geopolitical strategies to secure and maintain access to the world's oil supplies. One can hardly deny the obvious incentives that motivate these nations, namely, economic necessity and the political goodwill that low energy prices engender among the masses. Unlike other nations however, the United States has one additional and unique incentive of ensuring that both current oil supplies and future discoveries remain priced in U.S. dollars.

An examination of America's foreign policy efforts in the wake of the "oil shock" of 1973, and in the ensuing foundation of the petrodollar system in the mid 1970s, makes it painstakingly clear to any casual political observer that one of Washington's central goals has been to control global oil supplies, specifically in western Asia.[2]

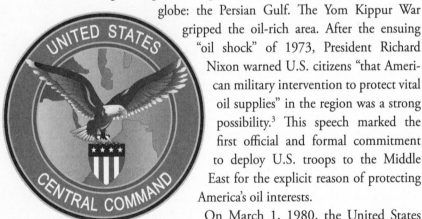

In 1973, in the wake of U.S. military involvement in the Vietnam War, Washington began turning its attention to another region of the globe: the Persian Gulf. The Yom Kippur War gripped the oil-rich area. After the ensuing "oil shock" of 1973, President Richard Nixon warned U.S. citizens "that American military intervention to protect vital oil supplies" in the region was a strong possibility.[3] This speech marked the first official and formal commitment to deploy U.S. troops to the Middle East for the explicit reason of protecting America's oil interests.

On March 1, 1980, the United States announced the creation of the Rapid Deployment Joint Task Force (RDJTF).[4] The stated mission of the Rapid Deployment Force was as a deterrent (primarily against the Soviets) and to "help maintain regional stability and the Gulf oil-flow westward."[5]

On January 1, 1983, Carter's Rapid Deployment Force morphed into a separate force known as the United States Central Command (USCENTCOM). USCENTCOM would be responsible for the Middle East and Central Asian regions.

Since 1980, the United States has feverishly built military bases all over western Asia. Understanding the petrodollar system will help explain the hundreds of U.S. military bases stationed in over 130 countries. After all, maintaining an empire dependent upon a "dollars for oil" system is no cheap task and requires careful monitoring and oversight of the world's oil supplies. Chief among the potential concerns for the petrodollar guardians are: 1) threats of restrictions on oil supplies, 2) new oil discoveries in potentially "anti-Western" oil fields, 3) the nationalizing of a country's oil supplies, and perhaps most importantly, 4) devising "permanent solutions" to the problems presented by nations who dare challenge the current "dollars for oil" system.

As the primary guardian of the petrodollar, the United States often finds its militaristic adventurism at odds with the goals of foreign nations who do not share the same enthusiasm for confronting sovereign nations over a system in which they share no real direct incentives.

Given these facts, let's now explore how the petrodollar system has affected America's foreign policy actions in the oil-rich region of western Asia. We will begin with a look back at the events of America's darkest hour.

Beating the Iraq War Drums — Before 9/11

On September 11, 2001, America's relations with the Middle East would be altered forever. The tragic events of that day still live on in the memory of every American. The dreadful carnage in New York City, Washington D.C., and Shanksville, Pennsylvania, was heart-rending to the billions around the world who watched the terror unfold before their eyes on live television.

Interestingly, just five hours after American Airlines Flight 77 crashed into the Pentagon, Secretary of Defense Donald Rumsfeld began ordering his staff to develop plans for a strike on Iraq — despite the fact that there was absolutely no evidence linking the country, or its leader Saddam Hussein, to the 9/11 attacks.[6] When reports later came in that three of the hijackers involved in the 9/11 attacks were connected to Al Qaeda, Rumsfeld reportedly became so determined to find a rationale for an attack on Iraq that "on 10 separate occasions he asked the CIA to find evidence linking Iraq to the terror attacks of September 11." The CIA repeatedly came back empty-handed.[7]

On September 12, 2001, despite zero evidence against Iraq, Defense Secretary Rumsfeld proposed to President George W. Bush that Iraq should be "a principal target of the first round in the war against terrorism."[8] Bush, along with his other advisors, including Deputy Secretary of Defense Paul Wolfowitz, strongly supported the idea that Iraq should be included in their attack plans. Colin Powell, then Secretary of State, urged constraint, however, stating that "public opinion has to be prepared before a move against Iraq is possible."[9]

In fairness, however, Washington had already been preparing for a new invasion of Iraq. The *Los Angeles Times* reported that one year prior to the attacks of 9/11, the United States began constructing Al Adid, a billion-dollar military base in Qatar with a 15,000-foot runway, in April 2000.[10] What was Washington's stated justification for the new Al Adid base, and other similar ones in the Gulf region? Preparedness for renewed action against Iraq.

In a March 2001 Pentagon document entitled "Foreign Suitors for Iraqi Oil Field Contracts," details of how Iraq's oil fields would be carved up and outsourced to Western oil companies are given two full years before the war.[11] It would later be revealed that an invasion of Iraq was at the top of the Bush administration's agenda[12] only 10 days after his inauguration, which was a full eight months before 9/11.[13]

In an explosive book entitled *Against All Enemies* by Bush's former counter-terrorism director, Richard A. Clarke, the author recounts life inside the Bush administration in the days immediately following the 9/11 attacks:

> The president in a very intimidating way left us, me and my staff, with the clear indication that he wanted us to come back with the word there was an Iraqi hand behind 9/11 because they had been planning to do something about Iraq from before the time they came into office. I think they had a plan from day one they wanted to do something about Iraq. While the World Trade Center was still smoldering, while they were still digging bodies out, people in the White House were thinking: "Ah! This gives us the opportunity we have been looking for to go after Iraq." [14]

On September 17, six short days after the 9/11 attacks, President George W. Bush named Osama Bin Laden as the "prime suspect" in the biggest terrorist act on American soil in history. Washington's response was swift.

On September 20, 2001, President Bush met with Britain's Prime Minister Tony Blair to coordinate war plans. In the meeting, Bush purportedly states his intention to attack Iraq immediately. Blair advises Bush to remain focused on Al Qaeda and to work on gaining international support for an invasion of Iraq. Bush reportedly agrees to "leave Iraq for another day."[15]

On October 7, 2001, Operation Enduring Freedom was launched. Thousands of U.S. troops were sent into the mountainous regions of Afghanistan. Washington's stated goal in this mission was clear: to capture Bin Laden, and to wipe out two groups intimately connected to him — Al Qaeda and the Taliban.

But the Bush administration had no plans of allowing a good crisis go to waste. While they had succeeded in their initial invasion plans of Afghanistan, Iraq was still at the forefront of the Administration's collective mind. Within a few short weeks after the Afghanistan war had begun, Washington began using the corporate-controlled mainstream media to build their case for a full-scale invasion of Iraq.

In the build-up to a separate war, U.S. officials began publicly claiming that Iraq, and its maniacal dictator Saddam Hussein, presented an entirely separate set of national security threats, despite the fact that no legitimate evidence linked Bin Laden to the country of Iraq. Despite this astounding lack of evidence, the Bush administration continued to whip the American public into a war-crazed frenzy with unfounded claims of Iraq's alleged development and possession of weapons of mass destruction. In addition, Iraq's intimate ties to international terrorist groups were highlighted, and hypnotically repeated, through the mainstream media outlets.

A deeply wounded post-9/11 America desperately sought answers and justice. In the moment of their deepest grief and fear, the Washington elites manipulated the masses to promote their desired foreign policy measures.

All of the stops were pulled out. Conservative radio and television talk show hosts began reading the Bush talking points verbatim over the air, warning the already fearful American public of the tremendous threats that Iraq posed to our national security.

Evangelicals, who openly claim to worship the "Prince of Peace," opted for bloodshed. Many Christians sought to justify the Iraq war by butchering their own "Just War" theory, and sought vengeance through a pre-emptive military strike on Iraq.[16]

It did not take long for America to become sharply divided on Washington's hasty insistence on launching another war in the volatile region of the Middle East. And while a majority of the American public supported a full-scale invasion of Iraq, others urged a more diplomatic approach.

But in the wake of the devastation of 9/11, few were in the mood for diplomacy. As the war drums over Iraq beat ever so loudly, legitimate questions concerning the merits of the war required Washington to provide specific answers to a confused and terror-weary public. Some of those pressing questions included:

> Was there any evidence that Iraq had plans to harm the American people or to invade the borders of our nation?

> Was there solid proof that Iraq had weapons of mass destruction?

> Was there any evidence linking Iraqi president Saddam Hussein to the vicious terror plot of 9/11?

The Bush administration and the corporate-controlled mainstream media wasted no time in answering those difficult questions with a resounding and overly confident yes.

Sadly, as we all know now, Saddam Hussein had no link to Osama Bin Laden, or the tragic events of 9/11. When asked by a White House correspondent directly about the connection between Iraq and the events of 9/11, President George W. Bush denied that any link ever existed.[17] Conveniently, this change of tone came from the administration after the war had already begun.

The Iraq-Petrodollar Connection

So why Iraq? Why the rush to war with a country who so obviously had no connection with the events of 9/11?

As I write this in the first half of 2012, it is a safe assumption that most Americans carry a suspicion, however slight, toward the reasons that they were told the United States needed to invade Iraq back in 2003. It is simply not possible to explain the depths of the corruption that exist at the highest levels of government today. Those who have bought into the mainstream media's portrayal of the American government as an institution that seeks the common good do well to recall the words of America's own first national leader:

> Government is not reason; it is not eloquent; it is force. Like fire, it is a dangerous servant and a fearful master. — President George Washington[18]

With that quote as a backdrop, let us dig deeper into our original question: Why did the United States appear so eager to launch an unprovoked war against Iraq? And why did the United States begin hatching these war plans many months prior to the events of September 11? After all, many other nations around the world have confirmed stockpiles of dangerous weapons. So why did the United States specifically target Iraq so soon after the Afghanistan invasion of 2001? Did the United States have some other motivation for seeking international support to invade Iraq?

William R. Clark was among those who questioned the status quo answers and Washington's stated motives regarding the invasion of Iraq. In his book *Petrodollar Warfare*, Clark claims that the 2003 U.S.-led invasion of Iraq was not based upon "violence or terrorism, but something very different, yet not altogether surprising — declining economic power and depleting hydrocarbons."[19]

Clark's work was heavily influenced by another author named F. William Engdahl and his book *The Century of War: Anglo-American Oil Politics and the New World Order*.[20]

According to research conducted by both Clark and Engdahl, the U.S.-led invasion of Iraq was not exclusively motivated by Iraq's connection to the terrorist groups who masterminded the 9/11 attacks. Nor was it out of a concern for the safety of the American public or out of sympathy for the Iraqi people and their lack of freedom or democracy. Instead, Clark and Engdahl both claim that the U.S.-led invasion was inspired predominantly by Iraq's public defiance of the petrodollar system. According to page 28 of Clark's book:

> On September 24, 2000, Saddam Hussein allegedly "emerged from a meeting of his government and proclaimed that Iraq would soon transition its oil export transactions to the euro currency."[21]

Not long after this meeting, Saddam Hussein began preparing to make the switch from pricing his country's oil exports in greenbacks to euros.[22] As renegade and newsworthy this action was on the part of Iraq, it was sparsely reported in the corporate-controlled media. Clark comments on the limited media coverage on page 31 of his book:

> CNN ran a very short article on its website on October 30, 2000, but after this one-day news cycle, the issue of Iraq's switch to a petroeuro essentially disappeared from all five of the corporate-owned media outlets.[23]

By 2002, Saddam had fully converted to a petroeuro — in essence, dumping the dollar.

On March 19, 2003, George W. Bush announced the commencement of a full-scale invasion of Iraq. According to Clark and Engdahl, Saddam's bold threat to the petrodollar system had invited the full force and fury of the U.S. military onto his front lawn.

Was the Iraq war really about weapons of mass destruction, al-Qaeda, fighting terrorism, and promoting democracy? Or was America's stated purposes to "liberate" the Iraqi people from a brutal regime actually a clever guise for making an example of a nation who dared threaten the existing petrodollar system?

I am no Washington elite. Nor do I claim to know the minds of men. However, the more that you consider all the facts, you will find that the invasion of Iraq was likely one of the first in a series of "petrodollar wars" designed to protect America's economic interests.

It should be noted that Iraq's proven oil supplies are considered to be among the largest in the world. However, some experts believe that Iraq's oilfields,[24] many of which have yet to be exploited, will catapult Iraq above Saudi Arabia in total proven oil reserves in the coming years.[25]

What's "Our" Oil Doing Under "Their" Sand?

Washington, of course, adamantly denied any and all accusations that the Iraq war was motivated by anything other than disarming Iraq and liberating its beleaguered people. According to the Washington elites, the Iraq war was not, nor was it ever, about Iraqi's oil supplies. Consider a small sampling of quotes from U.S. officials:[26]

> The idea that the United States covets Iraqi oil fields is a wrong impression. I have a deep desire for peace. That's what I have a desire for. And freedom for the Iraqi people. See, I don't like a system where people are repressed through torture and murder in order to keep a dictator in place. It troubles me deeply. And so the Iraqi people must hear this loud and clear, that this country never has any intention to conquer anybody. — (U.S. President George W. Bush)

> This is not about oil; this is about a tyrant, a dictator, who is developing weapons of mass destruction to use against the Arab populations. — (U.S. Secretary of State Colin Powell)

> It's not about oil and it's not about religion. — (U.S. Secretary of Defense Donald Rumsfeld)

> I have heard that allegation (of oil motives) and I simply reject it. — (Coalition Provisional Authority Paul Bremer)

> It's not about oil. — (General John Abizaid, Combatant Commander, Central Command)

> It was not about oil. — (Energy Secretary Spencer Abraham)

> It's not about the oil. — (The Financial Times reported Richard Perle shouted at a parking attendant in frustration)

> This is not about oil. — (Australian Treasurer Peter Costello)

> The only thing I can tell you is this war is not about oil. — (Former Secretary of State Lawrence Eagleburger)

This is not about oil. This is about international peace and security. — (Jack Straw, British Foreign Secretary)

This is not about oil. That was very clear. This is about America, and America's position in the world, as the upholder of liberty for the oppressed. — (Utah Republican Senator Bob Bennett)

There's just nothing to it. — (White House spokesperson Ari Fleischer on the U.S. desire to access Iraqi oil fields)

Condoleeza Rice, in response to the proposition, "If Saddam's primary export or natural resource was olive oil rather than oil, we would not be going through this situation," said, "This cannot be further from the truth. He is a threat to his neighbors. He's a threat to American security interest. That is what the president has in mind." She continued, "This is not about oil."

The government line was loud and clear: The Iraq war was *not* about oil.

Or . . . Is It About the Oil?

Despite the adamant denial by the Washington elites that their intentions were anything but pure, it did not take long for dissenters to emerge. Anti-war demonstrations filled the public squares of nearly every American town.

Interestingly, as the war with Iraq raged on, even those within Washington began to make revealing comments on the U.S.-Iraq-Oil connection.

In January 2003, British Foreign Secretary Jack Straw admitted that oil was *a key priority* to the West's involvement in Iraq, even more so than the supposed "weapons of mass destruction."[27]

In June 2003, Deputy Defense Secretary Paul Wolfowitz made the following comments after being asked why Iraq was being treated differently than North Korea on the question of a nuclear threat, while speaking to an Asian security summit in Singapore:

Let's look at it simply. The most important difference between North Korea and Iraq is that economically, we just had no choice in Iraq. The country swims on a sea of oil."[28]

In an August 2008 interview with *Business Week* magazine, Republican Vice-Presidential candidate Sarah Palin stated:

> We are a nation at war and in many [ways] the reasons for war are fights over energy sources, which is nonsensical when you consider that domestically we have the supplies ready to go.[29]

During a 2008 town hall campaign meeting, former presidential candidate and Senator John McCain, made the following statement:

> My friends, I will have an energy policy which will eliminate our dependence on oil from the Middle East that will then prevent us from having ever to send our young men and women into conflict again in the Middle East.[30]

Former chairman of the Federal Reserve, Alan Greenspan, stated the following on page 463 of his book *The Age of Turbulence*:

> I am saddened that it is politically inconvenient to acknowledge what everyone knows: the Iraq war is largely about oil.[31]

In an interview with Bob Woodward of the *Washington Post*, Greenspan elaborated on the comment in his book by saying that removing Saddam from power was "essential" to keep the "existing system" in place.[32]

Apparently everyone in Greenspan's circle "knew" that Iraq was about oil. However, the average American was told exactly the opposite by the Bush administration and the corrupt and derelict corporate-controlled mainstream media.[33]

In a televised interview with Frontline, former Secretary of State James A. Baker III made the following statement regarding U.S. national security policy:

> I have been a member of four (presidential) administrations. And in every one of those administrations we had written as a national security policy that we would go to war to protect the national energy reserves of the Persian Gulf, if necessary.[34]

General John Abizaid, who was formerly the commander of the USCENTCOM during the Iraq war, stated during an October 2007 round-table discussion entitled "Courting Disaster: The Fight for Oil, Water and a Healthy Planet" at Stanford University:

> Of course (the Iraq war) is about oil, we can't deny that.[35]

Former U.S. Ambassador and war hawk John Bolton publicly admitted in an interview on Fox News dated October 22, 2011, that the multiple wars that America has fought in the Middle East have been about securing oil supplies. Speaking of the U.S.-Middle East conflicts, Bolton stated:

> The critical oil and natural gas producing region that we fought so many wars to try and protect our economy from the adverse impact of losing that supply or having it available only at very high prices.[36]

Based upon the quotes above, we have no need to wonder if Iraq's oil supplies played a role in the 2003 U.S.-led invasion of that nation. After all, the global elites have told us in no uncertain terms[37] that the Iraq war was clearly about oil and maintaining the American empire's grip on the oil-rich region.[38] In 2011, this was further confirmed when a torrent of damning government documents were leaked.[39]

Finally, consider the following words from one of the chief architects behind the Iraq war, Vice President Dick Cheney. In an interview with C-Span recorded in 1994 — nine years prior to the 2003 invasion of Iraq — Cheney was asked about his opinion of the previous 1991 Gulf War. His answer is revealing.[40]

> Q: Do you think the U.S., or U.N. forces, should have moved into Baghdad?
>
> A: No.
>
> Q: Why not?
>
> A: Because if we'd gone to Baghdad we would have been all alone. There wouldn't have been anybody else with us. There would have been a U.S. occupation of Iraq. None of the Arab forces that were willing to fight with us in Kuwait were willing to invade Iraq. Once you got to Iraq and took it over, took down

Saddam Hussein's government, then what are you going to put in its place? That's a very volatile part of the world, and if you take down the central government of Iraq, you could very easily end up seeing pieces of Iraq fly off: part of it, the Syrians would like to have to the west, part of it — eastern Iraq — the Iranians would like to claim, they fought over it for eight years. In the north you've got the Kurds, and if the Kurds spin loose and join with the Kurds in Turkey, then you threaten the territorial integrity of Turkey. It's a quagmire if you go that far and try to take over Iraq. The other thing was casualties. Everyone was impressed with the fact we were able to do our job with as few casualties as we had. But for the 146 Americans killed in action, and for their families — it wasn't a cheap war. And the question for the president, in terms of whether or not we went on to Baghdad, took additional casualties in an effort to get Saddam Hussein, was how many additional dead Americans is Saddam worth? Our judgment was, not very many, and I think we got it right.

Apparently, Saddam's move to switch Iraq's oil sales from dollars to euros may have been enough to change Cheney's mind about sacrificing American lives.[41] Based upon the quotes above, and upon the mountain of evidence that we have today, it is obvious that oil had played some role in the U.S.-led Iraq invasion.

Sadly, innocent civilians in Iraq are the ones who paid the ultimate price for the U.S. invasion. As of this writing, over 105,000 Iraqi civilians have been killed since the war commenced in March 2003.[42] And many of these casualties were children.[43]

Let's take a look at what has transpired in the aftermath of the U.S.-led invasion of Iraq to see if the words and the actions line up.

The Rush for Post-War Iraqi Oil

In late 2002 and early 2003, the preparations for the Iraq war were well under way. As the United States sought international support for the war, several nations expressed opposition to the invasion. China, Russia, and France were among these nations. Many in the corporate-controlled American media portrayed these nations as "sympathizers" and "supporters" of terrorism due to their hesitancy to invade Iraq on groundless charges. However, what the corrupt media outlets failed to mention was that these nations had existing oil contracts with Iraq that would be endangered in the event that the West gained control of Iraq.

In an October 2002 interview with the Observer UK, a Russian official at the United Nations stated:

> The concern of my government is that the concessions agreed between Baghdad and numerous enterprises will be reneged upon, and that U.S. companies will enter to take the greatest share of those existing contracts. . . . Yes, if you could say it that way — an oil grab by Washington.[44]

With just a little bit of in-depth investigation, the clueless American elite media would have discovered that there was more to this than "sympathizing" with terrorists and that prior to the war, Russia was owed billions of dollars by Iraq. Russia had even billions more wrapped up in future contracts.

Together with France and China, Russia stood to gain billions in future oil contracts when, and if, sanctions were lifted against Iraq.

In a separate 2002 news article entitled "Oil After Saddam: All Bets Are In," Samer Shehata, a Middle East expert at the Center for Contemporary Arab Studies in Washington, was interviewed regarding the situation.[45] In the interview Shehata said, "Russia, China, France have the highest stakes in the Iraqi oil industry. Once Saddam is out, everything becomes null and void and there is no legal authority to enforce those claims."

Is it any wonder why much of the world hates America? Of course, we are told that nations hate us because we have "blue jeans" and "fast cars." We are told that foreign nations hate Americans because of our liberties. The same corrupt outlets that cram this garbage down the American public's throats are the same ones who lied to the American public about the real reasons for the war in Iraq. The truth is that very few foreign nations "hate" American citizens. Instead, they resent the actions of the American empire with its militaristic adventurism and its excessive intervention into foreign affairs.

The Most Damning Evidence of a Petrodollar Motive in the Iraq War

On June 5, 2003, the corrupt U.S. media missed one of the most important and revealing stories about the Iraq war. However, Carol Hoyas and Kevin Morrison from the London-based *Financial Times* reported on the story in a piece entitled "Iraq Returns to International Oil Market."[46] Here's an excerpt of the story:

> Iraq on Thursday stepped back into the international oil market for the first time since the war, offering 10m barrels of oil from its storage tanks for sale to the highest bidder. For some international companies it will be the first time in more than a year that they will do business directly with Iraq. . . . The tender, for which bids are due by June 10, switches the transaction back to dollars — the international currency of oil sales — despite the greenback's recent fall in value. Saddam Hussein in 2000 insisted Iraq's oil be sold for euros, a political move, but one that improved Iraq's recent earnings thanks to the rise in the value of the euro against the dollar.

Is it not rather interesting to note that within weeks of the invasion of Iraq, all Iraqi oil sales were switched from the euro — back to the U.S. dollar?

Was this war, as Clark and Engdahl suggest, the first "petrodollar" war? I think the evidence is clear that it was.

Think about this:

- If Iraq was not ultimately about oil, then how ridiculous is it that a nearly bankrupt nation like America could spend hundreds of billions of dollars on "spreading democracy" to foreign nations, like Iraq, when our own nation is in a steep economic decline?

- How are the American people able to afford such an altruistic foreign policy when they can't even afford to take care of their own citizens?

- And finally, since when has America become so interested in giving American lives and dollars for the benefit of foreign nations with nothing in return?

And speaking of return, what could Iraq possibly offer in return to America?

Perhaps Vice President Cheney answered that question best when he said in a 1999 speech at the Institute of Petroleum:

> The Middle East, with two-thirds of the world's oil and the lowest cost, is still where the prize ultimately lies; even though companies are anxious for greater access there, progress continues to be slow.[47]

Finally, consider Republican Senator Charles Hagel's rather blunt statement given in a 2007 speech at the Catholic University of America regarding the true purposes behind the Iraq War:

> People say we're not fighting for oil. Of course we are. They talk about America's national interest. What the hell do you think they're talking about? We're not there for figs.[48]

Quick Summary

✓   A proper understanding of the petrodollar system helps explain why there are hundreds of U.S. military bases stationed in over 130 countries.

✓   In order to protect the petrodollar system, the United States must be vigilant to deal with 1) threats to restrictions on oil supplies, 2) new oil discoveries in potentially "anti-Western" oil fields, 3) the nationalizing of a country's oil supplies, and 4) devising "permanent solutions" to the problems presented by nations who dare challenge the current "dollars for oil" system.

✓   On September 24, 2000, Iraqi President Saddam Hussein boldly determined to remove all of his oil sales away from the U.S. dollar and began accepting euros for his country's oil supplies in 2002.

✓   On March 19, 2003, the U.S. military invaded Iraq under false pretext. The American media provided a scarce amount of critical reporting.

✓   On June 5, 2003, Iraq's oil sales were returned to the petrodollar system.

✓   When pressed, U.S. politicians admit that our wars are often motivated by natural resources.

Endnotes

1. Smedley Butler, *War Is a Racket* (New York: Round Table Press, Inc., 1935), chapter 1.
2. http://ftmdaily.com/wp-content/uploads/2012/03/US-Saudi-Arabian-Joint-Commission-on-Economic-Cooperation.pdf.
3. http://www.historyofwar.org/articles/weapons_rdf.html.
4. http://www.rand.org/content/dam/rand/pubs/papers/2005/P6751.pdf.
5. http://www.historyofwar.org/articles/weapons_rdf.html.
6. http://www.cbsnews.com/2100-500249_162-520830.html.
7. http://archives.cnn.com/2002/ALLPOLITICS/05/06/time.out/.
8. http://classes.maxwell.syr.edu/hst341/WPost--InsideWhiteHouse2.htm.
9. http://classes.maxwell.syr.edu/hst341/WPost--InsideWhiteHouse2.htm.
10. http://articles.latimes.com/2002/jan/06/news/mn-20757/2.
11. http://ftmdaily.com/wp-content/uploads/2012/03/IraqOilFrgnSuitors.pdf.
12. http://articles.baltimoresun.com/2003-03-16/news/0303160268_1_president-bush-powell-hussein.
13. http://www.cbsnews.com/2100-18560_162-592330.html.
14. http://busharchive.froomkin.com/A14852-2004Mar22.html.
15. http://news.bbc.co.uk/2/hi/uk_news/politics/2915149.stm.
16. http://erlc.c
17. http://www.youtube.com/watch?v=f_A77N5WKWM.
18. http://en.wikiquote.org/wiki/George_Washington.
19. http://ftmdaily.com/go/petrodollarwarfarebook.
20. http://ftmdaily.com/go/centuryofwar.
21. http://ftmdaily.com/go/petrodollarwarfarebook.
22. http://www.time.com/time/magazine/article/0,9171,998512,00.html.
23. http://archives.cnn.com/2000/WORLD/meast/10/30/iraq.un.euro.reut/.
24. http://www.ft.com/intl/cms/s/0/af6cc05a-cf9a-11df-a51f-00144feab49a.html#axzz1oY0IMM6h.
25. http://www.ft.com/intl/cms/s/0/af6cc05a-cf9a-11df-a51f-00144feab49a.html#axzz1oY0IMM6h.
26. http://www.counterpunch.org/2007/09/19/oil-warriors/.
27. http://www.guardian.co.uk/politics/2003/jan/07/uk.iraq.
28. http://www.news24.com/World/Archives/IraqiDossier/Update-Iraq-war-was-about-oil-20030605.
29. http://www.businessweek.com/bwdaily/dnflash/content/aug2008/db20080829_272692_page_2.htm.
30. http://www.youtube.com/watch?v=cydX7uZaXMs&feature=related.
31. http://ftmdaily.com/go/ageofturbulence.
32. http://www.washingtonpost.com/wp-dyn/content/article/2007/09/16/AR2007091601287.html.
33. http://www.counterpunch.org/2007/09/19/oil-warriors/.
34. http://www.pbs.org/wgbh/pages/frontline/shows/saudi/interviews/baker.html.
35. http://fora.tv/2007/10/13/Security_Roundtable_Breyer_Friedman_Abizaid.
36. http://www.youtube.com/watch?v=rAgv6HaOHzM.
37. http://www.youtube.com/watch?v=bE_JFk_XIwA.

38. http://www.youtube.com/watch?v=b8z_g1Igz-k.
39. http://www.independent.co.uk/news/uk/politics/secret-memos-expose-link-between-oil-firms-and-invasion-of-iraq-2269610.html.
40. http://www.metacafe.com/watch/1193195/cheney_admits_in_1994_that_an_iraq_invasion_would_be_a_disaster/.
41. http://www.lewrockwell.com/paul/paul303.html.
42. http://www.iraqbodycount.org/.
43. http://www.mcclatchydc.com/2011/08/31/122789/wikileaks-iraqi-children-in-us.html.
44. http://www.guardian.co.uk/world/2002/oct/06/russia.oil.
45. http://www.msnbc.msn.com/id/3071521/
46. http://ftmdaily.com/wp-content/uploads/2012/03/ft_iraq-returns-to-international-oil-market.pdf
47. Full text of Dick Cheney's speech at the Institute of Petroleum Autumn lunch, 1999, http://www.energybulletin.net/node/559.
48. http://www.fpif.org/articles/the_costs_of_war_for_oil.

Chapter 6

The History of the Federal Reserve (or How America Lost the Revolutionary War)

From the Great Depression, to the stagflation of the seventies,
to the burst of the dotcom bubble in 2001, every economic
downturn suffered by the country over the last 80 years can be
traced to Federal Reserve policy.[1]

— U.S. Congressman Ron Paul

*OVERVIEW: Few Americans truly understand the complexities involved
with central banking. Most people throughout modern history have made
the terrible mistake of not understanding the relevance of their nation's
central banking scheme to their own wealth preservation. In this chapter,
I will highlight the devastating effects that central banking has had upon
the United States and its national wealth. But America is not unique in
this economic plunder, as private international banking interests have long
sought to collude with governments in an effort to gain the privilege of
controlling the issuance of the nation's currency. Historically, this hybrid
system of governments and the international banking cartel has followed
a predictable pattern that eventually leads to a devaluation of the nation's
currency system. These government-banking alliances, known as central
banks, ultimately lead to the destruction of the underlying nation's wealth
— leading to the bankruptcy of the nation itself. In order to come to a*

complete and full understanding of what is really happening in America's economy, and what will happen in the near future, we do well to "follow the money" throughout America's history of central banking.

On December 23, 1913, President Woodrow Wilson signed into law the Federal Reserve Act. With the stroke of a pen, Wilson created a government-endorsed banking cartel — otherwise known as a central bank. During the 18th century, America had experimented with the central banking concept. But these prior attempts by the international "banksters" would pale in comparison to the total monetary control that Wilson would grant to the Federal Reserve a century later.

In this section we will venture into the history of the Federal Reserve and witness the financial carnage inflicted on our nation through the marriage of government and banking. As we will see, its effect upon America's collective wealth has been devastating.

Despite the vast economic control wielded by the Federal Reserve over consumers, most Americans are not aware of the true purpose of the institution — let alone its sordid history. It is my hope that this chapter will help you understand America's attempts at central banking and *why it matters to you and your finances.* Some readers who have an intimate knowledge of the Federal Reserve may already know much of what is written here. Others, however, will learn more than they may expect. My ultimate goal is to expose the fatal flaws in America's central banking system and reveal how the corruption of sound monetary principles in our nation's banking sector has greatly contributed to financial excess.

The truth is that America's economic growth and prosperity has been made possible solely by debt.

The corrupt policies of the American federal government, along with those of the Federal Reserve Bank, have turned our once vibrant economy, based upon free market principles, into a zombie, debt-based economy that requires increasing debt in order to survive. Together, the government and the Federal Reserve have plundered our nation's wealth and have replaced it with IOUs. Put simply, Americans have been shepherded to the cliff of bankruptcy by the very individuals entrusted with our nation's economic protection.

> All the perplexities, confusions, and distresses in America arise, not from defects in their constitution or confederation, not from a want of honor or virtue, so much as from downright ignorance of the nature of coin, credit, and circulation.
> — John Adams[2]

Reasons for the Revolutionary War

Since grade school, we have been taught that one of the primary reasons America's founding fathers fled their British homeland in search of the New World was to escape religious persecution. While there is some truth to this story, there was another more important reason behind the mass exodus to America. This reason had less to do with religion and more to do with money.

The British Empire's rigid rule over its numerous colonies around the world is well-documented in history books. The 13 colonies birthed in America were no exception, as they were subject to many of the same rules as other British colonies of their day. The Americans, however, sought to overthrow their British oppressors who they felt stifled their economic freedoms. While the British Crown could hardly impose strict religious adherence to their subjects across the Atlantic Ocean, they could exact taxes from the burgeoning American colonies.

Until the mid-18th century, early American settlers were predominantly faithful to the wishes of Great Britain. This was true despite the fact that America's diverse religious beliefs often conflicted with the theology espoused by the Church of England. Early colonial America experienced great prosperity with massive exports of rum and tobacco. Their dependence upon free slave labor from Africa allowed the early Americans to maximize their profits. With virtually no income taxes and relatively little unemployment, America was economically well positioned. During this era, the American colonies began creating and using their own form of paper money. Unlike Britain, however, America's paper money was not being issued by central bankers for obscene profits. Regarding this golden economic era in early America, Benjamin Franklin wrote: "There was abundance in the Colonies, and peace was reigning on every border. It was difficult, and even impossible, to find a happier and more prosperous nation on all the surface of the globe. Comfort was prevailing in every home. The people, in general, kept the highest moral standards, and education was widely spread."[3]

On a later diplomatic trip to England in 1763, Franklin witnessed the squalid conditions of England. Franklin claimed that the streets of London were "covered with beggars and tramps." Upon further investigation, Franklin discovered that England was suffering from massive unemployment due to an exorbitantly high tax burden upon its citizens. England was suffering from the high costs of the Seven Years War and had little money left over to provide aid to the poor. British officials, who were acutely aware of America's growing economic prosperity, quizzed Franklin about the financial structure of America's economy. Franklin replied, "That is simple. In the Colonies, we issue our own paper money. It is called Colonial Scrip. We issue it in proper proportion to make the goods pass easily from the producers to the consumers. In this manner, creating ourselves our own paper money, we control its purchasing power, and we have no interest to pay to no one."[4]

Britain, which was suffering from a skyrocketing national debt, sought to outlaw America's Colonial Scrip and replace it with money issued by the Bank of England. This came in the form of the Currency Act of 1764. Within a year, according to Franklin, America's streets began to resemble London's, as America's money supply plummeted and unemployment rose dramatically. As Britain's economy continued to suffer, more taxes were placed upon commercial activity within the American colonies. These taxes included the Sugar Act, the Stamp Act, the Townshend Acts, and the infamous Tea Act, which ultimately led to the Boston Tea Party. America had little incentive to pay these taxes, as they no longer needed British military protection after France and Spain were defeated in the French and Indian War. As America grew more economically defiant, Britain passed the Intolerable Acts, which further damaged the fragile relationship between the two nations. To justify the taxes upon the American colonies, the British explained that America should rightly help shoulder the economic burden of keeping the new country in the Empire. America,

> **Did You Know?**
>
> On January 8, 1835, President Andrew Jackson became the first — and only — president to ever pay off the U.S. national debt.

however, defied Britain's attempts to confiscate its wealth through heavy taxes with the cry of "taxation without representation." Finally, after much deliberation, the tensions between the two nations sparked the American Revolutionary War. The Americans succeeded in gaining independence from the British "tyranny" that they so greatly despised.

Or so they thought.

Alexander Hamilton's Central Banking Scheme

Having escaped the economically diseased European continent, which had become dominated by destructive central bankers, America's founding fathers knew the importance of laying a sound economic foundation for their new nation. It did not take long, however, for the central banking community to come knocking at America's door.

The First Bank of the United States, a proposed central bank similar to the one in England, came at the suggestion of Alexander Hamilton in 1790, who argued for a strong centralized government. With England's economic machinations fresh in the minds of the American public, Hamilton's idea for a central bank quickly found numerous opponents. Few Americans were in the mood for a new private banking cartel that would loan newly printed money to the U.S. government at interest. Many early Americans were intimately aware of the dangers and potential devastation that these central banking systems could have upon their new nation. One such opponent was U.S. Secretary of State Thomas Jefferson.

Jefferson, who also authored the Declaration of Independence, believed that a central bank, such as the proposed First Bank of the United States, was clearly forbidden by the Constitution. According to the U.S. Constitution, the creation and issuance of the nation's currency was the sole privilege of the government. In defense of his argument, Jefferson wrote: "I believe that banking institutions are more dangerous to our liberties than standing armies. . . . If the American people ever allow private banks to control the issue of their currency, first by inflation, then by deflation, the banks and corporations that will grow up around them will deprive the people of all property until their children wake up homeless on the continent their fathers conquered. . . . The issuing power should be taken from the banks and restored to the people, to whom it properly belongs."[5]

Jefferson's quote is not prophetic. He was not predicting what he thought might happen. Instead, he was speaking from a wealth of experience. Jefferson was intimately aware of the failed history of central banking schemes. And he passionately warned of their effects upon a nation: "first by inflation, then by deflation. . . ."

This, in fact, is precisely how central banks manipulate the economies upon which they leach. First, they encourage borrowing by creating "cheap" money through a reduction in interest rates, which increases the overall money supply. Then, the central bank raises interest rates, leading to credit defaults, foreclosures, and bankruptcies. This allows the bankers to purchase properties, businesses, and smaller banks for "pennies on the dollar." *Sound familiar?*

Opponents of the proposed First Bank feverishly pointed to the Constitution in an effort to prevent private central banks from gaining control over their own government's monetary activities. Constitutional support for this opposition is taken from Article I, Section VIII of the Constitution where it states that the U.S. federal government is authorized "to coin money, regulate the value thereof, and of foreign coin, and fix the standard of weights and measures."

But while the Constitution may not give express permission to print paper money, Hamilton reasoned, it certainly did not restrict it.

Think about It —
Is the U.S. Dollar Unconstitutional?

Even a casual reading of the U.S. Constitution demonstrates that the Congress is only authorized to create coins with fixed "weights and measures" — not paper money. For this reason, many today believe that the fiat U.S. paper dollar is expressly forbidden by the U.S. Constitution!

And while the Constitution does permit the Congress to coin money, it does not give them permission to outsource this responsibility to an outside institution. According to some, this means that the Federal Reserve Bank is an unconstitutional institution — despite being passed into law by Congress! (For more on this, see the U.S. Supreme Court case Lewis v. United States, 680 F.2d 1239 (1982)

Despite vehement opposition to the First Bank of the United States, President George Washington signed the First Bank of the United States into law on April 25, 1791, along with a 20-year charter, set to expire in

1811. During its first five years of operation, the American government borrowed more than $8 million from the First Bank and prices rose by an average of 72 percent.[6] Just two years prior to the passage of the First Bank, President Washington had warned his countrymen: "No generation has a right to contract debts greater than can be paid off during the course of its existence."

Jefferson would later lament in 1798, "I wish it were possible to obtain a single amendment to our Constitution — taking from the federal government their power of borrowing."[7]

As the 20-year charter for the First Bank came up for renewal in 1811, Congress began debating whether to renew the First Bank's charter for another 20 years or to let it expire. After it was discovered that 70 percent of the First Bank's ownership was held by foreigners — namely England — pressure to allow the bank's charter to lapse became overwhelmingly strong. Nathan Rothschild, a powerful European central banker, was one foreign banker who had a strong, vested interest in the continuation of the First Bank of the United States. Gustavus Myers, in his 1936 book entitled *The History of the Great American Fortunes*, further confirms the Rothschild connection to the First Bank when he wrote, "Under the surface, the Rothschilds long had a powerful influence in dictating American financial laws. The law records show that they were the power of the old Bank of the United States."[8]

It is reported that Rothschild — eager for the renewal of the First Bank charter — issued a bold threat to the U.S. Congress: "Either the application for renewal of the charter is granted, or the United States will find itself involved in a most disastrous war."[9] But on March 3, 1811, after the bank's 20-year charter had expired, the Congress voted against renewing it.

In the following year, mounting conflicts between the British and the United States led to the War of 1812. The British war efforts were funded by none other than the Rothschild family.[10] Four years later, in the wake of the war, the United States was crippled by inflation and rising unemployment. Not surprisingly, the money-hungry Congress moved to charter the Second Bank of the United States.

This second attempt at a U.S. central bank occurred under the administration of President James Madison. Despite being deeply opposed to the idea of private central banking, Madison had little choice but to support the creation of the Second Bank of the United States in the face of high inflation and economic instability. The Second Bank included the same mandates as the First Bank: to issue currency and purchase government debt. The new Bank's charter was set for 20 years and would expire in 1836.

Similar to the First Bank, 80 percent of the Second Bank was privately owned by banks. One-third of these banks were foreign. True to form, the Second Bank quickly led the United States back into massive inflation. Within the first 18 months, the Bank had injected nearly $20 million into the U.S. money supply. As prices soared due to the increase in money supply, inflationary pressures began to harm American commerce. The bank reacted by cutting the money supply in half — from over $20 million to just $11.5 million.[11] This manipulation of the money supply rocked the economy. This would be the first of many infamous "boom and bust" cycles brought on by the central bank.

As the central banking scheme continued, Americans became wise to the Second Bank's attempts to loot the nation of its hard-earned wealth through crafty monetary policies that encouraged inflationary periods followed by deflationary periods.

President Madison, aware of the pitfalls of the Second Bank, warned: "History records that the money changers have used every form of abuse, intrigue, deceit, and violent means possible to maintain their control over governments by controlling the money and its issuance."[12]

Andrew Jackson — "I Killed the Bank"

In 1828, 12 years after the inception of the Second Bank of the United States, Andrew Jackson was elected president. President Jackson came into office with one mission: to kill the Second Bank of the United States. However, the bank's charter would not be up for renewal until 1836 — another eight years. To accomplish his goal would require Jackson to win a second term in office. During his first term, he fired nearly 20 percent of the employees of the federal government — many who had ties to the Second Bank.

In 1832, with his re-election approaching, the bank struck an early blow, hoping that Jackson would not want to stir up controversy. They asked Congress to pass their renewal bill four years early.[13]

Jackson swiftly vetoed the bill and stated, "It is not our own citizens only who are to receive the bounty of our government. More than eight millions of the stock of this bank are held by foreigners. . . . Is there no danger to our liberty and independence in a bank that in its nature has so little to bind it to our country? Controlling our currency, receiving our public moneys, and holding thousands of our citizens in dependence . . . would be more formidable and dangerous than a military power of the enemy."[14]

In Jackson's lengthy veto message, he explained why the Second Bank of the United States should be abolished. Jackson's reasons included the following:

- It concentrated the nation's financial strength in a single institution
- It exposed the government to control by foreign interests
- It served mainly to make the rich richer
- It exercised too much control over members of Congress
- It favored northeastern states over southern and western states[15]

After his successful 1832 re-election bid against his opponent, Henry Clay (who received $3 million in campaign contributions from the banks), Jackson continued his tireless campaign to permanently dissolve the Second Bank. He began by removing funds from the Second Bank to render it ineffective. These actions provoked strong opposition from the bankers. The president of the Second Bank, Nicholas Biddle, lashed out at President Jackson, saying, "This worthy President thinks that because he has scalped Indians and imprisoned judges, he is to have his way with the bank. He is mistaken."[16]

Jackson responded: "Gentlemen, I have had men watching you for a long time and I am convinced that you have used the funds of the bank to speculate in the breadstuffs of the country. When you won, you divided the profits amongst you, and when you lost, you charged it to the bank. You tell me that if I take the deposits from the bank and annul its charter I shall ruin ten thousand families. That may be true, gentlemen, but that is your sin! Should I let you go on you will ruin fifty thousand families, and that would be my sin! You are a den of vipers and thieves. I have determined to rout you out, and by the Eternal God, I will rout you out!"[17]

Jackson's courageous and controversial act of pulling funds from the government-controlled banking cartel, known as the Second Bank of the United States, led to the final demise of the central bank. When later asked what his greatest accomplishment had been during his two terms as president, Andrew Jackson confidently replied, "I killed the bank." He would later order that this phrase be engraved on his tombstone.[18]

The National Banking Act

After the death of the Second Bank of the United States, America soon began experimenting with various types of monetary systems. The period from 1837 to 1862 was known as the Free Bank Era. While the central bankers were still at bay, their influence was ever present in America's political system — and was threatening to creep back in.

As America entered the 1860s, the nation's economy was fractured, and the political climate between the North and the South reached a boiling point. Eleven Southern slave states declared their secession from the United States to form the Confederate States of America in 1861. On April 12, the Confederates led an attack upon a U.S. military installation in Fort Sumter, South Carolina. Thus, the first shots had been fired on what would become known as the American Civil War — the deadliest war in American history.

War is an expensive proposition for a nation. In search of an effective way to fund the costs of the war, President Abraham Lincoln authorized the National Banking Act. This act was similar in structure to the First and Second Bank of the United States. However, instead of vesting power into just one central bank, this new act made provisions for the federal government to control a number of national banks. These national banks were then responsible for purchasing federal government bonds with their own created bank notes.[19] The importance of this act should be noted, as it helped establish our current debt-based monetary system, which allows our federal government to create money out of thin air with the help of the Federal Reserve Banking system. In a letter sent to New York bankers in support of the 1863 National Banking Act, John Sherman wrote: "The few who can understand the system will either be so interested in its profits, or so dependent on its favors, that there will be no opposition from that class, while on the other hand, the great body of the people, mentally incapable of comprehending the tremendous advantages that capital derives from the system, will bear its burdens without complaint and perhaps without even suspecting that the system is inimical to their interests."[20]

Just before the passage of the National Banking Act, President Abraham Lincoln wrote a letter to William Elkin stating: "I see in the near future a crisis approaching. It unnerves me and causes me to tremble for the safety of my country . . . the Money Power of the country will endeavor to prolong its reign by working upon the prejudices of the people, until the wealth is aggregated in a few hands and the Republic is destroyed. I feel at this moment more anxiety for the safety of my country than ever before, even in the midst of war."[21]

Five months later, Lincoln would be assassinated. Controversy still surrounds his murder. Salmon P. Chase, the Secretary of the Treasury under Lincoln, later expressed regret at his role in the passage of the National Banking Act when he said, "My agency in promoting the passage of the National Banking Act was the greatest financial mistake in my life. It has built up a monopoly which affects every interest in the country."[22]

The national debate over the need for a centralized monetary authority continued to ebb and flow during the decades following the collapse of the Second Bank and the passage of the National Banking Act.

It was not until a series of bank runs known as "the Panic of 1907" that the American public became insatiably eager for a fresh round of banking and monetary reform. The Panic of 1907 would become the catalyst for the birth of the "Third" Bank of the United States.

The "Third" Bank of the United States

One year after the Panic of 1907, President Theodore Roosevelt launched the National Monetary Commission. Under the direction of Senator Nelson Aldrich (a friend of J.P. Morgan and the father-in-law of John D. Rockefeller Jr.), the commission members embarked on a tour of major European capitals in an effort to discover the inner workings of Europe's central banks. Senator Aldrich, who personally led the commission's team of experts, sought to gain insight into how

America could create its very own central bank. The group's findings became the basis for the Federal Reserve Act, which would lead to the creation of the Federal Reserve Banking System — "The Third Bank of the United States."

From its inception, the Federal Reserve Bank was shrouded in mystery. Many Americans mistakenly believe that the Federal Reserve Bank is simply an agency of the federal government that is regulated at the federal level. However, this is not true. While it is true that the Federal Reserve was created by an act of Congress, the bank is not a government entity. Instead, the "Fed" is a partnership between the federal government and the private banking system. In other words, the Fed is a government-controlled banking cartel. As such, it is as "federal" as Federal Express.

Although the Fed was created by an act of Congress on December 23, 1913, the idea for America's new central bank was not debated in the halls of Congress. Instead, it was secretly conceived among a group of bankers on a small island off the coast of Georgia, known as Jekyll Island.

On the night of November 22, 1910, Senator Aldrich and seven of his associates boarded a private rail car in Hoboken, New Jersey. They traveled south to Jekyll Island, Georgia. Details of the meeting were kept secret. Security was tight and the media was not invited.

It was not until 1919, six years after the Jekyll Island event, that B.C. Forbes of the famed *Forbes* magazine broke the story of the top-secret meeting. Forbes interviewed one of the meeting attendees, Paul M. Warburg. During the interview, Warburg described the experience: "Picture a party of the nation's greatest bankers stealing out of New York on a private railroad car under cover of darkness, stealthily heading hundreds of miles south, embarking on a mysterious launch, sneaking onto an island deserted by all but a few servants, living there a full week under such rigid secrecy that the names of not one of them was once mentioned lest the servants learn the identity and disclose to the world this strangest, most secret expedition in the history of American finance. I am not romancing. I am giving to the world, for the first time, the real story of how the famous Aldrich currency report, the foundation of our new currency system, was written."[23]

Warburg would later write this in his book, *The Federal Reserve System, Its Origin and Growth*: "The results of the conference were entirely confidential. Even the fact there had been a meeting was not permitted to become public. . . . Though eighteen years have since gone by, I do not feel free to give a description of this most interesting conference concerning which Senator Aldrich pledged all participants to secrecy."[24]

The strict cloak of secrecy under which the Federal Reserve was created should be alarming to all Americans. This intentional concealment on the part of our government and the banking elites begs the question: what were the creators of the Federal Reserve hiding? Why did they feel such a strong need for secrecy? What was there to hide?

Perhaps the answer lies in the following statement from another attendee of the secret meeting, Frank Vanderlip. In a February 9, 1935, article in the *Saturday Evening Post*, Vanderlip wrote, "If it were to be exposed publicly that our particular group had gotten together and written a banking bill, that bill would have no chance whatever of passage by Congress." According to Vanderlip, the Federal Reserve Bank, which controls our nation's money supply and our interest rate targets, was concocted in secret because Congress *would not have passed the bill if they had full knowledge of the bank's true intentions.*

Is this a legitimate reason for hiding the deliberations over this piece of legislation from the American public, and its elected leaders?

If monetary history has taught us anything it is that nations should cautiously guard who gains control over their money supply. Because of the extreme power that is attached to the issuance of a nation's money supply, it is not something that should be doled out to a secretive group cloaked in mystery.

A few weeks before his assassination in 1881, U.S. President James Garfield said these words: "Whoever controls the money of a nation, controls that nation. . . . Whosoever controls the volume of money in any country is absolute master of all industry and commerce. . . . And when you realize that the entire system is very easily controlled, one way or another, by a few powerful men at the top, you will not have to be told how periods of inflation and depression originate."[25]

Several U.S. political leaders vocalized their concerns about the true intentions of the Federal Reserve Bank. For example, Minnesota

Congressman Charles A. Lindbergh (the father of the famed aviator) said in 1913: "This [Federal Reserve Act] establishes the most gigantic trust on earth. When the President [Wilson] signs this bill, the invisible government of the monetary power will be legalized. . . . The worst legislative crime of the ages is perpetrated by this banking and currency bill."[26]

Fearing the ultimate control that the private central bankers would now have over the U.S. economy, Lindbergh added: "From now on, depressions will be scientifically created."[27]

Despite numerous warnings — and two past failures — the Federal Reserve Act was passed by the U.S. House of Representatives on December 22, 1913.

With the bill passed by the House, it went on to the U.S. Senate. Given the secrecy in which the idea was originated, there is little doubt that the timing of the proposed Federal Reserve Act — the same week as Christmas break — was intentionally designed to get the controversial bill through the Senate with as little debate as possible. The clever ploy succeeded, as the Senate vote was quietly scheduled for December 23, 1913. Just two days before Christmas, many senators had already gone home for the holiday break. As the bankers had hoped, the bill passed through the Senate with relatively little debate. Later that same day, President Woodrow Wilson signed the Federal Reserve Act into law.

As Ralph Epperson would later put it: "The American people, who had suffered through the American Revolution, the War of 1812, the battles between Andrew Jackson and the Second Bank of the United States, the Civil War, the previous panics of 1873 and 1893, and now the panic of 1907, were finally conditioned to the point of accepting the solution offered by those who had caused all of these events: the international bankers. That solution was a central bank."[28]

True to form and to history, the Federal Reserve Bank doubled the U.S. money supply from 1914 to 1919. These fresh injections of U.S. dollars into the economy created an era of widespread economic growth. By 1920, when the nation's money supply had become too robust, the banks began calling in loans, resulting in widespread bankruptcies and foreclosures. Over 5,000 banks failed during the ensuing recession of 1921, leading to a consolidation of the banking industry. This consolidation of the banking industry in 1921 allowed larger banks to purchase their former competitors for pennies on the dollar, giving more control to the nation's largest banks. This would become a common theme throughout the 20th century.

From 1921 to 1929, the Federal Reserve again increased the U.S. money supply, this time by over 60 percent.[29] This era, marked by increasing wealth and consumer excess, is often referred to by historians as the "Roaring Twenties." As the Fed increased the supply of money and credit, investors enjoyed the benefits of rising asset prices. An unfortunate side effect of this Fed-created distortion of the real economy was the belief by many Americans that the stock market, which had increased in value five-fold from 1923 to 1929, would continue rising indefinitely. Investor optimism led to wild speculation as hundreds of thousands of Americans sought to strike it rich in the stock market. By August 1929, stock brokers had loaned out over $8.5 billion to small investors — more than the entire number of U.S. dollars in circulation at the time.[30]

Few Americans were prepared for the cataclysmic event that awaited them. In the final week of October 1929, America's time of reckoning arrived as the U.S. stock market dropped precipitously, wiping out billions of dollars of American wealth in an instant.[31] Many Americans, fearing for the safety of any wealth they had left, began withdrawing funds from local banks. These events, known as "bank runs," led to the failure of over 10,000 banks — leading to an even further consolidation of the banking industry. The Federal Reserve did little to prevent the crash of 1929, and did even less to stabilize the economy once it had weakened. In the face of such desperate economic pressure, this inaction on the part of the Fed confirmed the deep-seated concerns that some American political leaders had regarding the central bank.

One case involved Pennsylvania Congressman Louis T. McFadden, who sought to bring conspiracy charges against the Federal Reserve Board in 1932. In a speech before the Congress, McFadden declared: "Mr. Chairman, we have in this country one of the most corrupt institutions the world has ever known. I refer to the Federal Reserve Board and the Federal Reserve Banks, hereinafter called the Fed. The Fed has cheated the government of these United States and the people of the United States out of enough money to pay the nation's debt. The depredations and iniquities of the Fed have cost enough money to pay the national debt several times over. This evil institution has impoverished and ruined the people of these United States, has bankrupted itself, and has practically bankrupted our government. It has done this through the defects of the law under which it operates, through the maladministration of that law by the Fed and through the corrupt practices of the moneyed vultures who control it. Some people think that the Federal Reserve Banks are United States government institutions. They are private monopolies which prey upon the people of these United States for the benefit of themselves and their foreign customers; foreign and domestic speculators and swindlers; and rich and predatory money lenders. There is not a man within the sound of my voice who does not know that this nation is run by the international bankers."[32]

McFadden's concerns were not unusual. Even President Franklin D. Roosevelt was intimately aware of the intense debate over the efficacy of the Federal Reserve. In a letter to Colonel Edward M. House dated November 21, 1933, Roosevelt admitted the extreme tension between the nation and the Federal Reserve Bank: "The real truth of the matter is, as you and I know, that a financial element in the larger centers has owned the Government ever since the days of Andrew Jackson — and I am not wholly excepting the Administration of W.W. [Woodrow Wilson]. The country is going through a repetition of Jackson's fight with the Bank of the United States — only on a far bigger and broader basis."[33]

Did You Know?

In 1933, America was still suffering through the worst of the Great Depression. In an effort to preserve their capital, many Americans were cashing in their gold-backed U.S. dollars in exchange for gold. As demand for gold became crippling, President Roosevelt issued Executive Order 6102, which authorized the confiscation of all privately owned gold held by U.S. citizens. In exchange for their gold, Americans would receive paper money. This despicable act was done under the guise of helping "bring an end to the depression." The penalties for violating this Gold Seizure Law: a $10,000 fine and/or ten years in prison.

While the average American was facing severe financial hardship in the wake of the Great Depression, the central bankers and their rich banking friends had seen the danger coming and had escaped the downturn. For example, Federal Reserve member Paul Warburg reportedly issued a warning in March 1929 to the central banking community that a U.S. stock market crash was nearing. In his book, *The Creature from Jekyll Island*, G. Edward Griffin writes: "Virtually all of the inner club [banking elite] was rescued. There is no record of any member of the interlocking directorate between the Federal Reserve, the major New York banks, and their prime customers having been caught by surprise."[34]

President Woodrow Wilson, the president who signed the Federal Reserve Act into law, would later openly express his concern that America was being controlled by a separate "invisible" government. The following three quotes are taken from the writings of President Wilson.

> We have restricted credit, we have restricted opportunity, we have controlled development, and we have come to be one of the worst ruled, one of the most completely controlled and dominated, governments in the civilized world — no longer a government by free opinion, no longer a government by conviction and the vote of the majority, but a government by the opinion and the duress of small groups of dominant men.[35]

> Since I entered politics, I have chiefly had men's views confided to me privately. Some of the biggest men in the United States, in the field of commerce and manufacture, are afraid of somebody, are afraid of something. They know that there is a power somewhere so organized, so subtle, so watchful, so interlocked, so complete, so pervasive, that they had better not speak above their breath when they speak in condemnation of it.[36]

> The government, which was designed for the people, has got into the hands of the bosses and their employers, the special interests. An invisible empire has been set up above the forms of democracy."[37]

Supreme Court Justice Felix Frankfurter would later express similar concerns when he stated in 1952: "The real rulers in Washington are invisible and exercise power from behind the scenes."[38]

Senator Barry Goldwater identified the international money lenders as the source of this "invisible power" when he stated: "Most Americans have no real understanding of the operation of the international moneylenders. The bankers want it that way. We recognize in a hazy sort of way that the Rothschilds and the Warburgs of Europe and the houses of J.P. Morgan, Kuhn, Loeb and Company, Schiff, Lehman, and Rockefeller possess and control vast wealth. How they acquire this vast financial power and employ it is a mystery to most of us. International bankers make money by extending credit to governments. The greater the debt of the political state, the larger the interest returned to the lenders. The national banks of Europe are actually owned and controlled by private interests."[39]

Sir Josiah Stamp, the president of the Bank of England in the 1920s and the second richest man in Britain, made this revealing comment: "Banking was conceived in iniquity and was born in sin. The bankers own the earth. Take it away from them, but leave them the power to create deposits, and with the flick of the pen they will create enough deposits to buy it back again. However, take it away from them, and all the great fortunes like mine will disappear and they ought to disappear, for this would be a happier and better world to live in. But, if you wish to remain the slaves of bankers and pay the cost of your own slavery, let them continue to create deposits."[40]

How America Lost the Revolutionary War

America's early history is one of struggle for economic and political freedom from edicts and policies issued by Great Britain. The conflict eventually led to an American declaration of freedom and independence by way of the Revolutionary War. But it did not take long for America's new-found economic freedom to be threatened by Europe's corrupt central banking system. After several battles with private banking interests throughout its history, America finally lost the war for their economic autonomy with the establishment of the Federal Reserve Banking System on December 23, 1913. I believe that on this day, America lost nearly all of the benefits they sought to gain from their earlier Revolution.

Today, the U.S. government is heavily indebted to private banking interests — both domestic and foreign. Similarly, U.S. citizens are no more than indentured servants beholden to the debts that have been created through years of poor fiscal and monetary choices. After all, "we the people" bear the ultimate responsibility for all of the debts incurred by our spendthrift government and their central banking schemes.

Since 1913, the U.S. government has opted to outsource its constitutional obligation to create currency. Instead of creating its own currency free of interest as it is instructed to do in Article I, Section VIII of the Constitution, it has chosen to *borrow its own currency from the privately held Federal Reserve — at interest!*

The U.S. government grants this private banking cartel — the Federal Reserve — the ability to print money out of thin air. In turn, the Federal Reserve banking system empowers American banks to do the same through the magic of "fractional-reserve banking," which we will discuss at length in the following chapter.

The greatest fears of America's founding fathers have come true: Our nation has become enslaved to private banking interests — and most do not even realize it.

Several questions remain as we prepare to delve deeper into this subject. These questions include the following:

- If the Federal Reserve is a private banking cartel that is independent from the government, *who are its owners?*
- Why does the government pay interest to the Federal Reserve for the currency that it creates when the government could save the interest by printing its own currency?
- How are America's banks able to create money out of thin air?
- And finally, what effect has this central banking scheme had upon you, the average American consumer?

In this chapter you have been introduced to a very brief history of a system that has been at the root of political debates, national struggles, and even wars. In the following chapter, you are going to discover how this system actually works and how it impacts your own finances.

Quick Summary

✓ The American Revolutionary War was rooted in a belief that the American colonies had a right to economic liberty and political autonomy.

✓ Despite vehement opposition to the First Bank of the United States, President George Washington signed the First Bank of the United States into law on April 25, 1791, along with a 20-year charter, set to expire in 1811.

✓ In 1816, after the War of 1812, the Second Bank of the United States was born with a 20-year charter.

✓ The policies of these early central banks led to a series of booms and busts, which are a common trait of an economy with a central bank.

✓ In 1828, Andrew Jackson was elected president. His one guiding mission was to "kill the Second Bank."

✓ After a long struggle, Jackson succeeded in destroying the Second Bank of the United States.

✓ The period from 1837 to 1862 was known as the Free Bank Era.

✓ Despite numerous warnings — and two past failures — the Federal Reserve Act was passed by the U.S. House of Representatives on December 22, 1913. The next day, just two days before Christmas, the Senate passed it and President Woodrow Wilson signed it into law.

✓ With the passage of the Federal Reserve Act, the greatest fears of America's founding fathers came true as our nation became *enslaved to private banking interests*.

Endnotes

1. From a speech by Representative Ron Paul, M.D., "Abolish the Fed," in the House of Representatives, September 10, 2002, http://www.lewrockwell.com/paul/paul53.html.

2. Charles Francis Adams, *The Works of John Adams, Second President of the United States* (New York: Little, Brown & Co., 1853), letter to Thomas Jefferson (August 25, 1787).

3. Ellen Hodgson Brown, *Web of Debt: The Shocking Truth about Our Money System* (Baton Rouge, LA: Third Millennium Press, 2007), p. 36.

4. http://www.planetization.org/prosperity.htm.

5. John McMurty, *The Cancer Stage of Capitalism: And Its Cure* (London; Sterling, VA: Pluto Press, 1999), p. 291.

6. Mike Hewitt, "America's Forgotten War Against the Central Bankers," http://www.financialsense.com/fsu/editorials/dollardaze/2007/1020.html.

7. Richard H. Palmquist, *Einstein, Money, and Contentment* (Bloomington, IN: AuthorHouse, 2005), p. 92.

8. Gustavus Myers, *History of the Great American Fortunes* (Chicago, IL: C.H. Kerr & Co., 1910).

9. Brown, *Web of Debt*, p. 77.

10. Ibid., p. 556. The Rothschilds long had a powerful influence in dictating American financial laws. The law records show that they were the power in the old Bank of the United States.

11. Hewitt, "America's Forgotten War Against the Central Bankers."

12. Olive Cushing Dwinell, *The Story of Our Money* (Boston, MA: Meador Publishing Co., 1946), p. 71.

13. *The Money Masters* (video), produced by Royalty Production Co.

14. "President Jackson's Veto Message Regarding the Bank of the United States," July 10, 1832, http://avalon.law.yale.edu/19th_century/ajveto01.asp.

15. Andrew Jackson; http://en.wikipedia.org/wiki/Andrew_Jackson.

16. Bray Hammond, *Banks and Politics in America from the Revolution to the Civil War* (Princeton, NJ: Princeton University Press, 1957), p. 433.

17. http://quotes.liberty-tree.ca/quote/andrew_jackson_quote_4f92.

18. Sandra and Harry Choron, *Money: Everything You Never Knew About Your Favorite Thing to Covet, Save & Spend* (San Francisco, CA: Chronicle Books, 2011), p. 43

19. Hewitt, "America's Forgotten War Against the Central Bankers."

20. The Rothschild brothers of London writing to associates in New York, 1863. http://www.themoneymasters.com/the-money-masters/famous-quotations-on-banking/.

21. Archer H. Shaw, editor, *The Lincoln Encyclopedia: The Spoken and Written Words of A. Lincoln* (New York: Macmillan Co., 1950), a letter to William F. Elkins, November 21, 1864, p. 40.

22. Mark Hill, *Shadow Kings* (Canada: Trafford Publishing, 2005), p. 107.

23. G. Edward Griffin, *The Creature from Jekyll Island: A Second Look at the Federal Reserve* (Westlake Village, CA: American Media, 1994), p. 9.

24. Paul M. Warburg, *The Federal Reserve System: Its Origin and Growth* (New York: The Macmillan Company, 1930).

25. http://en.wikiquote.org/wiki/James_A._Garfield.

26. Mike Kirchubel, "Abolish the Federal Reserve System, Treasury Bills, Notes, Bonds, and the National Debt," Independent Media Center, Dec. 10, 2008, http://www.indymedia.org/en/2008/12/917530.shtml.

27. Charles Merlin Umpenhour, *Freedom, a Fading Illusion* (Aurora, WV: Book-Makers Ink, 2005), p. 170.

28. A. Ralph Epperson, *The Unseen Hand: An Introduction to the Conspiratorial View of History* (Tucson, AZ: Publius Press, 1985), p. 169.

29. Hewitt, "America's Forgotten War Against the Central Bankers."

30. http://www.ft.com/intl/cms/s/7173bb6a-552a-11dd-ae9c-000077b07658,Authorised=false.html?_i_location=http%3A%2F%2Fwww.ft.com%2Fcms%2Fs%2F0%2F7173bb6a-552a-11dd-ae9c-000077b07658.html&_i_referer=http%3A%2F%2Fen.wikipedia.org%2Fwiki%2FWall_Street_Crash_of_1929#axzz1prO0Lxvm.

31. http://www.nytimes.com/1987/10/21/business/the-market-turmoil-past-lessons-present-advice-did-29-crash-spark-the-depression.html.

32. Brown, *Web of Debt*, p. 129.

33. Elliott Roosevelt, editor, *F.D.R.: His Personal Letters, 1928–1945* (New York: Duell, Sloan and Pearce, 1950), p. 373.

34. Griffin, *The Creature from Jekyll Island.*
35. *Woodrow Wilson, The New Freedom: A Call for the Emancipation of the Generous Energies of a People* (Englewood Cliffs, NJ: Prentice-Hall, 1961), p. 201.
36. Ibid., p. 17–18.
37. Ibid., p. 117.
38. Ibid., p. 118.
39. Barry M. Goldwater, *With No Apologies: The Personal and Political Memoirs of United States Senator Barry M. Goldwater* (New York: Morrow, 1979), p. 281.
40. Robert Harris Brevig, L. Fletcher Prouty, *Beyond Our Consent* (Canada: Trafford Publishing, 2004), p. 149.

Chapter 7

Modern Money Mechanics: What the Banksters Do Not Want You to Know

It is well that the people of the nation do not understand our banking and monetary system, for if they did, I believe there would be a revolution before tomorrow morning.[1]

— Henry Ford, echoing President Andrew Jackson

OVERVIEW: Ask most Americans if they believe that their nation has too much debt and the inevitable answer will be a resounding yes. But follow that question up by telling them that the money in their pocket itself is actually debt, and you will receive confused looks. This is because the American government, along with its banking cartel friend, the Federal Reserve, has done a fabulous job of deceiving the public into believing that the U.S. dollar is an asset. In this chapter, you will discover the explosive truth that will hopefully change your entire outlook on the U.S. monetary system. This truth summed up in a single statement is simply that money is debt.

In 2009, I was asked to teach an economics course at a local college. During one of my lectures I decided to help my students explore the nature of America's debt-based monetary system. I began the lesson by reaching into the pocket of my sports coat to grab a crisp new twenty dollar bill. I held the bill up high so that the entire class could see and exclaimed: "This is a piece of debt."

Some of the chuckles that followed were loud enough to stir a few sleeping students from their slumber.

Doing my best not to crack a smile, I repeated my statement, this time a bit more forcefully: "This piece of paper is nothing more than a piece of debt."

Suddenly, the smiles and laughter turned to confused and puzzled looks.

Since that moment, I have delivered the exact same message to audiences, both large and small, around the world. And every single time, the reaction is the same: Absolute astonishment, and sometimes even denial.

The truth that I am going to share with you in this chapter is admittedly shocking. However, without a true and proper understanding of the following facts, you will be highly vulnerable to those who have sought to keep you living in financial darkness.

Here is the hard truth: Money is debt.

It is an absurd statement, isn't it? In fact, if you believe me to be crazed, I do not think that I could blame you. After all, the very idea that "money is debt" seems to offend everything that you and I have been taught about money. Perhaps I would appear to be more sane if I said "black is white" or "high is low." I certainly do not expect you to immediately grasp this debt-based money concept, which is likely foreign to you.

So how can this be? And if it is true that money is nothing more than debt, then why would any American work 40 hours per week for money?

By the end of this chapter, my goal is to explain our debt-based monetary system in such simple terms that you will not only understand it yourself, but you will be able to explain it to others with ease.

Let's begin.

Modern Money Mechanics

Running a national government is an expensive endeavor. Like most nations, the U.S. government raises the money funds it needs to function in two ways. The first method of funding is through the collection of taxes, tariffs, and fees. The second way is to borrow money.

Since most U.S. citizens pay taxes, we are all at least somewhat familiar with the process of taxation. And given our current consumer debt levels, I think it is fair to say that Americans are experts at borrowing. When you or I need to borrow money, we simply use a credit card or contact our bank for a loan.

But to whom does the Federal government turn when it needs a loan?

When the government wants to borrow money, it turns to the U.S. Treasury Department. The Treasury Department responds to the government's request for money by printing treasury bonds, which it then sells to various buyers through public auctions.

Who are the buyers at these auctions? There are numerous kinds of buyers, including U.S. and foreign investors, domestic and international financial institutions, and foreign central banks. When these buyers make a purchase of treasury bonds through the auction process, they are using their own money, which is already in existence.

But what happens if the U.S. government wants to borrow $50 billion and the Treasury is only able to sell $30 billion worth of bonds? Is the government simply out of luck?

Not quite. Fortunately for our spendthrift government, they always have a willing lender in their own central bank — the Federal Reserve. In fact, as the government's "lender of last resort," the Fed is virtually required to step in and purchase all excess treasury bonds that are not sold to the public. As the nation's central bank, the Fed has discretion to loan money at interest to any institution it considers as "too big to fail."

Did You Know?
Who Owns the Federal Reserve?

The Federal Reserve Bank is privately owned by shareholders, who all happen to be private member banks of the Federal Reserve System. The U.S. government does not own any shares in the Federal Reserve. While the Federal Reserve was created by an act of Congress, and can therefore be ended by an act of Congress, it is not a federal entity. It is a government-run private banking cartel that controls the monetary policy of the U.S. federal government.

But what you may not know is that when the Fed purchases treasury bonds, it does not use its own hard earned money. Instead, *it simply prints the money, thus creating it "out of thin air."* So regardless of how well the bond auctions go, the government is virtually guaranteed to get every penny that it has requested — even if the money has to be printed.

Don't believe me? Then consider this quote from a document put out by the Boston Federal Reserve Bank called "Putting It Simply."

> When you or I write a check there must be sufficient funds in our account to cover the check, but when the Federal Reserve writes a check there is no bank deposit on which that check is drawn. *When the Federal Reserve writes a check, it is creating money.*

Can you imagine how much financial trouble many American citizens would get into if local banks started handing out credit cards with no credit limits? How do you think this would affect the public's spending habits? And yet, that is essentially what the Fed does for the United States government! The government can borrow nearly limitless amounts of money from the Fed, with the occasional annoyance of having to pass a debt ceiling increase, to pay for virtually anything it wants. It's no different than giving a financially irresponsible teenager a credit card with

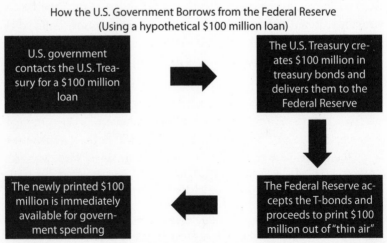

How the U.S. Government Borrows from the Federal Reserve
(Using a hypothetical $100 million loan)

U.S. government contacts the U.S. Treasury for a $100 million loan	The U.S. Treasury creates $100 million in treasury bonds and delivers them to the Federal Reserve
The newly printed $100 million is immediately available for government spending	The Federal Reserve accepts the T-bonds and proceeds to print $100 million out of "thin air"

FACT: U.S. currency is created out of government debt. MONEY=DEBT no credit limit and then telling him or her to be smart! Who in their right mind would do such a thing? Apparently the American public would.

Is it any surprise then that the government has racked up well over $15 trillion in debt — and $118 trillion in future debt obligations!

To simplify the process of how the government borrows money, consider the following diagram. It illustrates how the U.S. government borrows money from the Federal Reserve, via the U.S. Treasury. In this example, we will assume that the government needs to borrow $100 million.

As you can see, the process by which the U.S. government borrows money is quite simple. But allow me to point out a couple of key points regarding this process.

First, when the Treasury Department delivers the bonds to the Fed in exchange for the newly printed currency, the bonds are then listed as new debts on the government's balance sheet. This means that every dollar created by the Federal Reserve immediately becomes a debt obligation of the Federal government.

Second, the new currency created by the Federal Reserve and delivered for the government's use is created *out of thin air!* Put simply, the Federal Reserve accepts government IOUs in exchange for printing new U.S. currency.

> When the Federal Reserve writes a check for a government bond it does exactly what any bank does, it creates money, it creates money purely and simply by writing a check.[2] (Congressman Wright Patman, chairman of the House Banking and Currency Committee in the 1960s)

If all of this seems bizarre, you should take note that we have only scratched the surface of this *government-endorsed counterfeiting scheme.* The longer we peer behind the curtains of this system, the more *illegitimate* and *unreasonable* it becomes. Any government that relies upon a central bank to print its own money must pay back the borrowed money — plus interest — to the bank. You may be thinking: Why shouldn't the government pay interest to the bank that loans it money? After all, it is only reasonable that a bank would charge interest on money it has loaned. There is no reason to consider this process abnormal.

If you sympathize with the above reasoning, then consider these two important questions:

1) Why does the U.S. government insist on paying interest to borrow its own currency, when the currency could be created by the government itself, interest-free?

2) Where does the government obtain the interest owed to the Federal Reserve?

After all, the Fed only creates the *principal*, not the *interest*. So where does the money to pay the interest come from?

The answers to these two questions are vitally important and will help unveil the deception behind this very unconstitutional government-run banking cartel, known as the Federal Reserve.

Let us answer these two questions now.

Why Does the U.S. Government Pay Interest to "Borrow" Its Own Currency?

In 1913, the Fed was given congressional permission to print U.S. currency out of thin air. Ever since then, the U.S. government has chosen to borrow its own currency from the Fed, *at interest*. It should be obvious why the Fed desires to partner with global economic powers like the United States. The Fed, which is owned by several large private banks, profits greatly from the large and consistent income shoveled into its coffers by the government. For centuries, private bankers have known that national governments make the best clients. With their perpetual demand for large loans and national taxing power, which virtually guarantees the ability to never miss a loan payment, what else could a banker ask for? Perhaps only one thing could possibly make this relationship more profitable for the Fed: war.

How does the Fed financially benefit from war? Through the increased government demand for borrowed money that is generated by war. Wartime is to central banking what Christmastime is to retailers. Unfortunately, history is replete with stories of sinister involvement of central banking in national conflicts.

So the Fed's true incentive is crystal clear to any casual observer: to lend as much money to the government as possible.

But perhaps less obvious are the reasons why the U.S. government would be willing to borrow its own currency at interest from a central bank. If Washington wants to borrow limitless amounts of money, why not just cut out the middleman and print their own currency in the Congress? While this would not solve Washington's chronic spending problem, at least the government would not have to pay interest on every dollar that it printed.

The answer to this question has less to do with practicality and everything to do with perception. Public perception is everything in modern politics and economics. The Washington elites believe that there is something "wholesome" about the government being required to approach the central bank in order to "borrow" money. After all, the need to borrow from a bank at times seems familiar to a naïve American public. However, few Americans understand the concept of printing your own money when your bank account runs low.

Therefore, this veil of monetary normalcy serves to cloak the disturbing reality of the government-run banking cartel from the average American. But the use of economic sleight of hand to deceive an economically ignorant public does not make the current monetary arrangement moral, *or even legal.*

According to Article I, Section VIII of the U.S. Constitution, it is the Congress — not a central bank controlled by private banking interests — that is given sole power "to coin money, regulate the value thereof, and of foreign coin, and fix the Standard of Weights and Measures."

As we learned in the previous chapter, America's founders were intimately aware of the dangers inherent in allowing private banking interests to gain control of the national money supply. For this very reason the Constitution gives express authorization to the Congress alone "to coin money and regulate the value thereof." But in 1913, a derelict U.S. Congress delegated these exclusive constitutional powers to a private banking cartel, and the rest is history.

By voluntarily transferring monetary powers to an independent "federal" institution, the Congress has hoodwinked the American into thinking that its borrowing ability has been somehow limited to "responsible" levels. This is a completely false perception, but it has worked well.

In reality, the government's reckless borrowing from the Fed has subjected the American public to a new stealth tax called inflation. The "Federal" Reserve banking fraud serves as a clever front which disguises the real truth about money creation from the public.

I have never yet had anyone who could through the use of logic and reason justify the Federal Government borrowing the use of its own money. . . . I believe the time will come when people will demand that this be changed. I believe the time will come in this country when they actually blame you and me and everyone connected with Congress for sitting idly by and permitting such an idiotic system to continue.[3] (Wright Patman, Congressman 1928–1976, Chairman, Committee on Banking and Currency 1963–1975)

Where Does the Interest to Pay the Fed Come From?

This next question cuts right to the core of the issue, but leads to a mind-bending answer. As we have already stated, when the Fed loans currency to the government, it only creates the principal, not the interest. As we will see momentarily, *it is precisely this issue that imperils the entire American monetary system.*

Using our previous example, imagine that the Fed lends $100 million in new currency to the government. The government now owes the Fed $100 million, plus interest. But since the interest was not created and loaned out along with the initial principal, the government must raise other funds to repay the interest on the loan. Put simply, the government does not have the interest to pay back to the Fed because it was never created in the first place!

In recent years, the interest on the national debt has become an enormous burden as the annual interest costs have reached into the hundreds of billions. Because the debt levels have become so massive, the government has resorted to simply paying the interest due each month, *leaving the principal virtually untouched.* This is like making minimum monthly payments on a large credit card balance. In essence, the debt will *never* be repaid because only the interest is being paid each month.

The modern banking system manufactures money out of nothing. The process is perhaps the most astounding piece of sleight of hand that was ever invented.[4] (Sir Josiah Stamp, Director of the Bank of England, 1928–1941)

So far, we have examined the Fed's money creation process from a macro-level. Now we will move from the insanity of Washington to the seeming normalcy of the local banks found on Main Street, USA.

Does your local bank possess the ability to create money out of thin air like the Federal Reserve? The answer may surprise you.

Fractional-Reserve Banking 101

Have you ever asked yourself the question "Where does money come from?" As we have previously discussed, all you have to do is look at the front of a U.S. dollar bill to find the answer. It says in big bold letters at the top and center: Federal Reserve Note. The Fed is not bashful at all that it prints and issues the currency. The word "note" is the perfect definition for what every dollar bill is: *a piece of debt*. If you have a car *note*, you have a car loan. And if you have a Federal Reserve *Note*, you have a money loan. All Federal Reserve Notes are loaned out to the government and the Fed expects to be paid back for those notes *with interest*. It's all very simple, and yet totally absurd. And while every physical dollar bill that has ever come into existence was initially created by the Fed, the nation's banks are permitted to add even more money and credit into the American monetary system through something known as *fractional-reserve banking*.

To understand fractional-reserve banking, it helps to think of modern banks as *money factories*. While they do serve other purposes, a bank's primary purpose is to create money through lending. Banks are in the business of making loans. Without the ability to lend, banks would not be able to thrive in our modern economy. Most Americans believe that banks profit exclusively through a combination of banking fees (monthly maintenance fees, NSF fees, etc.) and the interest spread between loans and investments. For example, if a bank charges a six percent interest rate for a home mortgage loan and offers a three percent interest rate on a CD (Certificate of Deposit), the bank would

> **Did You Know?**
>
> Today, some of the Federal Income Tax that you hand over to the government each year actually goes to pay for the accumulated interest on the enormous U.S. national debt. Who receives this interest? Holders of the national debt, which includes the Federal Reserve. Is it a coincidence then that the Federal Income Tax Code was passed in 1913 — the same year as the Federal Reserve?

earn the three percent difference. It is true that the bank makes money on the interest spread and on the fees that they are able to charge. However, if these were the only two income streams for a bank, many would go out of business tomorrow. The system of fractional-reserve banking provides a far more powerful method from which banks can earn profits. Through this system, banks have been given the ability to create money out of thin air.

The most important ingredient for working their money creation magic requires customer deposits into the banking system. Banks need people, like you and I, to deposit their hard-earned money into their bank. When a bank does receive a deposit from one of its customers, it is then permitted to create new money *that did not exist before*.

In a nutshell, fractional-reserve banking is a system that permits banks to keep only a "fraction" of customer deposits in reserve. Who determines what this "fractional" amount will be? The Federal Reserve, of course.

In most Western nations, the amount of customer deposits which must be held in reserve, commonly referred to in the banking community as reserve requirements, typically range from anywhere as low as 0 percent, to upward of 10 percent.

Did You Know?
Reserve Requirements as a Fed Policy Tool

In addition to the setting of interest rate targets and purchasing government bonds on the open market, another policy tool available to the Federal Reserve is making adjustments to banking reserve requirements.

If the Fed is concerned that the economy is growing too quickly, it can raise reserve requirement ratios, which will tighten the money supply as banks have less money to lend.

But if the Fed believes that the economy may be slowing down, it can lower reserve requirements to increase the amount of money that the bank can lend to borrowers.

If, for example, a central bank sets the banking reserve requirements at 10 percent, banks must keep 10 percent of every customer deposit received. However, the remaining 90 percent of customer deposits are considered "new assets" on the bank's balance sheet. And because banks are allowed to loan out their "assets," the bank is able to immediately make new loans from their newly acquired "assets."

If you think this sounds strange, you should know that I am just getting started. . . .

Even more incredible, the new loans that the bank is able to issue from this 90 percent of customer deposits are also considered assets.

I repeat — *the new loans that the bank is able to make are considered "assets."*

Why are the loans made by the bank considered assets and not liabilities? Because when a bank issues a loan, it does so under the assumption that it will be paid back in full with interest. For this simple reason, they are considered to be assets of the bank. And banks are allowed to make loans from their "assets."

Through the bizarre logic employed by the fractional-reserve banking process, banks are able to create new money out of thin air. Admittedly, the intricacies of this money creation process can be somewhat confusing. Therefore, consider this very simple example in which we will assume a 10 percent reserve requirement.

Joe decides that he wants to purchase an automobile. After finding one that meets his criteria, he approaches his local bank, First Bank, for a loan in the amount of $10,000. Based upon Joe's good credit, the bank agrees to lend him the money. Upon signing the bank's loan contract agreeing to pay back the principal plus interest, Joe walks away with his $10,000 in cash.

Quick Note: After making the loan, First Bank inputs the data on Joe's new loan into a computer and instantly the money is created out of thin air. What gives the bank the ability to create this money from nothing? Based upon our current fractional-reserve banking system, banks are allowed to create money based upon the promise of the borrower to pay back the loan. *The signed loan agreement creates the money.* Another very important thing to note here is that the bank only creates the loan principal — not the interest. If the bank only creates the loan principal, who creates the interest? No one. *The interest does not exist.* Joe will have to obtain the money for the interest payments from the general economy, either through labor —

or by borrowing again. The fact that the interest on the new loan is not created along with the newly created loan principal will become an important point toward the end of the chapter.

Joe leaves First Bank to buy the car from Ann, the seller of the automobile. Ann agrees to sell her car to Joe for $10,000 in cash. Ann gives Joe the keys and the title and Joe drives off smiling in his new car. Ann immediately deposits the $10,000 cash into her bank, Second Bank.

> **Note:** When Ann deposits the $10,000 in cash into Second Bank, what happens to the money? Assuming a 10 percent reserve requirement, Second Bank is only required to keep $1,000 of the deposit, allowing it to lend the remaining 90 percent of the $10,000 deposit. That means that Second Bank has $9,000 in new available money that it can lend out to the next qualified borrower. Thanks to the fractional-reserve banking system, Second Bank is only required to keep a fraction of the deposit in bank reserves.

Because banks are able to gain such tremendous leverage on every customer deposit, this explains why at any point in time, all banks are technically bankrupt. The truth is that your bank has 10 percent, or less, of your deposited money at any one time. The American public's faith in the system is what is required to keep the illusion going.

But just because America's financial institutions are all bankrupt on paper does not mean that they will ever become physically bankrupt. Like the early goldsmiths who covertly loaned out their customer's gold, banks operate under the assumption that not every customer will need to withdraw all of their money at the same time. When the economy is good and consumer confidence is high, the fractional-reserve banking system appears to be efficient. But when the public's perception of the nation's financial system morphs from blind faith into primal fear, the fractional-reserve banking system is placed in jeopardy. Historically speaking, when bank customers are gripped by financial panic and fear for the solvency of financial institutions, they begin withdrawing their money from the system. These events, known as "bank runs," finally expose the overleveraged positions made possible by the fractional reserve banking scheme.

Did You Know

During the Great Depression era of the 1930s, thousands of bank runs occurred as fearful customers rushed to withdraw their money. In the end, over 10,000 banks collapsed, causing tens of thousands of Americans to lose their entire life savings.

In an effort to restore confidence in the general economy and the banking sector, the U.S. government responded to the bank runs by creating the Federal Deposit Insurance Corporation, also known as the FDIC. The FDIC was designed to prevent future bank runs by guaranteeing the safety of most U.S. bank deposits, up to a total of $100,000.[5]

The creation of the FDIC demonstrated the government's attempts to manage the American public's perception toward the monetary system. Since the 1930s, the FDIC, the Federal Reserve, and the nation's banking industry have all worked overtime to persuade the American public of the absolute safety of placing their hard-earned money into the nation's financial institutions. After all, the single most important ingredient required for maintaining the

FRACTIONAL-RESERVE BANKING 101

Assume that you deposit $100,000 into Bank ABC.
Based upon a 10% reserve requirement,
Bank ABC can lend $90,000 of your deposit.

Deposit	Reserve	Available for Loan
$100,000	$9,000	$90,000
($10,000 reserve)	$8,100	$81,000
	$7,290	$72,900
$9000,000 can be	$6,516	$65,610
created from a single	$5,904	$59,049
$100,000 deposit	$5,314	$53,145

The secret: Banks are allowed to consider new loans as "assets" on their balance sheets, once the loan applicant has signed the loan papers.

Therefore, your single $100,000 deposit can be converted into $900,000 in new bank loans! This $900,000 is created out of thin air. It never existed before your deposit!

fraudulent and diseased debt-based monetary system is the American public's continued "faith" in the nation's money-changers.

It should be added that in 2011, the FDIC announced that it was bankrupt. But fortunately for the millions of people who believe in FDIC fantasy, the Federal Reserve has agreed to provide the FDIC with as many U.S. dollars as they may need . . . at interest, of course.

> I am afraid the ordinary citizen will not like to be told that the banks can, and do, create and destroy money. The amount of finance in existence varies only with the action of the banks in increasing or decreasing deposits and bank purchases. We know how this is affected. Every loan, overdraft, or bank purchase creates a deposit, and every repayment of a loan, overdraft, or bank sale destroys a deposit. They [the banks] control the credit of the nation, direct the policies of governments, and keep in the palm of their hands the destinies of the peoples.[6] (The Rt. Hon. Reginald McKenna, former British Chancellor of the Exchequer — Chairman of the Midland Bank)

> The process by which banks create money is so simple that the mind is repelled.[7] (John Kenneth Galbraith)

> The important thing to remember is that when banks lend money they don't necessarily take it from anyone else to lend. Thus they "create" it.[8] (U.S. House of Representatives)

Money Is Debt . . . and Debt Is Money

In this chapter, I have done my best to explain the realities of fractional-reserve banking. It is a system that has allowed modern economies to prosper on paper, despite being technically bankrupt just under the surface. Through the powers of financial leverage, America's banking system has helped create an illusion of wealth that simply does not exist in reality. The deceitfulness of the system is further compounded when you consider that the banks are charging interest on money that they literally create out of thin air. It has been said that the darkest hour of a man's life is the moment that he sits down to ponder how he can get money without earning it. I can hardly think of a better definition for the illicit profits of fractional reserve banking.

Thomas Jefferson, during his struggles with early attempts at American central banking, once said, "No one has a natural right to the trade of money lender, but he who has money to lend."[9] The immorality of charging interest on money that is created out of thin air should be apparent, especially when the system is so completely rigged to benefit the banking class.

In his illuminating book on this very topic, *The Creature from Jekyll Island*, G. Edward Griffin writes: "When banks place credits into your checking account, they are merely pretending to lend you money. In reality, they have nothing to lend. . . . So what entitles the banks to collect rent (interest) on nothing? We are talking here, not about what is legal, but what is moral."[10] Griffin goes further by adding, "Every dollar that exists today, either in the form of currency, checkbook money, or even credit card money — in other words, our entire money supply — exists only because it was borrowed by someone. . . . That means all the American dollars in the entire world are earning daily and compounded interest for the banks which created them. . . . And what did the banks do to earn this perpetually flowing river of wealth? Did they lend out their own capital obtained through the investment of their stockholders? Did they lend out the hard-earned savings of their depositors? No . . . they simply waved the magic wand called fiat money."[11]

In summary,

1. Every time a bank makes a loan, it creates money.
2. The bank is allowed to charge interest on this newly created money.
3. When the debt owed on the loan is paid off, the money disappears from the system.

For this reason, debt is encouraged — and even required — in our debt-based monetary system.

In the August 31, 1959, issue of *U.S. News and World Report*, President Eisenhower's Secretary of the Treasury Robert B. Anderson was directly asked, "Do you mean that banks, in buying government securities, do not lend out their customers' deposits? That they create the money they use to buy the securities?"

The Treasury Secretary's reply is simply stunning: "That is correct. Banks are different from other lending institutions. When a savings association, an insurance company, or a credit union makes a loan, it lends the very dollar that its customers have previously paid in. But when a bank makes a loan, it simply adds to the borrower's deposit account in the bank by the amount of the loan. The money is not taken from anyone. It is new money, recreated by the bank, for the use of the borrower."

The absurdity of our financial system is well known by the Washington elites. And yet, isn't it interesting that the corporate-controlled mainstream media hardly ever reports on these topics?

Consider yet another astonishing example of America's monetary insanity: On September 30, 1941, Federal Reserve Board Governor Marriner Eccles appeared before the House Committee on Banking and Currency. During the hearing, Eccles was questioned by U.S. Congressman Wright Patman regarding a past Federal Reserve purchase of U.S. government bonds. Here's a partial transcript of the exchange.

Rep. Patman: "How did you get the money to buy those two billion dollars' worth of government securities in 1933?"

Eccles: "We created it."

Rep. Patman: "Out of what?"

Eccles: "Out of the right to issue credit money."

Rep. Patman: "And there is nothing behind it, is there, except our government's credit?"

Eccles: "That is what our money system is. If there were no debts in our money system, there wouldn't be any money."[12]

Stunning, isn't it? *If there were no debts in the U.S. economy, there would be no money.* That is because debt *is* money. And in our debt-based economy, money *is* debt.

Think about It

Imagine that our current president decided that completely paying off the national debt was in the national interest. Even if Americans agreed and voted to pay off the debt, *it would be impossible.* Why? Because the interest that must be paid back on every outstanding loan has never been created.

It is a sad truth that there is simply not enough money in our current system to pay the loan principal plus interest that is owed because only the principal has been created. The interest that is owed has never existed and cannot be created without incurring even more interest charges.

So where exactly does the money come from to pay the interest on our debts? Because the banks do not create the interest, the only way to obtain money to pay the interest is through human labor.

Therefore, human labor yields the banker's profit.

This cruel system pits every American against each other. With everyone in the system competing for the same limited money supply to pay off their debts, there are bound to be losers. In fact, our current system requires losers. It is mathematically impossible for everyone to win because the amount of debt, with interest, is greater than the amount of money in the system. The old children's game of musical chairs makes an apt illustration of this point. While the music is playing, there are no losers. But when the music stops, not everyone will find a chair.

Sadly, the losers in our society face *bankruptcies* and *foreclosures*. In fact, bankruptcies and foreclosures must occur due to the debt-to-money ratio imbalances that plague our modern monetary system. These are sad but inevitable components of one of the most fatal flaws inherent in the central banking scheme that has been foisted upon America.

> This is a staggering thought. Someone has to borrow every dollar we have in circulation, cash or credit. We are absolutely without a permanent money system. When one gets a complete grasp of the picture, the tragic absurdity of our hopeless position is almost incredible, but there it is.[13] (Robert H. Hemphill, Credit Manager, Federal Reserve Bank, Atlanta, Georgia)

In our final analysis, it is clear that debt is a necessary and required component of America's current monetary system. Our debt-based system has been built upon the faulty assumption that consumption and debt will always increase, thereby causing the economy to perpetually expand. Clearly, this is an unsustainable economic model. But it explains why, amid the fiercest economic turbulence, the government consistently encourages consumption and borrowing instead of savings and thrift. And perhaps it also reveals why Washington insists on solving its debt problems with the creation of new debt.

Quick Summary

✓ Modern fiat money is debt. Each U.S. dollar represents a loan that must be paid back with interest to the Federal Reserve.

✓ The Federal Reserve serves as the official "lender of last resort" to the U.S. government as well as to other institutions that it considers "too big to fail."

✓ When the Federal Reserve issues a loan, it creates the money out of thin air.

✓ Fractional-reserve banking legally allows banks to maintain only a fraction of their total customer deposits at any one time.

✓ The FDIC was created in the wake of the Great Depression to restore confidence in the nation's banking system.

✓ Human labor represents the banker's profit.

Endnotes

1. Ellen Hodgson Brown, *Web of Debt: The Shocking Truth about Our Money System* (Baton Rouge, LA: Third Millennium Press, 2007), p. ix.
2. Ibid., p. 25.
3. Congressional Record, House, Sept. 29, 1941, p. 7583.
4. Moriah Saul, *Plantation Earth: The Cross of Iron and the Chains of Debt* (Canada: Trafford Publishing, 2003).
5. FDIC insurance has been temporarily raised to $250,000 in the wake of the 2008 financial crisis.
6. http://www.michaeljournal.org/plenty23.htm.
7. John K. Galbraith, *Money: Whence It Came, Where It Went* (Boston, MA: Houghton Mifflin, 1975), p. 29.
8. Money Facts Subcommittee on Domestic Finance; Committee on Banking and Currency; U.S. House of Representatives, 88th Congress, 2nd Session, September 21, 1964, p. 7, http://www.scribd.com/doc/7547565/Money-Facts-Committee-on-Banking-and-Currency.
9. G. Edward Griffin, *The Creature from Jekyll Island: A Second Look at the Federal Reserve* (Westlake Village, CA: American Media, 1994), p. 190.
10. Ibid., p. 191.
11. Ibid.
12. Ibid., p. 188.
13. Irving Fisher, *100% Money: Designed to Keep Checking Banks 100% Liquid; to Prevent Inflation and Deflation; Largely to Cure or Prevent Depressions; and to Wipe Out Much of the National Debt* (New Haven, CT: The City Printing Co., 1945), p. xxii.

Chapter 8

America: The Greatest Debtor Nation in World History

Blessed are the young for they shall inherit
the national debt.[1]
— Herbert Hoover

I place economy among the first and most important virtues,
and debt as the greatest of dangers to be feared.[2]
— Thomas Jefferson

OVERVIEW: In 1980, America was the largest creditor nation in all of recorded history. Just over three short decades later, America now stands as the greatest debtor nation in world history. As of 2012, the United States has accumulated a national debt of nearly $16 trillion. Much of our national debt is owed to foreign countries that have purchased U.S. debt securities, including China and Japan. Our own projections show that America's national debt will cross the $20 trillion mark well before the year 2020. In addition to a ballooning national debt, the United States — as the world's largest consumer nation — has suffered from rapidly increasing trade deficits with its international trading partners. This chapter is filled with jaw-dropping statistics regarding the remarkable fiscal spending and overconsumption of the American government, including how we got here.

I am not your typical sports fan. While I enjoy playing sports, there are many other things that I would rather do than watch sports on television. However, I do enjoy attending a live sporting event from time to time. Recently, I had an opportunity to attend a baseball game near where I live. Before the game began, the audience was asked to rise for the singing of America's national anthem. As I sang along to the words, something dawned on me as the entire stadium sang the final lyrics: "O'er the land of the free and the home of the brave."

Those lyrics, which I normally sang without question, began to pierce my mind with questions. Is America really the "land of the free" as the song proclaims?

All of this brought to mind a familiar and oft-quoted biblical proverb that goes like this: "The rich rules over the poor, and the borrower is servant to the lender" (Prov. 22:7).

For centuries, people of faith have equated debt with a unique form of *slavery*. In ancient times, if you did not pay your debts, you could be imprisoned for a very long time. In those days, a few fortunate debtors were given the option of working as slaves for their creditors until it was determined that their debts were satisfied. But is it really any different today?

While it is true that no one in our modern American society is placed in the penitentiary for failing to pay his or her credit card bill, I would suggest that a modern form of debt slavery exists today among American consumers. Think about it: Many Americans spend their entire days working at a job they may or may not enjoy, simply to pay all of their creditors. Is this not even slightly reminiscent of the master-slave relationships of the past? Of course, it is. It is a much more sophisticated and subtle version. In an upcoming chapter, I will explore this topic of modern consumer debt slavery further, and will provide you with some very specific ideas and solutions for escaping what I call the Consumption Trap. But in this chapter I want to discuss the largest debt ever incurred in the history of the world. If you are an American citizen, pay close attention, because this debt belongs to you . . . and to your children . . . and your grandchildren.

It's called the national debt.

A Gift for Our Children: The Largest Debt in World History

The story of America's national debt spans the course of two centuries. But instead of providing you with an exhaustive examination, I will use this chapter to briefly explain what the national debt is, how it became so large, to whom it is owed, and why it all matters to you and those you care about.

America has carried a national debt since 1791. (The only exception is the year 1835 when President Andrew Jackson paid off the national debt and drove a stake through the bloodthirsty Second Bank of the United States. The details of this glorious story are found in chapter 6.) There is nothing uncommon about governments accumulating debt, as it is a normal economic activity in our modern economic era. The problem occurs when government borrowing is permitted to get out of control. Modern history provides a number of examples of governments allowing the practice of borrowing money at interest from the general public, and from foreign creditors, to become a dangerous game capable of destroying the nation's creditworthiness and economic credibility. A cursory examination of America's flirtation with debt over the last few decades is all that is required to realize the severe consequences that excessive government borrowing can cause.

For example, the entire U.S. national debt totaled a mere $900 billion in 1980. Fast forward to 2012, 32 years later, and you will find that the debt had skyrocketed over 1,622 percent to a jaw-dropping $15.5 trillion!

Before proceeding further, it is important to realize that this $15.5 trillion debt is not Washington's debt. (Wouldn't it be nice if it were? Then the American public could be insulated from all of the poor economic decisions made by the politicians.) Instead, this gargantuan debt belongs to every citizen of the United States.

But you may ask: "How can I personally be responsible for the national debt when I never wanted it in the first place?"

It is apparently time for a quick civics lesson. Here's the deal. When the government borrows money from *anyone*, at *any* time, and for *any* reason, you are the "co-signer." Like it or not, you and every other American citizen are on the hook for nearly $16 trillion. That works out to: $137,750 for every U.S. taxpayer.

How Did We Get Here?

The meteoric rise in America's national debt has been largely due to something economists call *deficit spending*. Put simply, deficit spending is an economic term for spending more than you earn. A government that relies upon deficit spending to grow its economy is like a man who pays for his groceries and his rent with a credit card. While this "buy now-pay later" attitude may work for a while, eventually the bill comes due. And when it does, it is often painful.

Search the pages of economic history and you will be hard-pressed to find another government that has relied so heavily upon deficit spending than the United States of America. Similarly, I cannot think of a constituency that has been more supportive of a government's out-of-control spending in all of history than the American public.

Did You Know?

America's $16 trillion debt is larger than the economies of the United Kingdom, Australia, and China . . . combined!

Because America enjoys a unique and enviable position in the global economy, our nation has been allowed to delay the inevitable day of reckoning. But the torch of economic supremacy can never remain in the hands of one empire forever. For this reason, we can know with all certainty that America's day of financial reckoning, which has been decades in the making, is nearer than ever before.

To help understand the magnitude of our current debt crisis, we will now pick up the story of the national debt from 1980 onward. In 1980, Ronald Reagan defeated President Jimmy Carter in the race for the White House. Reagan, who famously quipped, "Government is not the solution to our problem, government is the problem," won in a landslide victory. Ironically, from 1980–1986, the national debt did in just six short years under President Ronald Reagan what it had taken nearly 200 years to do: it doubled to $2 trillion. When Reagan's eight years of massive deficit spending were finally over, the national debt had soared a whopping 184 percent.

Reagan would later describe the massive debt increase as the "greatest disappointment" of his presidency. But unfortunately for America, the deficit spending under Reagan was just a warm-up for the coming debt marathon that lay ahead. Today, some 30+ years since the beginning of the "Reagan Revolution," the U.S. national debt has risen by over 1,600 percent!

After Reagan came George Bush Sr. Under the stewardship of President Bush, the national debt grew by a whopping 55 percent in just four short years. By the end of 1992, the national debt had grown to a total of $4 trillion.

Then, in 1993, America elected President Bill Clinton. One of the more priceless political memories that I have from that enchanting decade of the 1990s occurred during a presidential radio address on January 27, 1996. As Clinton was delivering one of his scripted commentaries to the nation, he made what had to be one of the most absurd statements ever uttered from the lips of a modern U.S. politician. While pandering to the masses about overhauling the federal government so that it "serves better and costs less," the first baby boomer president audaciously declared: "The era of big government is over."

While Clinton's remarks may now provide us with some much needed side-splitting humor, we do well to remember the context in which his ridiculous statement was made. The 1990s were a decade of political hope and economic enchantment. Much of the hope of this era was rooted in the sweeping changes occurring in the political landscape — namely, the "Republican Revolution." The GOP rose to power by making promises to massively reduce the size of government through draconian spending cuts. The details of these spending cuts were graphically portrayed and codified in a brilliant document written by Larry Hunter, Newt Gingrich, and several other GOP leaders, entitled the *Contract with America*. Through this proposed "contract," Republicans promised to demonstrate great "fiscal restraint" and to finally bring the era of "big government" to an end.

In 1994, with massive public support, the GOP gained majority control of the House of Representatives, which had been dominated by Democrats for nearly four straight decades. One year later, Republicans regained control of the Senate. Change was in the air and a growing sense of political optimism filled the country amid GOP promises to confront a bloated federal government that was ripe for the knife.

Ironically, this Republican-led "revolution" led to an *increase*, not the promised *decrease*, in government spending. Today, not only is the era of "big government" back, it never went away in the first place.

Did You Know?

The government spent more money in the year 2001 than it spent combined from 1787 through 1900 — even after adjusting for inflation.[3]

While the 1980s and 1990s witnessed staggering growth in the government sector, nothing could compare to the skyrocketing spending levels that would occur under President George W. Bush in the beginning of the 21st century.

One month after entering office, Bush confidently stated: "Many of you have talked about the need to pay down our national debt. I listened, and I agree. We owe it to our children and grandchildren to act now, and I hope you will join me to pay down $2 trillion in debt during the next 10 years. At the end of those 10 years, we will have paid down all the debt that is available to retire. That is more debt, repaid more quickly than has ever been repaid by any nation at any time in history."[4]

Not surprisingly, in Bush's first term in office, total government spending grew by *33 percent.*

By 2002, America's national debt stood at a staggering total of $6 trillion.

From 2002 to 2004, the debt grew by *another $1 trillion* for a total of $7 trillion.

By 2005, the total debt reached $8 trillion.

In 2007, the debt had risen to $9 trillion.

And in September 2008, the total national debt crossed the $10 trillion mark amid the global financial crisis.

Did You Know?

In 2008, the famous digital national debt clock located in New York City's Times Square ran out of space when the national debt crossed the $10 trillion mark. Why? The digital clock was designed back in 1989 when the national debt was just under $3 trillion. The clock's inventor, Seymour Durst, had never envisioned America's national debt being more than $10 trillion so he designed the clock to accommodate only 13 digits. A new replacement clock, which will be able to accommodate 15 digits, will reportedly replace the old outdated clock, and be able to reach the quadrillions. Geez, we all know that'll never happen. . . .

During George W. Bush's combined eight years as president, the total national debt increased by an *astounding 86 percent*, growing by an average of $662 billion each year he was in office.

In the wake of the Bush administration, the American public was growing tired of the economic and political status quo. In 2009, another promise of "change" was in the air. Barack Obama rode this sweeping public demand for change right into the White House. Little did the public realize that regardless of which political party in the White House, you still get the same results.

One month after entering office, President Barack Obama repeated the same tired mantra: "I refuse to leave our children with a debt that they cannot repay. And that means taking responsibility right now, in this administration, for getting our spending under control."[5]

While the people clapped and danced and thought they had finally found their political savior, President Obama was openly continuing the same destructive economic policies and disastrous foreign policy measures as his predecessors. During his first three and a half years in office, America's national debt skyrocketed from $10.9 trillion to its current level of around $15.5 trillion — growing by more than $200 billon per month! And as any casual observer can see, America's national debt is *not* shrinking.

The "Ludicrously Overgoverned"

The reasons behind the dramatic rise in the national debt are numerous, including explosive government-subsidized healthcare costs and excessive military spending on global wars. But I believe that Washington's excessive spending is simply a symptom of a much deeper problem facing our nation. While making cuts to government spending will help greatly, I would suggest that the real problem is rooted in America's philosophy of excessive governance and over regulation. Americans have forgotten the most basic principles of liberty and have allowed our elected political leaders to ignore the proper role of government as set forth in our founding documents. America's founders envisioned an extremely limited role for the federal government. *If they could only see America now. . . .*

In the early 1800s, providing basic services to the U.S. population cost the federal government roughly $20 per U.S. citizen per year.

Today, that number has increased to over $8,000 per person![6] The primary reason for this astronomical increase is due to a rise in government bureaucracies, which require a growing number of government employees.

In 2012, the U.S. Census bureau reported that the federal government had just over 3 million employees on its payrolls.[7] In addition, there were another 19.6 million Americans who were employed by various state and local governments.[8] *That's a combined 22.6 million Americans employed by federal, state, and local governments!* This is a remarkable increase from the paltry 4.5 million government employees in the 1940s.

Given the fact that there are roughly 312 million American citizens, these 22.6 million government employees represent approximately 7 percent of our nation's population.

That means that *1 out of every 14 Americans is employed by the government sector*, making it the largest employer of any industry in the national economy. I don't think this is the type of "limited government" that our founding fathers had in mind when they were forming our country!

And while the number of government employees is certainly concerning, let us also consider the excessive amount of taxpayer dollars that are literally wasted by the hundreds of government agencies each and every year.

In 2010, the U.S. Senate conducted an investigation into government waste. In a rather embarrassing finding, they discovered that the federal government had been issuing payments to over 250,000 deceased Americans. Benefit checks made payable to deceased Americans, some dead for over a decade, were being sent out from the federal government for prescription drugs, wheelchairs, rent subsidies, electricity bills, and more.[9]

And this is just one recent example. Entire volumes could be penned about government waste.

Clearly, our bloated and inefficient government, whether it is federal, state, or local, is costing taxpayers a fortune. Of course, no one has ever accused the U.S. government of being an efficient manager of capital and human resources. As former vice-presidential advisor Tom

Peters once said, "In the public (government) sector, we routinely have five people doing the work of one. It's a simple fact. Are we overgoverned in the United States? We are wildly, bizarrely, sickeningly, ludicrously overgoverned."[10]

Change the Incentives, Change the Behavior

Clearly, America has suffered at the hands of spendthrift politicians from both sides of the aisle for decades. One can only hope that Americans are *finally* beginning to realize that, despite their empty promises, neither Republicans nor Democrats are truly willing to do what it takes to solve our long-term fiscal problems. Instead, the leadership within both parties appears intent on continuing the welfare and warfare spending, despite the fact that doing so requires our country to borrow nearly $4 billion per day from total strangers.

Those who have become disillusioned with the failed two-party system would do well to consider the current *incentives* for America's politicians. I would suggest that America's political leaders have failed

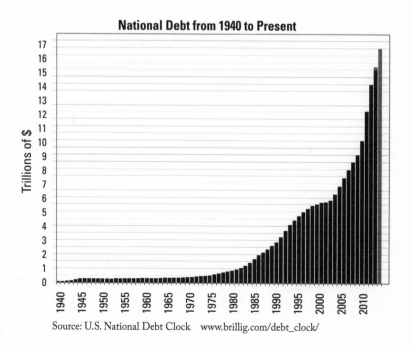

National Debt from 1940 to Present

Source: U.S. National Debt Clock   www.brillig.com/debt_clock/

to make good on their promises because they have no real incentive to do so!

Think about it: How does the American public reward politicians who threaten to make draconian spending cuts? They are often vilified by the corporate-controlled mainstream media and then their proposed spending cuts are used as a weapon against them by their political opponents. Isn't it much safer for politicians to just "go with the flow" and not rock the boat? Of course. And I would go even a step further and suggest to you that the only true incentive that a modern U.S. politician has is *getting re-elected*.

Stop for a moment. Don't read on before you really grasp that last thought.

I truly believe that a politician's only real incentive in our modern system is re-election. And if this is true, then which of the following options do you think politicians will choose:

1) to hand out benefits to their constituents while talking about the "importance" of cutting spending,

2) or propose real cuts to excessive government spending?

The answer is obvious. The politicians who pander to the American public by promising to "protect" current public benefits are rewarded with re-election. It is difficult to lay all of the blame upon politicians when the actions of American voters have helped reinforce their irresponsible behavior.

Unfortunately, the American public is becoming wise to this game. Why would I call the awareness of the American public to this fact unfortunate? Because instead of holding the political leaders accountable for doing nothing to solve our national crisis, the American public has sought to exploit politicians' perverse incentive structure for their own gain. After all, as rational economic creatures, most Americans will happily take all of the "free" benefits they can get. In short, the American public has learned that they can vote themselves *entitlements* through their local ballot box. And if that is what the American voter wants, that's what our modern political leaders, whose only motivation is public approval and re-election, will deliver.

Did You Know? Who Owns Our National Debt?

All of this talk about the national debt becomes more absurd, and even sinister, when it is discovered who owns America's debt. So, who holds our debt? The answer is a bit complicated, but it paints a disturbing picture as you will see below. Here is a breakdown of the top ten holders of the national debt, according to the data recorded in a January 2012 U.S. Treasury report.[11]

1. The Federal Reserve and Intergovernmental Holdings — U.S. Debt Holdings: $6.328 trillion

According to the data, the Federal Reserve owns $1.65 trillion of U.S. debt securities. The remaining $4.68 trillion is held by the government, including the Medicare Trust Fund and the Social Security Trust Fund.

2. China — U.S. Debt Holdings: $1.132 trillion

China is currently the largest foreign holder of U.S. debt securities, although recent purchasing data demonstrates that China's spending spree on U.S. debt has been slowing and actually decreasing. I expect this trend to continue as China looks for more stable places to stash its savings.

3. Other Investors/Savings Bonds — U.S. Debt Holdings: $1.107 trillion

This group includes a wide range of individual and corporate investors, government-sponsored enterprises, as well as U.S. Savings Bond purchases.

4. Japan — U.S. Debt Holdings: $1.038 trillion

Japan has been a long-time buyer of U.S. debt securities and is one of America's largest trading partners. However, Japan has publicly discussed the possibility of diversifying their debt holdings into Chinese government bonds in an effort to strengthen diplomatic and economic ties.

5. Pension Funds — U.S. Debt Holdings: $842.2 billion

Since pension funds are required to invest the large amounts of money they control into investments that are traditionally considered to be safe, they often invest the bulk of their money in U.S. debt securities.

6. Mutual Funds — U.S. Debt Holdings: $653.5 billion

This group includes money market funds, mutual funds, and closed-end funds.

7. State and Local Governments

U.S. Debt Holdings: $484.4 billion

State and local governments often hold their surplus funds in federal debt securities.

8. The United Kingdom — U.S. Debt Holdings: $429.4 billion

The UK's holdings of U.S. debt securities make it America's third-largest foreign creditor.

9. Depository Institutions — U.S. Debt Holdings: $284.5 billion

This group includes commercial banks, savings banks, and credit unions.

10. Insurance Companies — U.S. Debt Holdings: $250.1 billion

This group includes property-casualty and life insurance firms.

For lovers of liberty and small government, it is a sad day as both Republicans and Democrats compete to outspend each other to appease our entitlement-crazed generation. Thankfully, there are still a few renegade politicians naïve enough to suggest massive spending cuts. But their views are rarely encouraged by the corporate-controlled media. And they are typically rebuffed by their polished political peers who believe that pressing a revolver into the side of their temple and squeezing the trigger would likely be more comfortable than asking Americans to give up a single entitlement benefit.

The Magic of Compound Interest . . . in Reverse

Albert Einstein reportedly once called compound interest "the most powerful force in the universe." If you are an investor, compound interest is your friend as it causes your investments to grow exponentially over time. However, when you are a debtor, the tremendous power of compound interest actually works in reverse — against you. Sadly, this powerful force of compound interest is currently working its magic against the American taxpayer, and his government, through the explosive interest that is accumulating by the billions every single day on the national debt.

Can you even imagine what the monthly payments, plus interest, are on America's $15.5 trillion debt? (No wonder Washington wants the Federal Reserve to keep interest rates artificially low! I would want ultra-low interest rates too if I was $16 trillion in debt.)

Since most of us don't tend to think in terms of billions, let alone trillions, let me attempt to simplify the gravity of this situation with the following statistics.

In fiscal year 2011, the U.S. government spent $454,393,280,417.03 of their total income (translation: your tax dollars) on interest payments to the holders of the national debt.[12] That $454 billion is just the interest on our skyrocketing debt!

To help put this number in perspective, let's compare this amount to other important expenditures by the federal government. Consider the following items below from the U.S. Federal Budget from Fiscal Year 2012.

Federal U.S. Budget — Fiscal Year 2012[13]

- The entire annual budget for the Department of Labor in FY 2012: $12.8 billion
- The entire annual budget for the Environmental Protection Agency in FY 2012: $9 billion
- The entire annual budget for the NASA Space Program in FY 2012: $18.7 billion
- The entire annual budget for the Department of Energy in FY 2012: $29.5 billion
- The entire annual budget for the Department of Homeland Security in FY 2012: $43.2 billion
- The entire annual budget for the Department of Housing and Urban Development in FY 2012: $41.7 billion
- The entire annual budget for the Department of Interior in FY 2012: $12 billion
- The entire annual budget for the Department of State in FY 2012: $47 billion
- The entire annual budget for the Department of Education in FY 2012: $77 billion

It is truly shocking to discover that all of the above federal departments bear a total cost of just over $290 billion per year, which pales in comparison to the $454 billion that was spent on interest payments on the national debt alone during that same fiscal year!

Despite Washington's best attempts to keep interest rates artificially low, they will not be able to remain near zero forever. As interest rates rise, so will America's interest payments. In fact, the White House anticipates that interest payments on the national debt will quadruple over the next decade.[14] And by 2018, economists have projected that the interest on the national debt will cost more than Medicare on an annual basis.[15] Only defense spending and the Social Security program will cost more than America's interest payments on our explosive national debt.[16]

The Way Forward

When I was a financial advisor, I had a client who came to me drowning in debt. Together, he and his wife had accumulated over $150,000 in consumer debt. Because I knew this couple particularly well, I was profoundly shocked to discover how deep a hole they had dug for themselves as their minimum monthly payment to service the debt was higher than most people's mortgage payment!

Did You Know?
• U.S. National Debt •

If 16 trillion U.S. dollar bills were stacked on top of each other, they would create a pile that would reach 3.5 times the distance to the moon from the earth! If 16 trillion U.S. dollar bills were stretched out end to end, they would stretch from the sun to the orbit of Saturn!

In our first meeting, I asked them a series of questions in an effort to discover how this could have happened to them. To my amazement, my friend and his wife appeared clueless and refused to take any responsibility for their actions. They even attempted to place blame on one of their credit card companies who had recently raised their interest rate.

I knew this was an extremely delicate situation. My clients had come to me in an hour of great desperation and were looking for answers. I was determined to bring some much-needed truth into their financial situation. Through the process of several confidential meetings, I helped them realize that no one had put a gun to their head and forced them to borrow money. It was vital that they fully understood that their financial situation was of their own making. Until they were willing to take responsibility for their poor financial choices, it would be virtually impossible for them to change the behaviors that were destroying their finances, their credit, and the peace in their marriage.

Today, America is in a very similar situation. America's gargantuan debt is a nothing less than a national emergency requiring immediate attention. But very few of our nation's leaders are brave enough to face the fact that our nation's poor fiscal and monetary policies have driven our nation into a state of bankruptcy.

America is a nation in complete and total denial, seeking to blame others for our own poor economic decisions. As long as we remain in this state of denial, we will never be able to see past the illusion and thereby make the changes required to solve our nation's financial crisis.

The denial operating in some Americans is so deep that they have resorted to blaming *a single political party, or a single politician,* for our nation's exploding national debt. How absurd! This is what children do. Children seek to blame others. But mature adults learn to take responsibility for their own actions. Our debt is too large, and our economic crisis is too advanced, to be playing the political blame game.

> **Did You Know?**
> **• U.S. National Debt •**
>
> Astronomical numbers? There are 100 billion stars in our galaxy. While that number used to be considered large, it now represents less than 1 percent of the U.S. national debt!

Facts are stubborn things. Unfortunately, the facts won't change simply because we don't like them. And the fact is that we are ALL to blame for the economic mess that has been created on our watch. Like it or not, we all did this to ourselves.

So is America really "the land of the free" today, as we so boldly proclaim in the national anthem? I would suggest to you that we are certainly not, financially speaking.

As tragic as it may sound, if we use the biblical definition of borrowers being slaves, then America is no longer "the land of the free." Instead, by definition, America has become the greatest "slave" nation in all of recorded world history.

Conclusion

By the way, my clients with the $150,000 in debt finally dug their way out. How did they do it? Through a lot of sacrifice. They began selling a lot of their stuff online and on eBay. They tightened their spending, worked with their creditors to pay off their debts, and found ways to increase their income. Needless to say, they have much more peace now.

I wish I could say the same for our great nation. But it's not too late for America to begin the process of recovery from its excessive debts. There are no guarantees that we can succeed, given the sheer numbers

> **Did You Know?**
>
> When politicians increase or decrease federal government spending in an effort to influence the direction of the U.S. economy, it is known as fiscal policy. Conversely, attempts to influence the U.S. economy through the manipulation of interest rates by the Federal Reserve is known as monetary policy.

we are dealing with here. In fact, I would suggest that the deck is heavily stacked against us. However, I believe in the triumphant spirit that resides in the American people. I refuse to believe that our nation will simply raise the white flag of surrender and hand the entire bill for our massive overconsumption to the next generation. Despite our drunken financial stupor, I believe that we must make an attempt at fiscal sobriety; if not for our sakes, then for the sake of our children and our grandchildren. Of course, doing so will require a people who are no longer willing to live in absolute denial about their true situation.

It will take a courageous population of men and women who comprehend the futility of blaming others for their nation's own actions. This grand attempt at fiscal sobriety will also require a national spirit of unity and sacrifice, which will guide the American people to work harmoniously together toward a goal of restoring financial liberty to our nation.

While we cannot change others, we can change our own actions. Later in this book, I will explain what some of those positive changes are, and how you can begin implementing them in your own life.

For now, we turn to something I call the 2036 Crisis.

Quick Summary

- ✓ In 1980, America was the world's largest creditor nation. In 2012, America has become the world's largest debtor nation in all of recorded world history.
- ✓ America has carried a national debt every year since 1791, with the exception of 1835 when President Andrew Jackson paid off national debt.
- ✓ Some of the primary causes of our increasing in our national debt include a dependence upon deficit spending, excessive military spending, entitlement spending, and a dramatic increase in the number of government employees.
- ✓ History shows that both political parties have contributed to America's growing debt crisis.
- ✓ The only true incentive for a modern U.S. politician is re-election.
- ✓ As of 2012, the Federal Reserve is the single largest owner of America's $15.5 trillion national debt.
- ✓ In 2011, the U.S. paid $454 billion in interest payments alone on the national debt.

Endnotes

1. Francis X. Cavanaugh, *The Truth about the National Debt: Five Myths and One Reality* (Boston, MA: Harvard Business School Press, 1996), p. 25.

2. *The American Journal of Economics and Sociology,* Robert Schalkenback Foundation, v. 20 (1960/1961): p. 231.

3. Stephen Moore, "The Most Expensive Government in World History," The Institute for Policy Innovation, Policy Report 161, February 2002, http://ipi.org/IPI%5CIPIPublications.nsf/PublicationLookupFullTextPDF/0D0C62FBB3E9E3F586256B4D003F0AE2/$File/PR161-Moore-Size_of_Government.pdf?OpenElement.

4. "Address of the President to Joint Sessions of Congress," President George W. Bush, February 27, 2001, http://georgewbush-whitehouse.archives.gov/news/releases/2001/02/20010228.html.

5. http://www.politifact.com/florida/statements/2012/mar/08/lenny-curry/obama-promised-cut-deficit-half-end-his-first-term/.

6. Federal Government Civilian employment by Function, March 2010, http://www2.census.gov/govs/apes/10fedfun.pdf.

7. Annual Survey of Public Employment and Payroll Summary Report: 2010, Released January 2012, http://www2.census.gov/govs/apes/g10aspep.pdf.

8. Ibid.

9. http://www.washingtontimes.com/news/2010/oct/29/1-billion-paid-dead-people-senate-panel- finds/.

10. Cavanaugh, *The Truth about the National Debt: Five Myths and One Reality*, p. 25.

11. http://finance.yahoo.com/news/biggest-holders-of-us-gov-t-debt.html.

12. 2012 Federal Budget Summary. http://www.washingtonpost.com/wp-srv/special/politics/documents/2012budget-full-summary.html

13. Source:http://www.washingtonpost.com/wp-srv/special/politics/documents/2012budget-full-summary.html.

14. Ibid.

15. 2012 Federal Budget Summary, http://www.washingtonpost.com/wp-srv/special/politics/documents/2012budget-full-summary.html.

16. Interest Expense on the Debt Outstanding, TreasuryDirect.gov. http://www.treasurydirect.gov/govt/reports/ir/ir_expense.htm.

Chapter 9

The Retirement Crisis

They who have been bred in the school of politics fail now and always to face the facts. Their measures are half measures and make-shifts, merely. They put off the day of settlement indefinitely, and meanwhile, the debt accumulates.[1]

— Henry David Thoreau

In our every deliberation, we must consider the impact of our decisions on the next seven generations.[2]

— From the great law of the Iroquois confederacy

OVERVIEW: While the current U.S. national debt stands at over $15.5 trillion, this amount does not reflect what the federal government has promised to pay millions of Americans in entitlement benefits down the road. These future obligations put America's real debt figure at over $118 trillion — a staggering sum that is more than two times the total household net worth of the entire United States. According to the U.S. Government Accountability Office, if present trends continue in the form of reckless fiscal spending, the entire federal budget will be consumed by Social Security and Medicare payments alone by 2036. Failing government benefits, faltering pensions, longer life expectancies, and dismally low savings rates make this a noxious recipe for disaster. How are you preparing?

It was a day like any other as 61-year-old Kathleen Casey-Kirschling logged onto a computer in Washington, DC, on the morning of October 15, 2007. However, that day would also mark the end of an era. News reporters, both from the national and international media, had arrived in the nation's capitol to record a monumental moment in U.S. history.

Who is Kathleen Casey-Kirschling? And why was she important enough to command the attention of the global mass media? Is she a famous actress, a noteworthy scholar, or a determined politician? Well, not quite. And if you don't recognize her name, you are not alone.

She is not a famous actress, scholar, or politician. Instead, Ms. Casey-Kirschling is a retired school teacher living in New Jersey. And the reason behind her global debut was quite simple. As the nation's first baby boomer, born one second after midnight on January 1, 1946, she was the first to file for U.S. Social Security benefits. *The first of over 78 million baby boomers,* to be more exact.

The highly publicized event, performed online and hosted by the Social Security administration, sparked immediate national and international media coverage. In a speech given later that day, Ms. Casey-Kirschling, made a cryptic statement: "I think I'm just lucky to be at the top of the boom. I'm just one of many, many millions and am really blessed . . . to take my Social Security now."

For those unaware of America's massive entitlement crisis, this event would have seemed like just another news story. After all, why should an unknown retiring teacher from New Jersey be front-page news for the entire world?

The "Silver Tsunami"

The answer begins with a couple of brief definitions.

First, what is a *baby boomer*?

Demographers define a baby boomer as a U.S. citizen born between 1946 and 1964. It was the era of rock 'n' roll, TV dinners, and Dr. Spock. Elvis was the king and the Beatles took the nation by storm with their unique blend of vocal harmonies and driving rhythms. In addition, this era saw the decline of racial segregation with the likes of Rosa Parks, Martin Luther King Jr., and the historic *Brown vs. the Board of Education* Supreme Court decision.

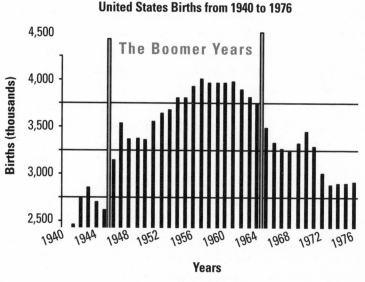

United States Births from 1940 to 1976

Source: 2.bp.blogspot.com/_VyTCyizqrHs/TSCeHWM1ggI/AAAAAAAAJ6s/lcWmQb-s5cUo/s1600/baby_boomers_statistics_graph.gif

But this era was also marked by an explosion, or a "boom," in the national birth rate. Beginning in the post–World War II era, birth rates skyrocketed across the country as the economy fully recovered from the Great Depression of the previous decade. An article from *Time* magazine dated February 9, 1948, demonstrates the early awareness of the unique nature of this demographic shift. "The U.S. had been expected to reach its population peak of 155–165 million by the end of the century. But the 'present surge of births' . . . indicates that the peak will actually be from 10 to 25 million higher and the crest of the growth curve has now been pushed beyond the year 2000."

Time magazine's prognostications concerning the future U.S. population were a little off, to say the least. Instead of ending the century with just fewer than 200 million, the United States Census Bureau estimated the number was closer to 300 million — 281,421,906 to be exact.

This unexpected explosion in U.S. births caused massive upheaval in demographic trends. The economic ripple effects of these trends will become much larger and more pronounced as we continue forward into the 21st century.

According to U.S. government birth records, which have been officially kept since 1910, there are roughly 80 million baby boomers alive today. Many of these 80 million Americans have paid large amounts through payroll deductions into government insurance programs designed for retirement, like Social Security and Medicare.

Here is where it gets interesting. . . .

Until recently, these millions of baby boomers were the primary payees into the Social Security and Medicare systems. That is, their payroll deductions were funding the benefit payments to current U.S. retirees.

However, this all began to change in 2008 as the first wave of baby boomers — 3.2 million in all — began turning 62 years of age. And just like Ms. Casey-Kirschling, they were eligible to begin applying for early retirement benefits from Social Security. Instead of "paying" into the system, these boomers could now begin "taking" from the system by receiving a monthly Social Security check for the rest of their lives.

In 2011, this first wave of boomers began turning 65 years old. At this age, they become eligible for subsidized healthcare benefits under the Medicare system. And in 2012, the remaining boomers who opted not to take early retirement benefits at age 62 will reach age 66. At this age, they qualify for their full share of Social Security benefits.

And this first wave is just the beginning.

From 2011 through 2030, 78 million of baby boomers — *or 10,000 people every single day* — will retire and become financial and medical dependents of the current U.S. taxpayers.[3] They will retire, and they will certainly demand their fair share of the assortment of government benefits, including Social Security, Medicare, and Medicaid.

In 2012, these three entitlement programs alone currently make up over 40 percent of the federal government's annual budget. And this percentage is expected to explode upward as millions of baby boomers begin moving into retirement.

If all this sounds like it is going to cost the U.S. government a lot of money, you would be wrong. The enormous bill created by this entitlement crisis is going to fall squarely upon the U.S. taxpayer. How much money will this entitlement crisis cost?

Over $118 trillion.

Now you are probably thinking: *Didn't we just learn in the last chapter that America's total national debt is $15.5 trillion?*

That's true. However, the official U.S. national debt figure of $15.5 trillion is only the tip of the iceberg because it does not include the government's future obligations and unfunded liabilities. These future benefits include:

- Social Security payments for tens of millions of American retirees over the next two decades
- Healthcare and prescription drug benefits for the millions of new retirees who will be qualifying for Medicare over the next two decades

When these additional obligations and liabilities are calculated, and the value of related federal assets is subtracted, the grand total of America's debt rockets to well over *$118 trillion!*

To help put this mammoth number in perspective, America's total household net worth stands at $67 trillion, as of this writing. That means that America's unfunded liabilities on government entitlements alone are nearly twice our entire national net worth!

Consider further that GDP of the *entire world* in 2011 was $62 trillion. Therefore, to pay off the entire reported accrued U.S. debt of $118 trillion would require the entire GDP of two planet earths!

Is it any surprise that the conservative think tank, the Heritage Foundation, has called this looming entitlement crisis "the single greatest economic challenge of our era"?[4]

When you stop and think about it, it is simply tragic that every new American baby boy and girl born this year each inherited this incredible amount of debt.

The fact that our children and grandchildren — both born and yet unborn — have been saddled with these outrageous debts tells me that this crisis is based on more than just pure economics. I would suggest to you that America's reckless overconsumption and addiction to credit represents a moral issue. I will discuss the moral implications near the end of this chapter. For now, let's figure out how we got here.

Think about It

America's promise to future retirees in Social Security, Medicare, and other benefits currently equal $118 trillion. The government currently has no plan on how to pay for these unfunded liabilities. If the repayment of this $118 trillion debt were to be spread out evenly over all current U.S. taxpayers, your individual share of this debt would be $1,043,772! That's like having five $200,000 mortgages, but no home equity to back them up!

Washington's New Four-Letter Word: M-A-T-H

Social Security is an unfunded income transfer scheme where current benefit payouts are financed by the contributions made by current workers. When the U.S. Congress passed the Social Security Act in 1935, as a part of the New Deal, an estimated 42 workers paid into the system for every retiree. By 1950, this ratio had decreased to 16.5 workers for every retiree.

Today, only 1.75 workers are paying into the system for each one of the 43 million retirees currently drawing a Social Security check.

The demographic trends are no kinder to the Medicare system. Today, there are 47.5 million Medicare recipients. But in 2030, that number will nearly double to 79 million.

According to most projections, Social Security will remain solvent until around 2036. However, current projections for the Medicare system are more bleak. It is estimated that Medicare will become insolvent sometime between 2016 and 2024. Here is how it all breaks down if current trends continue:

- In its 2011 annual report to Congress, the Social Security Board of Trustees projected that incoming tax revenues will fall below program costs in 2023. And in 2036, the Social Security Trust Fund will be completely exhausted. At that time, there will be sufficient tax revenue coming in to pay about 77 percent of benefits.[5]
- In its 2011 annual report to Congress, the Medicare Board of Trustees reported that its hospital insurance trust fund, which is funded through payroll taxes, will become insolvent in 2024.[6]

Considering the size and scope of the economic problems facing America's entitlement programs, you would expect that the federal government would be scurrying around the Beltway attempting to salvage the system that they have created. But are they? No.

Here's the hard, honest truth: U.S. policymakers have yet to create a viable plan to prevent our entitlement crisis from wreaking havoc on the U.S. economy.

Consider these words from Newt Gingrich way back in 1994 upon becoming Speaker of the House: "I think Social Security is off the table for the foreseeable future. We have so many other, more pressing and more immediate problems, and we ought to focus on the ones that are immediate, not the ones that are 20 years out."[7] If a $118 trillion "future problem" is not worthy of current consideration by our nation's leaders, we have more problems than we could ever imagine.

I don't believe that Washington wants Social Security and Medicare systems to fail. In fact, lawmakers have made a few attempts at propping up the failing entitlement systems through tax increases in Medicare and FICA taxes. But these measures will always fail because they place the money directly into the hands of America's spendthrift politicians, which is about as safe as placing your small child in the middle of a busy street. The tax dollars that are collected under these tax increase schemes are typically raided for other "important projects." And in their place are worthless IOUs that will likely never be repaid.

On March 3, 2001, a freshly minted President George W. Bush optimistically stated: "We're going to keep the promise of Social Security and keep the government from raiding the Social Security surplus."[8]

But just a few short years (and gray hairs) later, Bush's former idealism had morphed into realism: "Some in our country think that Social Security is a trust fund — in other words, there's a pile of money being accumulated. That's just simply not true. The money — payroll taxes going into the Social Security are spent. They're spent on benefits and they're spent on government programs. There is no trust fund."[9]

Bush was right. The Social Security Trust Fund is a double oxymoron: *it is not "funded" and it should not be "trusted."*

• The Real National Debt •
Did You Know?

If 118 trillion U.S. dollar bills were stretched out end to end, they would stretch from the sun to Pluto!

These demographic trends of America's entitlement crisis are startling and will demand tough choices. And tough choices demand tough political leaders who are not afraid of uttering words like "sacrifice" in the public square. But they must be addressed and solved.

But even if the nation's leaders could collectively muster the type of courage required to confront these pressing issues, it is not likely that we can avoid a head-on collision with a disastrous fiscal future. If recent history is any indicator, it is highly probable that America's entitlement crisis will have to degenerate into total economic chaos before the politicians will even begin to discuss it seriously, let alone confront it. Of course, most politicians would rather play catch with a live grenade than tackle this hot topic.

Perhaps the complete absurdity of America's entitlement crisis is best summed up by examining a possible solution put forth by the nation's former chief accountant, former U.S. Comptroller, David M. Walker. To avoid this impending fiscal nightmare, Mr. Walker states that "the U.S. economy would need to grow by double digits every year for the next 75 years."[10]

But given the fact that since 1970, U.S. GDP growth has averaged around 3 percent per year, after inflation, how likely is it that our nation's economy will grow by at least 10 percent every year for the next 75 years?

Clearly, our refusal to acknowledge our nation's $118 trillion entitlement crisis is going to be very painful, financially speaking. Instead of trying to solve our economic problems through the creation of sustainable solutions, Washington has tried to paper over our nation's debt problems with even more spending. Their logic goes something like this: By spending more money on government programs, we can grow our economic productivity and output to levels that will help us pay off our massive debts.

However, attempting to solve a massive debt crisis with more debt is like trying to extinguish a raging fire with a barrel of gasoline. It is illogical.

Trying to fight a debt problem with more debt is like giving a bottle of vodka to an alcoholic with a bad hangover. Sure, more alcohol may make his headache go away temporarily. But eventually, the pain will return and it will be even worse than before.

Let's face it. America is not going to grow its way out of our $118 trillion entitlement crisis. Or, as Mr. Walker is fond of saying: "Anyone who believes that we can grow our way out of this problem either does not know economic history, or is bad at math."

Now, for the Bad News . . .

Just as the demographic trends have created an entitlement crisis, poor financial planning, coupled with the effects of the global financial crisis, has left many of America's baby boomers with little money as they head into their golden years. So in addition to facing an entitlement crisis, America has a retirement crisis to worry about. According to one recent study, Americans as a whole are $6.6 trillion short of the amount of money they need to retire.[11] Many of these Americans, who have failed to save enough money during their working lives to prepare them for retirement, are faced with plummeting home values while others still have portfolio losses from the earlier 2008 financial crisis.

According to a 2011 survey by the Employee Benefit Research Institute, 46 percent of all American workers have *less than $10,000* saved for retirement, and 29 percent of all American workers have *less than $1,000* saved for retirement.[12] In addition, pension plans around the country are facing massive shortfalls putting millions of American retirement benefits at risk.

Many Americans have responded to all of this bad economic news by delaying their retirement plans, or just giving up on retirement all together. According to a recent study conducted by AARP, 40 percent of boomers "plan to work until they drop."[13]

It is no wonder that 88 percent of Americans nearing retirement are concerned about "maintaining a comfortable standard of living in retirement."[14]

Of all of the crises that face America, the greatest in my estimation is this retirement crisis. Failing government benefits, faltering pensions, longer life expectancies, and dismally low savings rates make this a noxious recipe for disaster.

Will a new generation of hard-working, U.S. tax-paying citizens be able to foot the bill for the retirement and medical benefits for the largest wave of retirees in American history? Only time will tell how this crisis unfolds. However, time is not on the side of any of us. That is why I have taken action in my own personal financial life to create multiple streams of income that I can rely upon both now and in retirement. In our final chapters, I will discuss how I am creating these income streams, and how you can, too. It is not too late if you are willing and able.

Quick Summary

- ✓ The U.S. Congress passed the Social Security Act in 1935 as a part of the New Deal.
- ✓ A baby boomer is defined as an American born between 1946 and 1964.
- ✓ There are approximately 78 million baby boomers in America.
- ✓ Over 10,000 Americans will reach the age of 65 every single day from 2011 to 2030.
- ✓ The unfunded entitlement liabilities for these 78 million Americans total $118 trillion.
- ✓ In 1935, an estimated 42 workers paid into Social Security for every retiree. By 1950, this ratio had decreased to 16.5 workers for every retiree. In 2012, only 1.75 workers are paying into the system for each one of the 43 million retirees currently drawing a Social Security check.
- ✓ U.S. lawmakers have not created a plan to save America's entitlement programs from insolvency. It is projected that the Social Security system will become insolvent in 2036. Medicare will become insolvent even earlier, in 2024.
- ✓ Failing government benefits, faltering pensions, longer life expectancies, and dismally low savings rates make this a noxious recipe for disaster.
- ✓ My personal financial strategy for weathering the retirement crisis is through the creation of multiple streams of income.

Endnotes

1. Henry David Thoreau, "Slavery in Massachusetts," http://www.thoreau-online.org/slavery-in-massachusetts.html.
2. www.solarhaven.org/Quotes.htm.

3. http://www.washingtonpost.com/wp-dyn/content/article/2010/12/31/AR2010123104109.html.

4. http://www.usatoday.com/news/washington/2007-10-08-boomers_N.htm.

5. http://www.socialsecurity.gov/OACT/TRSUM/index.html.

6. Ibid.

7. Laurence J. Kotlikoff and Scott Burns, *The Coming Generational Storm: What You Need to Know about America's Economic Future* (Cambridge, MA: MIT Press, 2005), p. 87.

8. Radio address of the president to the nation, March 3, 2001, http://www.ssa.gov/history/gwbushstmts.html#radio030301.

9. Max B. Sawicky, "Debt and Taxes," The American Prospect (Feb. 11, 2005), http://www.prospect.org/cs/articles?article=debt_and_taxes.

10. http://paul.house.gov/index.php?option=com_content&task=view&id=1118&Itemid=69.

11 http://www.cnbc.com/id/39177278.

12. http://www.ebri.org/pdf/surveys/rcs/2011/FS2_RCS11_Prepare_FINAL1.pdf.

13. http://www.aarp.org/about-aarp/press-center/info-12-2010/boomers_turning_65.html.

14. http://www.usatoday.com/money/perfi/retirement/story/2011-10-05/retirement-worries/50676604/1?loc=interstitialskip.

Chapter 10

The Coming American Hyperinflation and Dollar Collapse

Without the confidence factor, many believe a paper money system is liable to collapse eventually.[1]

— Federal Reserve Bank of Philadelphia

You earn wages, only to put them in a purse with holes in it.

— Haggai 1:6; NIV

OVERVIEW: In 1971, Richard Nixon detached the U.S. dollar from the gold standard. Since then, the amount of currency within the American financial system has skyrocketed to unprecedented amounts. The dollar, like all fiat currencies that have preceded it, will collapse eventually. It is currently being propped up by the petrodollar system, global U.S. debt demand, and a lack of a real currency competitor. However, all of these facts are changing. Poor monetary and fiscal policies are leading us to a period of hyperinflation that will be followed by a collapsing dollar.

As a kid, I used to enjoy hearing stories from my grandparents about how much cheaper things used to be in their "day." For example, a movie ticket today costs on average $8.00, but the average price for that same ticket in 1968 was a mere $1.31! Or a McDonald's hamburger, which costs around $1.00 today, cost only 15 cents in 1966! Those stories of how much things "used to cost" always fascinated me. Perhaps it was this fascination with prices that led me to a professional study of economics. However, it was not until I began studying the inner workings of the economy that I realized how drastically the prices of goods and services in America have increased over the last several decades. The prices of goods and services are certainly affected by a wide variety of factors, including technological advancements and the costs of doing business, among others. However, one of the primary determining factors of prices is related to the purchasing power of a nation's currency. In America, the purchasing power of the U.S. dollar has been declining, rather dramatically, for decades. In fact, the U.S. dollar is now worth less than 10 percent of what it was in 1945!

The declining value of the U.S. dollar has been, in part, caused by poor U.S. monetary policies, which give the government the ability to print money as often as they wish. Of course, this is precisely the problem with fiat currencies: the government can print them, as often as they like, with no accountability.

This decline in the purchasing power of the U.S. dollar has been felt greatly outside our own borders. Open any newspaper and you will

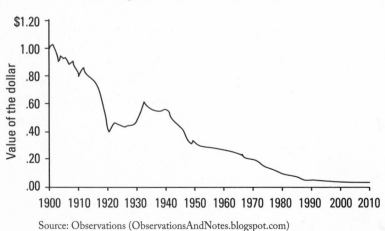

Purchasing Power of the U.S. Dollar Since 1900

Source: Observations (ObservationsAndNotes.blogspot.com)

see nearly every week that your hard-earned dollars are hitting all-time lows against other global currencies.

The U.S. dollar is in a long-term downward trend against other currencies. Of course, average, everyday Americans may not notice these massive currency fluctuations, especially if they do not travel outside the country. However, one thing everyone notices is gasoline prices and food prices. Have you noticed the price of groceries lately? They are going up rather quickly.

The price of gold is hitting an all-time high, as is the price of oil. Gasoline is going up. Food prices are rising. It appears that the price of everything is going up. Of course, the U.S. federal government has told us that inflation is steady. But the prices of gold, oil, and food don't lie.

The Death of the Dollar

Throughout this book we have learned:

- Since its inception in 1913, the Federal Reserve has been systematically devaluing the U.S. dollar through poor monetary policies.

- In 1971, the U.S. dollar became a fiat currency no longer backed by gold.

- In 1973, America's petrodollar system was created in an effort to maintain artificial demand for the U.S. dollar. The petrodollar system, which permits Washington to print excessive amounts of money with relatively few economic repercussions, has come under attack in recent years as the global economic community seeks an alternative to the dollar.

- Washington's attempts to protect and preserve the artificial dollar and government bond demand created by the petrodollar system have included full-scale military invasions of foreign nations under a variety of false pretexts.

- Washington's massive deficit spending on the welfare and warfare state has made it the largest debtor nation in all of world history. As of this writing, America's official national debt is $15.5 trillion, but when future unfunded liabilities are included, the total amount owed rises to a staggering $118 trillion.

- Out-of-control deficit spending coupled with dreadful demographic trends now threaten to destroy America's social safety net programs including Social Security, Medicare, and Medicaid.

We have also demonstrated that throughout history, all fiat currencies collapse due to political mismanagement and most often by hyperinflation.

A few years ago, when I wrote the first edition of this book, the idea that America could be confronted with widespread hyperinflation was not a mainstream idea. Today, however, more Americans are waking up to the financial realities facing our nation. Sadly, it took the worst financial crisis in a generation to stir many from their slumber.

In this chapter, I will present my case for why hyperinflation is coming to America as a result of both poor monetary and fiscal policies combined with the coming breakdown of the petrodollar system. I will also explain why this coming hyperinflation will destroy the global credibility of the dollar.

Today, the mighty U.S. dollar is still the world's reserve currency. But its days are numbered. *I firmly believe that we will witness the downfall of the U.S. dollar system within the next decade.* As the old saying goes: "If something is unsustainable, then it can't last forever."

The dollar's fate is literally hanging by three threads:

1) the artificial demand created by the petrodollar system
2) the global demand for the perceived safety of U.S. debt securities
3) no current competitor to the dollar

While these three things have benefited the U.S. dollar, they are all unsustainable.

We are witnessing massive shifts to the petrodollar system as several nations, including India, Iran, China, Russia, and others have been moving away from the dollar in their global oil transactions.

Meanwhile, an extended period of artificially low interest rates on U.S. debt securities have led several nations to seek out alternatives. Gold and foreign government bonds have been two of the primary beneficiaries of the new global search for higher rates of return.

Consider also that both Europe and China are aggressively seeking to create liquid government debt markets that will eventually rival the United States in attracting global investment funds. And it is no secret that both the euro currency and the Chinese yuan are both growing in global trade. The global economic community is already on edge as they perceive that Washington is willing to print excessive amounts of dollars to continue its welfare and warfare spending policies. It is only a matter of time before another currency, considered to have more stability than the dollar, will be viewed as a viable replacement for the dollar in global trade.

But what economic events would have to occur for the global economic community to forsake the U.S. dollar? While I believe that the dollar's reign is gradually nearing its end, a sudden decision by the majority of oil-producing nations to use another currency than the U.S. dollar for all of their oil transactions could spark a rapid collapse of the dollar. Such a collapse of the petrodollar system, which I believe will occur sometime within this decade, will make the 1971 Nixon Shock look like a dress rehearsal.

Since 1980, America has devolved from being the world's greatest creditor nation to the world's greatest debtor nation. But thanks to the massive artificial demand for U.S. dollars and government debt made possible by the petrodollar system, America is able to continue its spending binges, imperial pursuits, reckless wars, and record deficits. In America today, we are living proof that having the world's most important currency translates into a higher standard of living than most nations.

At one point in America's history, our largest export was a variety of manufactured goods, made right here in the United States. *Today, America's largest export is the U.S. dollar.* And the dollar costs us practically nothing to create. How long will it be before the world figures out the dollar fiasco is a fraud? Instead of viewing U.S. dollars as worthless paper backed by nothing (as they should), foreign oil producers and consumers were convinced — *and required* — to hold U.S. dollars in order to purchase oil back in the 1970s. However, this demand for dollars is not genuine. It is purely artificial.

The world currently consumes nearly 90 million barrels of oil per day. According to some projections, global oil demand will reach well over 100 million barrels per day by 2015. And thanks to the petrodollar

Source: ftmdaily.com

system, growing global demand for oil leads to an increase in U.S. dollar demand. This artificial demand for U.S. dollars has provided remarkable benefits for the U.S. economy. It has also required the Federal Reserve to keep the dollar in plentiful supply.

If the artificial global dollar demand, made possible by the petro-dollar system, were ever to crumble, foreign nations who had formerly found it beneficial to hold U.S. dollars would suddenly find that they no longer needed the massive amounts that they were holding. This massive amount of dollars, which would no longer be useful to foreign nations, would come rushing back to their place of origin . . . America. Obviously, an influx of dollars into the American economy would lead to massive inflationary pressures within our economic system.

It is difficult to overstate the importance of this concept as the entire American monetary system literally hinges on this "dollars for oil" system. Without it, Washington would lose its permission slip to print excessive amounts of dollars. Therefore, it should come as no surprise that America has a vested interest in maintaining the petrodollar system at all costs. And, if you are an American citizen, so do you.

What Would Happen if the Petrodollar System Ended Tomorrow

Here is a brief scenario describing the events that would likely transpire if oil-producing nations were to suddenly decide to abandon the petrodollar system.

- A secret meeting would be held among oil producing nations.

- These oil producing nations would then publicly announce their intentions to abandon the dollar in all future oil transactions for another preferred currency beginning on a particular date.

- Foreign nations would begin exchanging their current dollar holdings into the new preferred currency.

- All of these exchanged dollars would come like a flood back to the United States.

- The Federal Reserve, which would normally print more dollars to handle such a severe economic situation, would be forced to find another solution.

- The Treasury secretary and the Federal Reserve chairman would meet to determine the best course of action now that they have lost their ability to print more dollars.

- That action would involve an immediate and dramatic increase in interest rates to reduce America's money supply and to attract foreign capital.

- Hyperinflation would ensue temporarily while the interest rates took time to take full effect.

- All oil-related prices, including gas prices, would reach outrageous levels.

- Washington would soon realize that the total amount of money in the system would have to be dramatically slashed even further, leading to an even higher increase in interest rates.

- The clueless American public would demand answers. *Those on the left would blame the right. The right would blame the left.* And both political parties would seek to blame the Federal Reserve.

- People with adjustable rate debts would be crushed and massive layoffs would occur, as businesses would be suffering from the high interest rates.

- Asset prices across the board would plummet in value.

- Amid the financial carnage, an economic recovery eventually would begin to take place. But this new American economy would be tremendously smaller due to a drastically reduced money supply.

The Difference between "Billion" and "Trillion"

A few years ago, in an effort to place the number "one billion" into perspective for the American public, an advertising agency stated the following:

- A billion seconds ago it was 1959.
- A billion minutes ago Jesus was alive.
- A billion hours ago our ancestors were living in the Stone Age.
- A billion dollars ago was only 8 hours and 20 minutes, at the rate Washington spends it.

While those numbers are obviously incorrect now in 2012, their impact has not changed.

To help understand the gravity of our modern economic crisis, let's consider a few similar illustrations. You have heard the old saying, "Time is money." According to our traditional measurement of time, one million seconds is roughly equivalent to 12 days. That makes 118 million seconds equal to 1,416 days. Compare that with 118 billion seconds, which is equal to 3,740 years! So how many years is 118 trillion seconds? Almost 3.8 million years!

    118 million seconds = 1,416 days
    118 billion seconds = 3,740 years
    118 trillion seconds = 3,776,000 years

As you can see, the increase is exponential when you move from the word "billion" to "trillion."

Let us illustrate this point further with another example. Imagine that you were to receive a letter from the U.S. government addressed to you. Inside the letter you find this message:

Dear Mr. Reader,
    We, the United States government, have selected your name at random and will begin paying you $1.00 per second beginning tonight at midnight for our own undisclosed purposes.
                      Sincerely,
                      The Federal Government

Now assuming you lived another 20 years after receiving this incredible notice, your inheritance from the government would equal approximately $630 million. That's a healthy payday for doing nothing. But would it surprise you to know that the U.S. government spends that amount every 13 hours just in interest payments on our $15.5 trillion national debt?

That's right: every 13 hours your government spends over $600 million on INTEREST on the national debt.

Let's consider another illustration: Suppose that the Congress made a big decision to begin putting aside money to help pay for our $118 trillion in unfunded liabilities. And let's assume that they would begin paying off this

$118 trillion debt using our same imaginary rate of $1.00 per second that we used earlier. Assuming that this $118 trillion was not compounding with interest daily, how long would it take our government to pay off $118 trillion dollars at this imaginary rate of $1.00 per second?

Only 3,776,000 years.

According to this repayment plan, America could completely deal with the entitlement crisis facing us in 2036 by the year A.D. 3,778,012!

Are you beginning to see how large these numbers truly are? Think about that the next time you hear some slick-haired, shiny-shoed politician utter the word "trillion."

This brief nightmare scenario is far from exhaustive and is probably very incomplete. But I provide it to help you understand the great economic damage that you and I, and our nation in general, would sustain if the petrodollar system were to collapse suddenly. I personally believe that the demise of the dollar will occur over a longer period of time, but no one can rule out the possibility of the dollar losing value overnight. While it is likely no sane nation wants to provoke a dollar collapse, it is certain that no nation wants to be the last one holding the bag when it does collapse. When global fears rise over a currency collapse, not only does it spark a run on the currency by fearful nations, it also gives rise to wild currency speculation. As we know from history, such collapses have occurred with a depressing regularity in the terminal stages of a fiat currency. And without a doubt, the dollar is its terminal stages as the life span of virtually every fiat currency has been around 40 years. The U.S. dollar officially became a fiat currency in 1971. Therefore, the fiat dollar turned 40 years old in 2011.

The Washington elites are intimately aware of how serious the economic situation could become if the petrodollar system were to suddenly collapse. After all, they were the architects and masterminds of the entire system.

Dr. Bulent Gukay of Keele University puts it this way:

> This system of the U.S. dollar acting as global reserve currency in oil trade keeps the demand for the dollar "artificially" high. This enables the U.S. to carry out printing dollars at the price of next to nothing to fund increased military spending and consumer spending on imports. There is no theoretical

limit to the amount of dollars that can be printed. As long as the U.S. has no serious challengers, and the other states have confidence in the U.S. dollar, the system functions.[2]

Pay particular attention to Dr. Gukay's comment regarding "serious challengers" to the United States. As the global economy continues to evolve, a whole host of competing currencies will rise to challenge the current dollar hegemony. In fact, that movement is already afoot.

Considering Washington's policies since the mid-1970s, it is evident that they have no intention of allowing the petrodollar system to fail. In fact, I would expect a full-scale U.S.-led world war on "terror" before such an event as I described above were ever allowed to occur.

What does that mean for you? In essence, expect more perpetual wars against faceless and nameless enemies. And expect the theater for these conflicts to conveniently be staged in Western Asia — where the majority of the world's oil supplies lies waiting for their Western "liberators."

The Certainty of Uncertainty

Every day Washington continues its out-of-control spending, it brings us one step closer to our nation's impending day of financial reckoning. Through a myriad of poor fiscal and monetary policies, Washington has completely distorted our financial system. These distortions often breed uncertainty, which the financial markets despise. Adding to this financial uncertainty is the coming wave of 78 million baby boomers who are preparing to launch into the realm of retirement villages, entitlement benefits, and subsidized healthcare. Without a crystal ball, no one can say for sure how the economy will be impacted. It is only logical to assume, however, that these millions of retirees will be cashing out of the stock market and downsizing their living arrangement which could lead to a glut of new homes on the market in the coming years. And given the economic realities facing our nation's entitlement systems, it is only logical that they will continue to get worse not better. I believe that without a strong dose of fiscal discipline, coupled with political realism and intestinal fortitude, the American social safety net that shields our nation's growing segments of the poor and the elderly will falter before our eyes in the coming years.

America is living in the eye of a massive economic hurricane. The amount of funding required to keep Social Security, Medicare, and Medicaid afloat will devastate the U.S. economy. Add to this the military costs involved in protecting and preserving our dollar hegemony and you will find that there is no light at the end of this financial tunnel. America's financial demise will occur due to inadequate planning, military overextension, unrealistic political promises, dreadful demographics, poor leadership, and skyrocketing medical costs. Or as the first baby boomer, Ms. Casey-Kirschling, puts it, "I can't imagine what's going to happen with our children and our grandchildren. They're not going to be able to retire."[3]

During a 2005 speech in Colorado, President George W. Bush expressed his growing concerns about the looming entitlement crisis by stating: "Some of you may think there's what they call a Social Security trust: the government collects the money for you, we hold it for you, and when you retire, we pay it to you. But that's not how it works. You pay your payroll tax; we pay for the people who have retired, and if there's any money left over, we spend it on government. That's how it works. And what's left is an empty IOU, a piece of paper."[4]

If your goal is financial freedom, it is vital that you wake up to the economic realities facing our nation. The truth is, America is bankrupt.

We can no longer afford to be the policeman of the world. We need to stop worrying about the national borders in Central Asia and worry about solving our border issues here in America.

Our Social Security system is broken. Medicare is facing insolvency within a few years. Our politicians have no solutions and yet most American people still vote down party lines believing that somehow things will get better eventually. The American people have been completely deceived by the corporate-controlled mainstream media. The tax burden upon the American people will only go up from here. Our $118 trillion entitlement crisis is real and there are no easy answers. But there are answers. Two that immediately come to mind are:

1. reducing benefits

2. increasing taxes

While I would prefer a cut in benefits over a hike in taxes, the question becomes who should have their benefits cut? Should baby boomers take all the blame for our entitlement crisis? They paid into the system and were promised a certain set of benefits in exchange. What did they do wrong?

If we are going to cut benefits, it should be across the board. And we should start by cutting the luxurious congressional pension plans. Take away the posh retirement benefits from the Congress and make them dependent on Social Security like the rest of America. Suddenly, solving the problems of Social Security and Medicare will become a top priority in Washington.

Kicking the Can Down the Road

Finding financial solutions that everyone can agree on is nearly impossible within a declining empire living in denial. It is no secret that our current generation is notorious for its intolerance for any — and all — types of economic pain. If a politician runs for elected office on a platform of cutting benefits to all segments of the population, his chances of success are absurdly low. On the flip side, if a politician runs on a platform of increasing taxes, he has a political death wish.

The most astute politicians have rightly understood that the American public wants:

- Cheap gasoline prices and government policies that protect the environment

- Free healthcare and low taxes

- Low interest rates and even lower inflation

- Low unemployment and less government regulation

Who cares that this combination of goodies is economically unsustainable in the long run. . . . We will leave those problems for the next generation to sort out.

So if politicians are not willing to save money (reduce benefits) or increase income (raise taxes), then how are they able to keep the American financial illusion fully operating? This brings us to a third option that has historically proven to be less painful in the short-term, but most disastrous in the long run.

What is this third potential answer to America's entitlement crisis? To answer this stumper, think: *What is the typical American response to a financial dilemma?* While some Americans may get a second job or try to cut their spending, more often than not, they borrow money.

When Americans wish that they had the largest flat-screen television or the nicest lawn on their block, most of them turn to their three favorite money lenders: Visa, Mastercard, and Discover.

But satiating financial desires through borrowing money at interest has not been restricted to the U.S. consumer. To the contrary, a $118 trillion promised future obligations testifies to the obsession that our federal government has with abusing credit.

Therefore, the third option for confronting the nation's growing economic problems, including the current entitlement crisis, is and will likely continue to be borrowing the money.

We borrow for everything else in this country, so why not just borrow the money we need to pay for our $118 trillion entitlement crisis? And from whom will we borrow the money? Oh, dear reader, you have completely forgotten that this question does not matter to a deluded empire in decline. Take your pick: China, Japan, Germany, Britain, or even the Federal Reserve. Who really cares which foreign country or institution coughs up the cash? As long as *they* pay for *our* debts, then we can keep our economic illusion going, Americans can continue living in ignorant bliss, and the "hard-working" politicians can keep their jobs.

After all, how could the international economic community resist the chance to lend us more of their hard-earned money in exchange for our unsustainable debts at extremely low interest rates? And besides, these countries don't have anything better to do with their money than propping up our debts, right?

In retrospect, this third option of borrowing the money appears to be the preferred way of handling the mounting economic crises facing our nation. After all, it prevents Americans from having to be bothered with those pesky things like "tax hikes" and "spending cuts."

If the above reasoning comes off as absurd to you, the reader, imagine how it sounds to those foreign nations who get the honor of picking up the tab.

Consider the words from former Treasury Secretary Paul O'Neill regarding the three options facing us: "Because the Social Security trust fund does not consist of real economic assets, we are left to rely on the federal government's future decisions to either raise taxes, reduce spending, or increase borrowing from the public to finance fully Social Security's promised benefits."[5]

To fully understand why I believe that a period of high and sustained inflation lies on the horizon for America, let's briefly examine each of these three economic options, one at a time.

Option #1 — Raise Money by Increasing Tax Revenues

In America today, it is becoming nearly impossible for families to get ahead financially on one income. This has forced many women into the workforce, and some spouses even work two jobs just to make ends meet. But unlike the modern American family, the federal government can't earn more money by delivering pizzas on the weekend. Instead, the way it raises extra cash is by raising tax rates on the U.S. taxpayers. As I have demonstrated, the problem with this option is obvious.

First, you may recall that the American Revolution was inspired by "unfair taxes." (A three pence tax on tea was enough to drive America's founders to the point of madness.) Besides our historical resistance to taxes in general, modern U.S. taxpayers are rational economic creatures. As such, they naturally do not like giving up more of their income in the form of taxes than is necessary. Raising taxes has become risky business in modern politics, and few modern politicians are interested in risk, especially when it could cost them a re-election. It is likely that any future tax hikes will be on the nation's "wealthiest" citizens to limit the political fallout. Unfortunately, Washington's illogical definition of "wealthy" includes many of the nation's small business owners. By raising taxes on the nation's largest employers, Washington will ensure a net decrease in tax revenues and a higher unemployment rate.

Summary: Raising taxes is the wrong solution because Washington does not have a revenue problem — it has a spending problem. Giving more money to the same people who manufactured this crisis through poor financial stewardship will not solve our economic crisis. And because U.S. taxpayers do not typically elect, or re-elect, politicians who seek to raise taxes, politicians will recommend tax increases to the American public at their own risk.

Option #2 — Raise Money by Cutting Spending and Entitlement Benefits

The New York subway system is a modern marvel. The intricate transit system covers a total of 842 track miles, which if laid out end to end would stretch from New York City to Chicago! In between, or just outside the subway tracks, lies something called *the third rail*. The third rail provides a staggering 625 volts of electricity, which powers the entire NYC transit system. Without the third rail, the trains go nowhere. Occasionally, some poor ignorant fellow will accidentally touch the third rail. The result: *instant death by electrocution.*

Similarly, astute politicians have recognized "third rails" that they try to avoid touching at all costs. A political "third rail" is an idea or a topic that is so highly charged that one's political career is jeopardized simply by "touching" it. One of the most notorious "third rails" in American politics is the topic of entitlement benefits. Just ask the late U.S. Senator Barry Goldwater.

While running for president against Lyndon B. Johnson in 1964, Goldwater had the audacity to question whether the Social Security system should be a *voluntary* program. Bad move, Goldwater. Apparently, there are just some things in this country that you do not question. Goldwater lost the election in a landslide. Those who dare to venture into the forbidden forest of entitlement spending cuts do so at their own risk.

Is America's attitude toward entitlement spending any different today than it was in 1964? If anything, I would suggest that America's attitude has become galvanized toward not giving up any government benefits. Should the baby boom generation be asked to sacrifice any part of their promised entitlement benefits? I do not believe so. They paid into the system and deserve the benefits they were promised. Reducing entitlement benefits to existing beneficiaries, and to those near retirement, would not only be immoral, it would be highly impractical as well. However, a political plan must be implemented to protect younger Americans from the impending colossal failure of America's entitlement systems. The political will needed for this, however, is absent. Why? Because entitlements are a political "third rail."

One of the chief concerns in cutting the amount of benefit payments to the baby boom generation is their sheer lack of savings as we discussed in a previous chapter. I would suggest the reason that so few boomers are adequately saving for retirement is because our entitlement systems create an economic disincentive. Compare America's ridiculously low savings rate (less than 5 percent) to the much higher rate in China (more than 40 percent). Why is there such a big difference? The answer lies in the fact that the Chinese population does not have a social safety net in retirement like we have in America. Therefore, they must save.

Note the irony. America's entitlement benefits, which were created to help lift the poor and needy out of extreme poverty, have created a population that has failed to save for their golden years. But even if some boomers are prepared for the financial demands of retirement, are they prepared to finance a *long* retirement? Thanks to medical advances, Americans are living longer than ever. According to Croker, boomers who reached age 65 in the year 2011 can expect to live at least another 18 years on average. And some will live even longer. Maintaining the lifestyle that millions of retiring boomers have become accustomed to during their working years will be a very expensive proposition.

So any politician foolish enough to suggest spending cuts for millions of retiring boomers would be better off placing his wet hand on the third rail of the New York City subway system.

Summary: Politicians will delay cutting entitlement benefits as a long as possible because their only incentive is re-election. Modern elections require the support afforded by the 78 million baby boom voters. Americans will continue to demand more benefits, not fewer, and any suggestions to cut spending for entitlements will be met by a formidable boomer voting bloc.

Option #3 — Raise Money by Borrowing

The third option, given by Mr. Paul O'Neill, is to "increase borrowing from the public to finance fully Social Security's promised benefits." At last, you say, a reasonable option that doesn't involve economic pain. You are right, at least temporarily. It is a near certainty that America will attempt to delay the economic pain caused by the entitlement crisis for as long as possible. And the most obvious way to postpone the financial day of reckoning will be to export the debt to anyone who will buy it through the issuance of treasury securities. According to Alan Greenspan, the former head of the Federal Reserve, this is exactly what the federal government plans to do. In a speech given on April 27, 2001, Greenspan stated the following: "When the baby boom generation retires, and as the population subsequently ages further, these contingent liabilities [Social Security] will come due and — barring an offsetting surplus in the remainder of the government's budget — will be met by the issuance of Treasury securities, shifting much of total federal liabilities from contingent liability to debt to the public. At that point, of course, the unified budget will be in deficit."[6]

In other words, Washington will take the political low road by borrowing the money it needs to pay for the entitlements that it has promised to millions of Americans. In keeping with our national obsession of avoiding sacrifice at all costs, the path of least resistance will be all too appealing to desperate politicians.

If you are shaking your head, wondering how all of this could be happening in America, it is an indication that you now fully understand the full nature and severity of the crisis that America is facing. At one time in this nation's history, it would have been considered implausible that the government would do something so reckless as to fund incredible amounts of entitlement spending with borrowed money.

How would you feel about a man who walked into the finest restaurant in town, spent exorbitant amounts of money on a lavish dinner, and then told the waiter to mail the bill to his infant son? Or even worse, his unborn grandson? This is exactly what America is choosing to do by financing its current expenses and future debt obligations through borrowing. Apparently, there is no alternative for politicians motivated by re-election, and the entitlement-crazed generation they have spawned. Both blindly refuse to embrace the concept of short-term sacrifice for longer-term security.

Summary: The Federal Reserve has admitted that the entitlement crisis will be financed through federal borrowing. After all, creating debt is what Americans do best. Why would they apply any other logic to the entitlement crisis?

Why Massive Inflation Is Coming

On August 5, 2011, the New York-based credit rating agency, Standard & Poor's, downgraded America's AAA credit rating for the first time. S&P lowered the nation's credit rating one level to AA+, and further warned that it may cut America's credit rating to an even lower AA by 2013 if the nation fails to reduce spending, or attempts to cut taxes or raise interest rates.[7]

What few Americans yet realize is that our nation is living off the kindness of strangers. We are recklessly borrowing record amounts of money to continue funding unnecessary wars and a broken entitlement system. Our national obsession with avoiding any and all financial pain will be our undoing. Refusing to foster a mature dialogue on the economic challenges that currently face us will eventually lead to a collapse of our creditworthiness, and our currency.

When our currency collapses, a period of stubborn hyperinflation will ensue. The only true remedy for hyperinflation is a reduction in the money supply, which typically occurs through a dramatic increase in interest rates. Of course, an increase in interest rates would devastate U.S. consumers, borrowers, businesses, and asset prices. Through a series of poor fiscal and monetary choices, America has put itself in a classic "catch 22" situation.

I would suggest to you that a massive bout of inflation is simply unavoidable for America. To fully appreciate why I believe a coming hyperinflation is going to strike America's economy, it is vital to understand the Federal Reserve's role as "the lender of last resort." As the government's lender of last resort, the Fed is obligated to step in and buy government debt when public interest in that debt wanes. In 2011, the Fed purchased 61 percent of all of the debt securities issued by the government, and as of this writing, the Federal Reserve is the largest single holder of our national debt.[8]

And as I explained in an earlier chapter, when the Fed lends money, it does so with money that it creates out of thin air. It is the beauty of the fiat currency system. When times get tough and the government is in debt up to its eyeballs, just print more money!

Obviously, when the Fed is pumping new amounts of money into the economy, it leads to a devaluation of the current dollars in

The Greenspan Doctrine

The Fed's reliance upon printing money to solve financial crises is something that I refer to as the "Greenspan doctrine." During his tenure as Federal Reserve chairman, Alan Greenspan's response to financial crisis was to inflate his way out of them:

- In the stock market crash of 1987, Greenspan inflated the monetary base.
- During the 1994 Mexican peso crisis, Greenspan inflated.
- During the 1997 Asian crisis and LTCM debacle, Greenspan inflated.
- During the 1998 Russian ruble crisis, Greenspan inflated.
- In the wake of the dot-com crash in March 2000, Greenspan inflated.
- After 9/11/01, Greenspan inflated.

Later, in June 2003, Greenspan lowered key U.S. interest rate targets to one percent for an entire year.

Since Federal Reserve Chief Ben Bernanke took over the helm in 2006, little has changed.

Mr. Bernanke is following the same pattern, and for the past few years, he has maintained artificially low interest rates. By keeping interest rates low, the Fed has encouraged massive speculation and enormous debts.

Instead of attempting to save the fragile U.S. currency, the Fed has been guilty of devaluing it through extremely poor monetary policies. It is my belief that the Fed should be ended immediately, as it is a leach on our economy. It creates the boom-bust cycles that it claims to help us avoid.

circulation. Just as the discovery of a viable new source of oil puts downward pressure on the price of petroleum, creating money "out of thin air" with the printing presses only serves to devalue the existing currency base.

Printing new money *today* makes every dollar worth less *tomorrow*.

And while the government has become dependent upon the Fed for buying much of its debt, this dependency has been muted by the fact that foreign nations have still been willing to lend money to the United States.

Currently, foreign nations hold trillions of U.S. dollars in the form of U.S. Treasury bonds. Among the most voracious of U.S. debt purchasers are several Asian and European countries. According to a March 2012 report issued by the U.S. Treasury, China is America's largest foreign creditor, owning $1.132 trillion of U.S. Treasury bonds. China's ownership of American debt indicates our nation's growing reliance upon economic subsidies from Beijing. According to this same report, Japan is the second largest foreign holder of U.S. debt at $1.038 trillion as of March 2012.

As of this writing, foreign nations own nearly $5 trillion, or 33 percent, of America's $15.5 trillion national debt.[9] That means that one out of every three dollars that we have borrowed is owed to foreign creditors!

According to a March 2012 official report issued by the Federal Reserve, there is total of $1.1 trillion of U.S. dollars in circulation.[10] This means that America owes foreign creditors nearly five times the total amount of U.S. currency in circulation!

As long as foreign nations are willing to continue financing America's reckless overspending, *and* as long as the petrodollar system remains intact, the worst-case scenario of hyperinflation can be delayed. But these are both very large assumptions!

American dependence upon foreign creditors to continue financing our overconsumption is a fool's game and is clearly unsustainable. How can the government do all that it has promised if we are dependent upon foreign creditors? And especially if these foreign creditors are beginning to doubt our ability to pay back the debts that we owe. Proof of this sentiment is seen in China's holdings of our debt, which decreased by over 3 percent in just six months, from July to December 2011.

Foreign governments are acutely aware of America's economic problems. Knowing this, many of them are biding their time by actively looking for alternatives to U.S. dollar-denominated assets for investment purposes. In the months and years ahead, other global currencies, such as the euro and the yuan, will be strong competitors for these same global investment dollars. In recent months, we have already witnessed small-scale changes in investment flows toward Europe and away from the U.S. dollar. These shifts will increase over time until we witness a full-blown collapse of the U.S. dollar. Sadly, when this foreign financing of American debt begins to wane, it will generate great fears within the community of America's creditors (i.e., China, Japan, etc.). If one creditor were to begin massive sell-offs of American debts, it would spark a panic among America's debt holders. While no nation may want to be the first to sell their dollar holdings, they certainly will not want to be the last!

Meanwhile, America's deficits are hitting all-time highs, the credit crisis continues to worsen, and the U.S. money supply is expanding at a record pace, triggering widespread fears of inflation. And these are just a few of the problems currently facing our economy. Sadly, most Americans remain clueless as to the problems and issues that will inevitably face them and their children. The facts are clear. The current economic situation in the United States is completely unsustainable. A financial day of reckoning awaits this country, and its arrival will serve as a rude awakening to all who are not prepared. If you think that America has seen the worst of the financial crisis, consider yourself forewarned. The real financial crisis awaiting America will begin when the U.S. dollar collapses. Unfortunately for American citizens, the U.S. government is doing little to prevent this impending dollar collapse. As long as the debt-loving, interest-rate cutting, currency-printaholic Feds can't seem to find the "off" switch on the printing press, the dollar will continue to decline in value and in purchasing power.

The obvious structural problems facing the American economy, including a failing currency, a soft economy, an entitlement crisis, an unemployment crisis, and a housing crisis, are far from minor issues. *To the contrary, they are enormous problems.* And because investment capital tends to flow to the rate of highest return for the least amount of risk, some foreign investors are eagerly seeking to find replacements

---

Did You Know?

Most informed Americans are increasingly aware that America's foreign creditors have been recently expressing concern over Washington's ability to make good on their future debt payments. In fact, America's creditworthiness among foreign nations is becoming more suspect by the day. This concern among America's creditors was most noticeably witnessed during a 2009 speech by current U.S. Treasury Secretary, Timothy Geithner. In response to a question about the safety of U.S. debt securities after a speech at Peking University, Geithner assured the audience that Chinese investments into U.S. debt were "very safe." His answer was received with loud laughter from his student audience.[11]

for their holdings in U.S. debt securities. The mounting domestic and international fears surrounding the growing U.S. government debt will mean one thing: fewer borrowers. And fewer borrowers will mean less money for the federal government to use in shoring up the entitlement crisis that it has created. This trend is confirmed in a December 2011 report issued by the U.S. Treasury.[12]

According to the report, Russia's total holdings of U.S. debt securities fell by 42 percent, from $151 billion to $88 billion in a 12-month period ending December 2011.

During that same 12 month period:

- India cut its U.S. debt holdings by 15 percent, from $40.5 billion to $34.2 billion

- Hong Kong reduced their U.S. debt holdings by 16 percent from $134.2 billion to $112 billion.

- Singapore cut their holdings by over 14 percent from $72.9 billion to $62.5 billion.

- Mexico reduced their holdings by more than 18 percent from $33.6 billion to $27.4 billion.

- And Israel cut their holdings of U.S. debt by over 23 percent from $20.6 billion to $15.8 billion.

What does all of this mean? It means that foreign countries are no longer just questioning the wisdom of holding and hoarding U.S. debt instruments, *but they are beginning to actively look for alternatives.* China, for example, has recently been cutting its U.S. debt holdings and has been seeking diversification through other currencies, like the euro, and even in hard assets like gold, farmland, and foreign mining operations.[13]

With fewer borrowers for its debts, America will become increasingly dependent upon its "lender of last resort": the Federal Reserve. And how will the Federal Reserve go about purchasing the debt? Through the creation of freshly printed paper money. And because the Fed's money-printing process increases the money supply, it leads to a further dilution of the value of the currency. The result? Massive inflation.

The idea that America can forever spend and borrow its way into prosperity is a delusion that is promoted by the government and the corporate-controlled mainstream media. It is a lie and its effects are going to harm millions of unsuspecting Americans who continue to believe the deception.

Admittedly, this is a gloomy scenario. But it is based upon facts, and facts are stubborn things. Only those who are aware, can prepare.

Quick Summary

✓ The artificial demand and perceived safety of the U.S. dollar and debt securities, created by the petrodollar system, are the primary reasons behind the dollar's continued global status.

✓ I forecast that by the end of this decade, a currency other than the dollar will replace the U.S. dollar as global reserve currency.

✓ The fall of the petrodollar system is the key leading indicator of the coming collapse of the U.S. dollar.

✓ The three possible solutions to our nation's debt crisis are to raise taxes, cut spending, or borrow money. It is not feasible for an individual or the government to spend its way out of debt.

✓ One of the responsibilities of the Federal Reserve is to act as the federal government's "lender of last resort," buying U.S. debt securities when there are no investors left.

✓ Many foreign nations, including China, Russia, and India have recently reduced their holdings of U.S. debt securities, indicating that foreign nations are keenly aware of our nation's financial woes.

✓ When the desire to hold U.S. debt securities declines, and when no one needs U.S. dollars to purchase oil, massive inflation will soon follow.

Endnotes

1. David Wiedemer, Robert Wiedemer, Cindy Spitzer, and Eric Janszen, *America's Bubble Economy: Profit When It Pops* (Chichester, England: Wiley-Interscience, 2007), p. 234.

2. "The Beginning of the End of the Petrodollar: What Connects Iraq to Iran by Bulent Gokay," March 15, 2006; http://www.mathaba.net/news/?x=530827.

3. Richard Wolf, "Social Security Hits First Wave of Boomers," *USA Today*, http://www.usatoday.com/news/washington/2007-10-08-boomers_N.htm.

4. "President Discusses Strengthening Social Security in Colorado," March 21, 2005; http://georgewbush-whitehouse.archives.gov/news/releases/2005/03/20050321-13.html.

5. Jeannine Aversa, "Treasury Secretary: 'Social Security Has "No Assets," ' " *Augusta Chronicle*, July 10, 2001, http://chronicle.augusta.com/stories/2001/07/16/bus_318998.shtml.

6. http://www.federalreserve.gov/boarddocs/speeches/2001/20010427/default. htm.

7. http://www.bloomberg.com/news/2011-08-06/u-s-credit-rating-cut-by-s-p-for-first-time-on-deficit-reduction-accord.html.

8. http://online.wsj.com/article/SB10001424052702304450004577279754275393064.html, http://ycharts.com/indicators/us_currency_in_circulation#series=type:indicator,id:us_currency_in_circulation,calc:&zoom=10&startDate=&endDate=&format=real&recessions=false.

9. http://www.treasury.gov/resource-center/data-chart-center/tic/Documents/mfh. txt.

10. http://www.federalreserve.gov/releases/h41/Current/.

11. http://www.reuters.com/article/2009/06/01/usa-china-idUS-PEK14475620090601.

12. http://seekingalpha.com/instablog/1110090-the-gold-informant/324361-dumping-the-dollar-for-what.

13. http://online.wsj.com/article/SB1000142405270230382310457639162135252 8138.html.

Chapter 11

Maxed Out:
The New American Slavery

The rich rules over the poor, and the
borrower is servant to the lender.

— Proverbs 22:7

None are more hopelessly enslaved than those who
falsely believe they are free.[1]

— Johann Wolfgang von Goethe

Americans pride themselves on being a free people. But in reality, Americans are enslaved. The word "slave" conjures up a very negative image, perhaps of a poor soul being sold on an auction block to the highest bidder. This is an example of physical slavery. Today, approximately 27 million people are physical slaves.[2] Being enslaved, however, can occur in more than one form and is not always visible. A human being becomes a slave when he loses, or willingly gives up, the control over his own life to someone or something else. For example:

We are slaves to our culture . . . when we go against our better judgment and refuse to question the status quo.

We are slaves to religion . . . when we are fearful of questioning the validity of our own beliefs and values and permit others to tell us what we believe and why we believe it.

We are slaves to entertainment . . . when our lives are spent in a reckless pursuit of pleasure and a complete avoidance of anything resembling pain.

We are slaves to our politics . . . when we adopt political persuasions based upon our culture, the media, or other persuasive individuals or groups, instead of from our own convictions.

We are slaves to a paycheck . . . when we feel trapped in a job that pays us just enough to survive, but not enough to ever break free financially.

We are slaves to money . . . when the pursuit of it becomes our primary obsession.

We are slaves to consumerism . . . when the clever marketing messages concocted by corporations and the media dictate our appetites and spending patterns, which then trap us in a vain search for an increased amount of self-worth through the purchase of mere objects.

And we are slaves to debt . . . when we sabotage our own financial futures in order to obey the commands of our corporate masters through overconsumption with borrowed money.

I would suggest that each of us can identify with at least one of the above forms of slavery. Given the fact that our nation has a debt-based monetary system, it should be no surprise that one of the largest forms of enslavement in America today is debt slavery. America's consumer debt levels have skyrocketed over the last several decades as corporations and the credit industry have worked hard to convince the entire collective culture that the "buy now, pay later" mentality will bring them happiness.

Today, America's public education system churns out tens of thousands of young adults without ever providing them with even a basic financial education, leaving financial literacy rates among young adults at dismally low levels. The corporations and the credit industry, which are acutely aware of this education gap, have stepped in to become America's financial educators. Unfortunately, their noxious brand of financial education involves teaching people how to become consumers, not producers. Through the media, American consumers are encouraged to take on massive debts in order to enrich corporations and the credit industry.

Meanwhile, our elected leaders in Washington are the perfect model of the "buy now, pay later" mentality, having accumulated well over $15 trillion in debt and adding another $1 trillion in debt annually.

Sadly, even those Americans who have been able to avoid becoming enslaved to debt are not "debt-free." Becoming "debt-free" in America is a complete illusion. In truth, you and your children are ultimately responsible for the debts incurred by Washington's financial excesses.

The debt that the American government owes is *yours — you are America*.

The Congress and the Senate are not spending "Monopoly" money to drop bombs in foreign lands and to bail out the rich. They are borrowing it from others, with you as the co-signer.

Washington's frivolous spending is done with the checkbook of the U.S. citizenry. Think about it: How can you be free and at the same time be a citizen of the greatest debtor nation in world history? And likewise, how can a man be free if he *owes* money on everything that he "owns?"

> There are two ways to conquer and enslave a nation. One is by the sword. The other is by debt.[3] — (President John Adams)

"The Present Must Be the Minimum"

At the very foundation of America's economic problems lies a profoundly flawed assumption that our present level of consumption and economic growth must always be the absolute minimum. Just watch how Americans react when gas prices increase. It is as if they believe that their economy should not be touched by basic supply and demand concerns.

Did You Know?

Shopping centers
have become
the new houses
of worship in
America. Seventy
percent of
Americans visit a
mall each week —
more than attend
church.

This illusion, which should have been annihilated in the wake of the 2008 financial crisis, continues to plague our nation's financial psyche. Today, millions of Americans blame others for their own personal financial woes while still falsely believing that they have no need to change course in their personal financial lives because everything will all just work itself out in the end.

Millions of others falsely believe that America will remain the world's sole superpower in the 21st century and that foreign nations will always want to lend money to America.

Others falsely believe that by getting a "good education" and then a "good job," they can build a secure financial future.

Some Americans become outraged when there is an inevitable increase in the cost of living without understanding that inflation will only continue to increase under our fiat monetary system. Others even falsely believe that U.S. inflation rates and interest rates will never get out of control! Some Americans believe that tax rates should always remain low, that the stock market will always go up in the "long run," the grocery stores will always be stocked full of food, and that gasoline should always be cheap.

It is time to wake up from the illusion.

Our nation's grand experiment with a debt-based monetary system is nearing its end. The collapse that will result will only be made worse by a massive population that lives in denial of reality.

America's Addiction to Consumption and Credit

The enslavement of the American population has been further perpetuated by the emphasis not just upon consumption, but "overconsumption." Overconsumption has become a way of life for Americans as they have been programmed by the corporations, the credit industry, and the mass media to believe that happiness can only be found by having "more."

More money.

More sex.

More food.

More alcohol.

More work.

More gadgets.

More houses.

More cars.

More wealth.

And nothing is holy or off-limits to this corporate-inspired mind-set of overconsumption. Marketers play up their messages using patriotic themes designed to provoke Americans who love their country into believing that supporting their nation requires going into debt to commit random acts of consumption.

Perhaps even worse, the concept of "more" has seeped into the halls of America's churches. Christianity, a religion historically considered to be rooted in the concepts of self-sacrifice and the denial of self, has birthed entire industries in America designed to satiate the consumer cravings of the faithful.

Some clever Christian movements have even sought to closely associate a person's ability to overconsume with "godliness." Those who consume "more" corporate goods and services are considered to be more "blessed" by God than their more Spartan counterparts.

What deception!

The financial excesses attached to this corporate-inspired gospel of consumption directly compete with the most noble of human activities, including: developing relationships, wise stewardship, charitable giving, and economic self-reliance.

Without a doubt, times are tough in America today and will continue to get tougher for those who do not begin implementing some financial common sense. Unfortunately, for millions of Americans, excessive spending is a dangerous form of therapy designed to help them cope with the increasing amounts of stress caused by the American way of life. Of course, this shopping therapy creates a vicious circle, as the more we consume, the less money we have. Continuing the consumption requires us to work longer hours, which then leads to increasing amounts of stress.

In addition to working more hours, Americans are also borrowing more money than ever before. They have had to borrow more money

Think about It

This topic of overconsumption reminds me of a trip I took to the Mediterranean Sea while writing the first edition of this book. I was invited to Greece, Turkey, and Israel to speak about the global financial crisis and decided to take full advantage of the many sightseeing opportunities. While roaming through the ancient ruins of Athens, Ephesus, Jerusalem, and Galilee, it became very clear to me that I was literally seeing what the people of these ancient cultures held to be important and valuable. The ancient ruins of Greece and Ephesus displayed a strong reliance upon superstition, with numerous statues of gods and goddesses that the Greeks worshiped. Jerusalem and Galilee gave strong hints of a former Roman occupation. During my excursion, the thought occurred to me: if America's buildings and cities were suddenly to be covered by a super volcano and reduced to ruins, only to be discovered 2,000 years from now, what would archaeologists discover about our country? How would future travelers view our civilization and what could be determined about America's values based upon what exists today? The Greeks worshiped a number of gods, including Zeus and Athena. The Jews worshiped the Hebrew God. What God, or gods, would America be accused of worshiping by future discoverers of our artifacts and ruins?

The answer should be evident: Americans serve the god of money and consumerism. Archaeologists might mistakenly believe our houses of worship to be the shopping centers that exist on virtually every corner of town. They would also find banks, which fuel these acts of consumptive worship, peppered throughout every community. They would find that the tallest skyscrapers in every major American metropolis were banks. In my opinion, America's worship of money and overconsumption will be what future observers notice most when examining our nation's ruins.

to afford the luxuries they see everyone else enjoying. Trying to keep up with the Joneses is expensive. The truth that no one seems to understand is that the Joneses are going broke. This is because no one, not even the Joneses, can continue to spend more than they earn forever. At the end of 2011, Federal Reserve data showed that total U.S. household debt stood at a whopping $13.2 trillion.[4] This total includes all mortgage and credit card debt, bank loans, student loans, auto loans, loans from finance companies, etc.

While driving down the road, I saw a bumper sticker that said: "Winning is dying with your credit cards maxed out." Maybe so, but

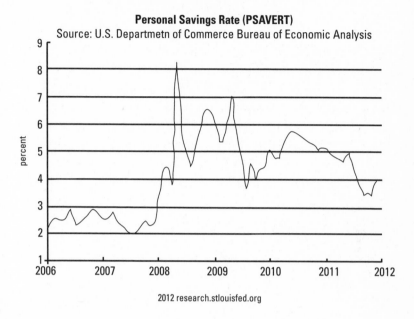

Personal Savings Rate (PSAVERT)
Source: U.S. Departmetn of Commerce Bureau of Economic Analysis

2012 research.stlouisfed.org

try telling that to the 1,467,221 U.S. consumers and businesses that filed for bankruptcy in 2011.[5]

How the U.S. Government Discourages Personal Savings

Today, it has become socially acceptable — even a cultural norm — for Americans to consume more than they need. To some, over-consumption may even feel like second nature. Sadly, our nation has become so obsessed with consuming corporate goods and services that we have forgotten the practical wisdom and discipline of saving even a small portion of our money. This financial insanity has led the majority of Americans into living a "paycheck to paycheck" lifestyle. In fact, many of these American families live with tremendous financial pressure and even fear, knowing that they are just one paycheck away from bankruptcy or foreclosure. And given our looming current retirement crisis, things will only get worse before they get better.

But how can all of this be possible in America? How can so many people work so hard all their lives only to reach retirement with so little to show for it?

As I have attempted to point out in this book, things have changed greatly in America over the last few decades. We are simply living in a very different era. Gone are the days of job stability and pension plans. Today, most employees are left to fend for themselves. The extent of financial planning for many Americans consists of shooting a quick question via e-mail to their Human Resources Department at work. Others turn to the mainstream financial media. The entertaining "stock jockeys" send these poor souls to the glorious casino of Wall Street. With few retirement dollars in hand, and thousands of different choices before them, it is no wonder so many Americans feel discouraged. The odds are stacked against an uninformed public. According to the U.S. Commerce Department, 40 percent of American households now believe they could accumulate $500,000 more easily through the lottery than by savings.[6]

However, America's favorite pastime of overconsumption is not solely to blame for its aversion to saving money. The U.S. federal government itself discourages personal savings through its policies. How? Consider the U.S. Tax Code. It has an inherent bias toward consumption by penalizing savings and investment. If you take your paycheck and decide to do the responsible thing and save it, you will pay a penalty in the form of a tax on interest. If you choose to invest it, you will also be taxed on any eventual gains. However, if you take your paycheck and blow it on a big-screen television, the federal government never gets directly involved. If the government would stop levying big taxes on productivity and investing, and instead tax consumption more heavily, Americans would be properly incentivized to become better financial stewards within our national economy.

And what about Social Security? By creating the false impression that their retirement expenses will be covered, the government provides a strong disincentive for Americans to save money for their future.

Did You Know?

The U.S. Tax Code was developed in 1913, the same year as the Federal Reserve. When it was originally written, it was a mere 400 pages. Today, it consists of over 72,000 pages, making it well over 50 times longer than the King James Bible!

This is not to say that a social safety net in retirement is wrong by any means. But when you consider it within the context of all of the government's other policies, it only makes sense that Americans consume big and save little. Their own government rewards this behavior.

The Real Problem: "Debt-Based" Wealth

Over two-thirds of the American economy is built upon consumption. This means that the future economic growth of America is dependent upon growing amounts of consumption. But is it possible to increase our consumption forever? Is this a sustainable model for future economic growth?

The answer is clear — without our continued consumption, our economy would collapse. We are held hostage by our own way of life. We are a nation dependent upon borrowing and consumption. We are slaves to debt. One Christian financial radio show that I have heard invites its listeners to call in and scream: "I'm debt free!" when they pay off all of their debts. And while their plight is better than most, they are still on the hook for the massive debts our nation has created through obsessive spending and reckless borrowing.

As we discussed in chapter 10, our modern banking system creates money out of debt. This debt-based money is then loaned out to the American public in the form of loans and lines of credit. However, when a consumer borrows money from a bank or other financial institution, they are only borrowing principal. The interest that will need to be paid back on that loan is not created by the lender. Lenders only create the principal of the loan — *not the interest*. This means that all borrowers in our nation are trying to pay back a *large* pool of principal plus interest from a smaller pool of only principal. For this reason, bankruptcies, repossessions, and foreclosures are guaranteed. According to the current banking system of debt-based money, *losers are required*. Not everyone can win. Only those who can go out into the marketplace and find the interest to pay back on their loans have a chance at coming out even. Like musical chairs, there are never enough chairs for everyone who is playing the game. Likewise, there is never enough money in the system for everyone to pay back both *principal and interest* — because only the principal exists.

The Tax Man Cometh

So far, we have established that many Americans are encouraged by corporations, the credit industry, the media, and even government policies to take on large amounts of consumer debt. Additionally, these debt-ridden Americans are living within a debt-based monetary system that has inflation, bankruptcies, and foreclosures as its byproducts. If all those heavy chains were not enough to lie upon a "free" people, Americans are also subject to a whole host of taxes and fees from their federal, state, and local governments.

Here is a list of some of the taxes to which most Americans are subject:

Accounts receivable tax
Automobile registration tax
Building permit tax
Capital gains tax
CDL tax
Cigarette tax
Corporate income tax
Court fines (indirect taxes)
Dog license tax
Estate tax
Federal unemployment tax (FUTA)
Fishing license tax
Food license tax
Fuel permit tax
Gasoline tax
Hunting license tax
Inheritance tax interest expense (tax on the money)
Inventory tax
IRS interest charges (tax on top of tax)
IRS penalties (tax on top of tax)
Liquor tax
Local income tax
Luxury taxes
Marriage license tax
Medicare tax

Parking meters
Property tax
Real estate tax
Septic permit tax
Service charge taxes
Social security tax
Road usage taxes (truckers)
Sales taxes
Recreational vehicle tax
Road toll booth taxes
School tax
State income tax
State unemployment tax (SUTA)
Telephone federal excise tax
Telephone federal universal service fee tax
Telephone federal, state, and local surcharge taxes
Telephone minimum usage surcharge tax
Telephone recurring and non-recurring charges tax
Telephone state and local tax
Telephone usage charge tax
Toll bridge taxes
Toll tunnel taxes
Traffic fines
Trailer registration tax
Utility taxes
Vehicle license registration tax
Vehicle sales tax
Watercraft registration tax
Well permit tax
Workers compensation tax

And that is just to name a few. . . .

There is also one more important tax that I forgot to mention in the list above that all Americans are required to pay: the *federal income tax*. Every April 15, Americans have a rendezvous with reality. This is the day when all Americans are required to give an accounting to their government of how they performed financially throughout the year.

No hiding allowed. If you think you are not a slave, try evading your taxes for a few years. If you are caught, the penalties will be severe.

Inflation — the Hidden Tax

There are many eroding factors that are attacking your money from every angle. One of these eroding factors is inflation. In his book *Lifetime Economic Acceleration Process*, Robert Castiglone states: "Math is not money, and money is not math."[7] This is true, as money is not static, but instead it is tangible. A U.S. dollar is more like a commodity than a mere number.

For example, if I placed an apple and a U.S. dollar on my kitchen table and then came back ten years later, what do you think I would find? Well, the apple would likely have completely disintegrated. And what would have happened to the U.S. dollar? Would it still buy a dollar's worth of goods? No, part of its value would also have been lost. How? Inflation.

Inflation is a stealth tax, and the fact that it is hidden makes it even more dangerous to your wealth potential. Every time the Federal Reserve increases the money supply higher than the nation's overall productivity, it creates inflation. Inflation eats away at your savings — and it does so invisibly. The American economist Milton Friedman put it best when he said, "Inflation is one form of taxation that can be imposed without legislation."[8]

Over the course of their working lifetimes, most American citizens will lose a large majority of their income to three things:

1. Interest
2. Taxes
3. Inflation

Interestingly, each of these three are created and collected by the federal government and their controlled banking cartel, the Federal Reserve.

- Banks collect interest on money that they do not have.
- Governments extract taxes and fees from their citizens on a consistent basis.
- As the Federal Reserve increases the money supply it creates inflation.

Only through proper financial planning can you even attempt to begin sheltering your wealth from all of the eroding factors on money. In our next chapter, I will explain the concept of the consumption trap even further and will provide you with several strategies for breaking free.

Quick Summary

✓ Many forms of slavery exist, including slavery to culture, entertainment, money, and debt.

✓ No American citizen can claim to be completely debt-free, as America's national debt belongs to its citizens.

✓ At the foundation of America's economic problems lies a flawed assumption that our present level of consumption and economic growth must always be the absolute minimum.

✓ In my opinion, America's worship of money and overconsumption will be what future observers notice most when examining our nation's ruins.

✓ The federal government encourages consumption (even overconsumption) and discourages personal savings via the U.S. Tax Code.

✓ Inflation is a stealth tax, and the fact that it is hidden makes it even more difficult to overcome.

Endnotes

1. Johann Wolfgang von Goethe, Otto von Wenckstern, translator, *Goethe's Opinions on the World, Mankind, Literature, Science, and Art* (London: J.W. Parker and Son, 1853), p. 6.
2. http://www.freetheslaves.net.
3. Ellen Hodgson Brown, *Web of Debt: The Shocking Truth about Our Money System* (Baton Rouge, LA: Third Millennium Press, 2007), p. 47.
4. http://www.federalreserve.gov/releases/z1/Current/.
5. http://www.uscourts.gov/News/NewsView/11-11-07/Bankruptcy_Filings_Down_in_Fiscal_Year_2011.aspx.
6. Lottery, Not Saving, Seen As The Ticket To Wealth. Cox News Service. October 29, 1999. http://articles.chicagotribune.com/1999-10-29/news/9910290204_1_net-wealth-household-wealth-consumer-debt
7. Robert Castiglone, *Lifetime Economic Acceleration Process* (Canada: Castle Lion Publishers, 2005).
8. Jay M. Shafritz, *The HarperCollins Dictionary of American Government and Politics* (New York: HarperPerennial, 1992), p. 296.

Chapter 12

Breaking Free from the Consumption Trap

I think it is a man's duty to make all the money that he can, to keep all that he can, and give away all that he can.[1]

— John D. Rockefeller, Sr.

Business is the art of extracting money from another man's pocket without resorting to violence.[2]

— Max Amsterdam

It all started when I was watching a football game. With my feet propped up in my nice new reclining sofa, I sipped on bottled water and ate from a bag of potato chips. As I sat there zoned out, staring at the TV screen, something occurred to me. The thought was so provocative that it literally jolted me to my core. I muted the television and began to look around me. The question that kept reverberating in my mind was simple, and yet very profound: "What do I produce?"

Obviously, I was consuming many things made by others. But what was it that I was producing?

I looked at the bottled water in my hand and realized that I had no idea where it had been produced. I had outsourced the job of making my clean drinking water to total strangers.

I felt the couch underneath my body and it occurred to me that I had no idea where it was made, nor did I even care for that matter. I had outsourced the production of my furniture. My eyes darted up to the television screen. It dawned on me that I was outsourcing my entertainment "needs" to my local cable company for an obscene monthly fee. I quickly got up from the couch in a slight panic with a mission of finding something in my own home that I had created.

I headed into the kitchen and opened the pantry. Everything staring back at me was neatly packaged straight from the grocery store shelves. I opened my refrigerator only to find the same thing.

It was an epiphany for me to realize that the production of everything that I owned — my clothes, shoes, tools, electronics, and even my home itself — had been outsourced to others. Slowly, I began to realize that I produced nothing! Instead, I was a specialist in consuming!

"I Never Had a Choice . . ."

As I attempted to come to terms with the facts that were entering fast and furious into my mind, a question occurred to me: at what point did I choose to outsource all of my production to complete strangers? I realized that I had never consciously made that choice. Instead, the choice was made for me by the culture. Think about it.

- When did you decide that you were going to choose to buy your food from the grocery store?
- When did you decide that you were going to buy your clothes from the department store?
- When did you decide that you were going to outsource your entertainment to the cable company?
- When did you decide that you were going to allow the utility company to produce your electricity?

I would suggest that you never made that choice consciously either. Instead, your culture simply decided it for you. Even worse, I also realized that my sense of wealth was directly related to how much of my production I could *outsource*. This was a truly shocking revelation for me. It was then that I began developing a name for this process which has been legally stealing wealth from Americans for decades. I call it the Consumption Trap.

Welcome to the Consumption Trap

In order for you to reach true financial freedom, you must first understand the three very powerful forces that are currently working against your future wealth.

Every single day, you and I are confronted by these three powerful forces that exist to devour our hard-earned money. Each one of these forces is powerful, in and of itself. However, when these three forces are combined, their strength is *exponentially increased.*

First, let me be clear that each of these forces is morally neutral. That is, they are not evil, bad, or wrong in any way. In fact, they all provide necessary functions in our modern era. However, over the years, these three forces have learned to work in a unified way to slowly erode your wealth on a consistent basis. The three powerful financial forces that make up the Consumption Trap and that are working against you are:

1) **Corporations**
2) **Media/advertisers**
3) **Financial institutions**

Corporations are in business to find a need in the marketplace and then fill it with an appropriate product or service.

The media is in business to promote the products and services created by corporations.

And financial institutions are in business to loan money on products and services created by corporations that have been promoted by the media.

You may be thinking to yourself: *Really? How can these three industries cause any lasting harm to my financial plan?*

The truth is that they cannot. At least, not without your permission. And discovering how to gain your permission has been exactly what these three industries have been studying meticulously for the last several decades. And as soon as you grant them permission in your mind, your future wealth instantly begins transferring to their bank accounts. *Nothing could be easier.*

And do you know what is so amazing? Most people today do not even realize the extent of the destruction to their financial futures that these three powerful forces are causing because our society tells us that it is what we are supposed to do! Just like I used to think that outsourcing all of my production was the only way to survive, most Americans hand over their hard-earned dollars systematically to this unholy trinity without even realizing they have a *choice*.

> When consumption becomes involuntary, as it has in our modern era, the result can lead to financial devastation.

How the Consumption Trap Works

I have created the graphic below to explain the process.

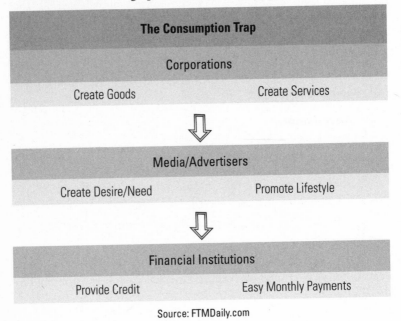

Source: FTMDaily.com

Now let me break this process down.

The Consumption Trap begins with *corporations*. Simply put, corporations are *producers*. They become successful by scanning the market place for problems that their products or services can solve for consumers. After they identify a consumer need, they carefully position their product or service offering in front of a pre-determined market, presenting it as the "solution."

However, bringing a product or service to the market can be a daunting task. Therefore, corporations seek marketing expertise for their products and services through *media and advertising companies*.

The role of these companies is to assist the corporation in creating a *need or a desire* for the new product or service. This is often accomplished by showing how the benefits of this new product or service will enhance the consumer's lifestyle.

Finally, there are the *financial institutions*, which I often call the credit industry. Among other things, these companies are in business to loan money to consumers for products and services that have been created by corporations and that are being promoted by the media. This is especially true if these products or services are big-ticket items. If so, the corporations and the media companies will work directly with financial institutions in order to provide the willing consumer with a line of credit with "easy low monthly payments."

Why the Consumption Trap Is Dangerous To Your Financial Health

It should be clear from the above description that these three powerful financial forces are aligned against you and your wealth-creating potential. I am not saying that consumption is bad. Instead, it is when consumption becomes involuntary, as it has in our modern era, that it can often result in financial devastation. For example, how many American families are living just one paycheck away from foreclosure or bankruptcy because of the Consumption Trap? The answer is too many to count.

Today, the Consumption Trap has convinced our society that every product and service that you use should be *outsourced* to corporations. I do not mean just *some* goods and services. I mean *all* goods and services.

If you do not believe me, take this quick quiz:

Of the following items, which do you currently produce on your own?

- **Food and water.** (Do you have your own food and water sources, or do you *choose* to outsource those items to corporations?)
- **Utilities.** (Do you generate your own utilities, or do you *choose* to outsource that task to corporations?)
- **Entertainment.** (Do you have your own means of entertainment, or do you *choose* to outsource that task to the cable company, Hollywood, and others?)

- **Clothing.** (Do you create your own clothing, or do you *choose* to outsource that to a corporation?)

Of course, I could on, but you get the point.

Now, if you believe that any of the above goods or services are impossible not to outsource, then you have been completely infected by the Consumption Trap. My goal with the above questions is not so much to get you to build a windmill or take up sewing, but instead to open your eyes to the extent that you have outsourced your basic necessities to those who are willing to produce.

> It is not going to get any easier for those who want to rely upon corporations for every good and service that they consume.

And do you know what? The "producers" are the ones in our society who are becoming wealthy in this entire process. Meanwhile, the "consumer" has bought into the mentality that they simply need to get an education, get a job with one of the nation's top "producers," and then outsource all of their needs and wants to "producers."

In fact, isn't the modern concept of financial success sold as being able to outsource all of our production? Interestingly, this concept of outsourcing all of our production is foreign to much of our nation's history.

Sure, businesses that produce goods and services have always been around and there has always been a need for trade and barter. But our modern producer-consumer system is unparalleled in human history. At no time in world history have humans lived in an era in which they are so completely dependent upon others for their basic necessities.

The Consumption Trap has enslaved countless Americans to jobs that they despise. And it has bound them to debts that they can barely pay. Why? All in the name of not having to produce anything at all — thus, giving them even more time for consumption! Are you beginning to see the irony here? The truth is that the producers are the ones who are getting ahead financially in our society. Meanwhile, the consumers are getting crushed, and will continue to get crushed.

In the near future, as inflation rises due to a mixture of poor monetary policies and growing global resource demand, producers will be able to pass on their rising costs to consumers. But who can the consumer pass on his rising costs to? No one. Believe me, it is not going to get any easier for those who want to rely upon corporations for every good and service they consume.

So, What Can You Do?

As an economist, I have a particular interest in consumer behavior, finance, and business in general. But fortunately, you do not need to know or even care about any of those things to escape the Consumption Trap. All you need is a desire to achieve real and lasting financial freedom . . . and a little discipline.

To conclude this chapter, I am going to give you four strategies that have helped me and countless others escape the Consumption Trap. If you will commit to applying each of these principles to your life, I truly believe you can begin the process of achieving lasting financial freedom.

1. Distinguish the difference between "wants" and "needs."

When I say learn the difference between your wants and needs, I am not lecturing you on the necessity to "live below your means," to "stop spending money," yada, yada, yada. . . . That kind of advice drives me crazy. It is like telling an overweight person that he needs to stop eating food. Gee thanks, but that is not helpful information for someone who needs to lose weight. Instead, the overweight person needs to be taught real strategies that will help him stop eating too much food.

When it comes to the Consumption Trap, what I am referring to is the brainwashing that has affected you since you entered this world. I am talking about your need to wake up to the financial deception that the Consumption Trap has created in your life. Let me give you an example.

I have a friend named Matt who despises his job. He recently told me that he hates his job so much that in order to get out of bed every morning, he has to repeat a series of positive words to himself. Even though I am no longer in his position, I can still greatly sympathize with him because I remember feeling trapped in a job that I greatly disliked.

After he told me how depressed he was by his "dead end" job, I asked him about his current spending habits. In just a few minutes, I heard him reference a new car, his big mortgage payment, his children's private school, his huge entertainment bill, and so on. I was speechless.

My friend's destiny has been hijacked by the Consumption Trap. He actually believes that he "needs" all of the goods and services that he is paying for every month. He actually cannot understand that they are optional and that, by refusing to stop consuming them, he perpetuates his misery.

In my mind, Matt is a modern-day slave dutifully serving his corporate masters. My friend's belief that he must outsource everything to others has enslaved him to a job that he hates. But because he is brainwashed into believing that his "wants" are actually his "needs," he is wasting his life in a job that he despises. If something does not change soon, my friend will no longer just be a victim; he will become a casualty of the Consumption Trap.

His situation reminds me of the old, but very true statement: "When your outgo exceeds your income, your upkeep becomes your downfall."

If you are stuck on life's treadmill, the quickest way off is to re-evaluate your "needs" and your "wants."

2. Drop the "entitlement mentality" and adopt an "enterprise mindset."

In case no one has told you lately, let me remind you: *no one owes you anything*. Never forget this. Why? Because, the people who ultimately fail in this economy are the ones who actually believe that they are entitled to something. They believe that they are owed a job. They believe that they are owed the ability to outsource all of their production. This is the trap. It has been set for anyone who will fall for it, and today, that means virtually everyone.

The longer you allow yourself to think you are owed a nice car, a new flat-screen TV, the latest electronic gadgets, or whatever else the engineers behind the Consumption Trap are currently trying to push on you, the longer you will remain in financial chains. Remember, it is the "producers" who are getting ahead today, not the "consumers." Therefore, if you are going to financially succeed, you must drop the entitlement mentality that pervades our modern society and, instead, develop an "enterprise mindset."

What do I mean by an "enterprise" mindset? I mean that you need to begin to think less like a "consumer" and instead, more like a "producer." You see, producers are not excited at the thought of buying all of the latest and greatest technological gadgets at the electronics store. Instead, they get excited about creating the next high-tech gadgets that consumers will buy. It is the thought of consumers, not consumption, that excites a producer.

Producers do not lay awake at night trying to figure out when they can retire. That is what consumers worry about. Instead, what keeps a producer awake at night is figuring out how to sell more of their products and services to consumers. So how do you begin to develop an enterprise mindset? By choosing to think like a producer. This does not mean you must start up a corporation and begin producing, but you must change your mindset from consumer to producer. Let me give you an example.

I personally love to watch late-night infomercials, not because I want to buy the garbage that is being promoted on them, but instead, because I enjoy learning new ways of marketing my own goods and services.

Here's another example. Every time I walk into a department store (or even a grocery store, for that matter) I consider it a lesson in marketing. These big retailers spend a pretty penny on their marketing efforts. And I get to walk in and learn for free. My wife and I both enjoy this because we are both producers.

It is time for you to start thinking like a producer. Believe me, it is the only way that you can stop being a victim to the corporate-inspired brainwashing that all of us have received since birth.

3. Begin producing for yourself first, then for others.

The easiest way to re-program your mind to think like a producer is to actually *become one.*

To get started, go through your entire monthly budget and examine every single good and service that you currently buy and decide if it is worth continuing. Most of us have become so brainwashed by the Consumption Trap that we actually buy goods and services that we do not even need, but that we have been told that we cannot live without. Be methodical. Make a list and then cut the fat.

The next step is to ask yourself this question: what am I currently buying and consuming from corporations that I can actually produce myself?

For example, perhaps you are 1) paying the cable company $60 a month so that you can outsource your entertainment and 2) have been trying to find time to take up gardening as a new hobby. Why not save $60 per month by turning off the cable and then go buy some gardening tools? Not only will you be saving money, you will also be decreasing your dependence upon corporations for your family's food supply.

After you have carefully examined and solved your own consumption and production outsourcing issues, it's time to ask yourself this question: what can I produce that others would be willing to consume? This leads us into my next point.

4. Commit to developing multiple streams of income.

In our modern-day society, it has become increasingly difficult to "get by" on a single income. I grew up in a single-parent family. I honestly do not know how my mother took care of both herself and me on her tiny income. I remember many evenings when I would eat macaroni and cheese and she wouldn't eat anything because she was "not hungry." I now know that the real reason was that we often did not have enough money for both of us to eat dinner.

I feel for those who are living under financial hardship because I have been there too. Today, we are all living in tough times. That is why the first thing that I tell people who ask me for financial advice is to sit down and create a comprehensive plan for cutting spending and increasing income.

Now, to be honest with you, I don't know anyone who can achieve true financial freedom simply by cutting back on some of their consumption. Remember, it's the producers who are getting rich, not the consumers. Today, the only sure-fire way that I know of for the average American to achieve true financial security is through the creation of multiple streams of income.

Several years ago, when I was a financial advisor, I was told that there were 11 possible streams of income that could be created in retirement. However, with my own experience as an entrepreneur, I have discovered that there are at least 7 more streams, for a total of 18 potential streams of income!

I am not just a staunch advocate for creating multiple streams of income, but I practice what I preach. Today, I have developed over one dozen streams of income that flow into my bank account each and every month. And each day that I go to work (in my home office) my tasks involve improving and maintaining our current income streams, as well as creating even more! The ways in which we can earn money in the Internet age are virtually limitless when we really begin to think about it.

It was in 1995 that I woke up and realized that I needed to begin creating multiple income streams. In those early days, I did not have the numerous income streams that I do now. It has taken a lot of hard work and dedication to get to where I am today. And, believe me, I have learned my fair share of lessons over the years.

I have owned appliance service companies, laundromats, rental real estate, and several Internet companies, among other things. I have learned what works and what does not for my personality type.

Quick Summary

- ✓ There are three forces working against your future wealth: corporations, media/advertisers, and financial institutions.
- ✓ Corporations are in business to find a need in the marketplace and then fill it with an appropriate product or service.
- ✓ The media is in business to promote the products and services created by corporations.
- ✓ Financial institutions are in business to loan money on products and services created by corporations that have been promoted by the media.
- ✓ When consumption becomes involuntary, as it has in our modern era, the result can lead to financial devastation.
- ✓ At no time in world history have humans lived in an era in which they are so completely dependent upon others for their basic necessities.
- ✓ Those who specialize in producing something in our economy succeed at the expense of those who specialize in consumption.
- ✓ If you are stuck on life's treadmill, the quickest way off is to re-evaluate your "needs" and your "wants."
- ✓ The easiest way to re-program your mind to think like a producer is to actually *become* one.
- ✓ To begin creating multiple streams of income, ask yourself this question: "What good or service can I produce that others would be willing to consume?"

As a follow-up to this book, I am writing a smaller e-book that will explain the many income streams that you can develop in your own financial life. This e-book will contain the list of the *18 different income streams* that you can create for yourself both now and in retirement, along with details on how to get each of them started. You can request more information about this book by going online to http://www.ftmdaily.com/incomebook.

In conclusion, you should know that the Consumption Trap is real, but it does not have to enslave you and keep you from enjoying financial freedom. You can overcome it and succeed by thinking less like a consumer and more like a producer. Don't settle for a life as a financial hostage to the latest trends and fashions pushed on you by the clever corporations. Instead, learn to use the system to your advantage.

Endnotes

1. http://www.strategicbusinessteam.com/famous-small-business-quotes/john-d-rockefeller-quotes-famous-business-quotes-from-the-worlds-richest-man-ever-in-history/.
2. http://www.englishclub.com/ref/esl/Quotes/Money/Business_is_the_art_of_extracting_money_from_another_man_s_pocket_without_resorting_to_violence._2728.htm.

Strategies

Financial Wisdom for
Uncertain Times

In this section, we will introduce our own systematic wealth creation and preservation strategies. We will teach you how to create, build, and preserve true wealth, regardless of your current financial situation. In addition, you will also learn:

- How to inflation-proof your portfolio with our P.A.C.E. investing philosophy (P.A.C.E. = Precious Metals, Agriculture, Commodities, and Energy)

- How to diversify your income sources by creating multiple streams of income

- Eight key strategies for protecting your finances

OVERVIEW: America has enormous financial problems that are not going away any time soon. These problems require solutions, yet, unfortunately, our nation's leaders appear unwilling to take the political risks necessary to confront them. It is safe to assume these financial problems will have to inflict massive amounts of economic pain upon a largely unprepared American public before the nation's political leaders will lift a finger to solve them. If you believe that Washington will solve any of these crises before they begin to impact you and your community, you are sadly mistaken. As Winston Churchill once quipped: "You can always count on Americans to do the right thing — after they've tried everything else."[1]

After reading the preceding chapters, the phrase "ignorance is bliss" should take on an entirely new meaning in your mind. By now, you know the brutal truth. But understanding the problem is just the first step. The next step is to prepare. After all, what good is it to see the writing on the wall if it does not stir us to take action?

In the Book of Proverbs, wise King Solomon writes, "A prudent man foresees evil and hides himself, but the simple pass on and are punished" (Proverb 22:3). My hope is that you will heed the obvious signs of America's financial meltdown by becoming proactive. The time for debate is over. Now is the time for preparation.

Endnotes

1. jpetrie.myweb.uga.edu/bulldog.html.

Chapter 13

An Introduction to the P.A.C.E. Investing Philosophy

The art of prophecy is very difficult, especially with respect to the future.[1]

— Mark Twain

The people who were honored in the Bible were the false prophets. It was the ones we call the prophets who were jailed and driven into the desert.[2]

— Noam Chomsky

OVERVIEW: In this chapter, I will explain our P.A.C.E. investing philosophy, which relies on hard assets such as precious metals, agriculture, commodities, and energy investments to hedge against the coming inflation.

As I have explained at length in this book, the size and scope of the economic problems facing America are enormous. And, in my opinion, these problems will result in widespread inflation. Several years ago, in an effort to develop my own investment strategy to weather the coming inflation, I designed something now known as the P.A.C.E. investment philosophy. P.A.C.E. is a simple acronym that stands for: P= Precious

219

Metals, A= Agriculture, C=Commodities, E= Energy. Historical data demonstrates that these four asset classes, also known as hard assets, have performed extremely well during times of inflation. These hard assets are tangible investments that you can physically touch and handle. As an investor, I have been focused on these areas for several years, and the overall returns have been stellar. Of course, no investment goes up in a straight line. My strategy has been to add to my positions aggressively during periods when the assets have declined in price.

Since 2006, I have been urging individuals just like you to consider broad investment diversification to include these areas. In 2012, due to a growing demand, I hired a well known faith-based certified financial planner to launch an actively managed P.A.C.E. investment fund. This investment portfolio is composed of 20 stocks that I personally own. To learn more about the stocks in the P.A.C.E. investment fund, please visit http://www.ftmdaily.com/pace.

Allow me to share some of the reasons why I like these four asset classes.

P = Precious Metals

Precious metals have enjoyed a prolonged and dramatic increase in value over the last several years. And just when everyone believes that gold and silver prices cannot possibly rise any higher . . . they increase even more. This is particularly true with gold, which has increased in price every year for 11 straight years. This has led some investors to worry if gold prices are nearing their peak. In fact, when I speak around the country on the topic of the economy and investing, one of the most common questions I am asked is whether or not I believe that gold and silver prices are going to continue rising. My answer has been the same for years: YES. See the following chart.

The reasons for my answer have not changed throughout the years. Put simply, precious metals are a direct beneficiary of poor monetary policies. Those who trust governments and their worthless paper currencies should avoid precious metals. But if you believe, as I do, that the economy is going to get worse before it gets better, then precious metals should be a part of your portfolio.

Concerning the question of whether gold prices are in a bubble, it is interesting that despite all of the marketing and hype, relatively few

Source: goldprice.org

Americans have actually taken the plunge and purchased physical gold or shares in gold mining companies. Across the globe, investors now own the largest amount of liquid "paper" wealth in recorded history. Of all of the liquid assets owned worldwide, gold makes up just over 1.4 percent. According to Anthony Allison from the PFS Group, "If just one or two percent of the world's liquid wealth moved into gold in future years, the price rise would be explosive."[3]

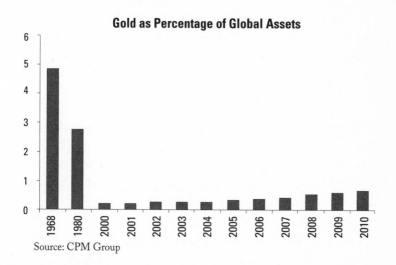

Source: CPM Group

Precious metals have long been scorned by governments that churn out paper (fiat) currencies. For example, U.S. dollars are printed at will and devalued as needed. The government's disdain for precious metals is obvious, as the metals have served to restrain the overproduction of paper currencies. But regardless of the government's opinion, gold and silver will continue to easily outperform most assets as a direct result of economic calamity created by poor fiscal and monetary policies. And if anything is certain, it is that the outlook for the global economy in the coming years is uncertain. The uncertainty that currently plagues the global financial markets breeds fear, which serves to benefit precious metals. As America's economy, in particular, continues to worsen over the coming months and years, I expect more investment dollars to pour into precious metals, thus driving their prices up to extremely high levels. Today, gold is being purchased in large quantities by hedge funds, central banks, and emerging nations. I expect this trend to continue. Given all of these factors, I personally expect gold prices to rise above $3,500 per ounce amidst the coming inflation.

Likewise, the supply shortages coupled with the enormous investment and industrial demand for silver indicates that prices will continue to trek higher. I expect silver prices to peak at over $125 per ounce in the coming years, potentially making this a "once in a lifetime" investment opportunity.

Finally, I am also bullish on palladium. This metal benefits from a strong and growing global demand. (It is used predominantly in catalytic converters in automobiles.) Anticipated supply shortages in the months and years ahead should cause the price of this metal to double in the coming years. I expect palladium prices to eventually peak above $1,150.

Five Ways to Invest in Precious Metals

In years past, American citizens knew how to buy gold and silver. In today's paper-driven economy, buying gold bars or silver coins is almost a foreign concept. Below, I will provide you with several ways that you can gain exposure to each of the precious metals that I discussed above. In addition, I will tell you how I personally buy and hold each of these metals.

- **Physical bullion**. This is the most direct form of ownership and, in my opinion, the best way to own precious metals for those with long-term inflation protection objectives.

- **Numismatic coins**. These are coins that are considered to be rare or collectible. These will typically have extremely high premiums over the spot price of gold. These types of coins are often aggressively marketed through television and radio advertisements. I do not buy numismatics because my investing goals with gold are related to inflation protection, not building a coin collection.

- **Shares of mining companies**. Investing in gold and silver mining companies can be very risky. However, I believe strongly that mining companies will outperform most sectors over the next 3–5 years. The P.A.C.E. investment portfolio contains several mining stocks. These names are published in our investment newsletter. I would only suggest investing in mining stocks after laying a foundation of gold bullion within your portfolio.

- **Mining exchange-traded funds**. While I am not a fan of ETFs that track the price of physical metals (like GLD, SLV), I do like gold and silver equity-based ETFs, as they can provide excellent diversified exposure to the mining industry for a relatively low fee. Three of my favorite mining ETFs include:
  ~ *Market Vectors Gold Miners ETF (Ticker: GDX)* Established in May of 2006, GDX was the nation's first gold shares ETF and is currently composed of investments in 31 of the world's largest gold mining companies. GDX is a pure play on gold mining and its investors with a small income, as many of the fund's underlying holdings pay a dividend. For those looking for a pure play on mining, but who are concerned about investing in one single mining company, GDX offers a unique and diversified approach.
  ~ *Market Vectors Junior Gold Miners ETF (Ticker: GDXJ)* Many fortunes have been made — and lost — through investments made into "up and coming" mining companies. For investors

looking for high risk/reward opportunities, there are few better places to look than small-cap (junior) mining companies. GDXJ is currently invested in a basket of 86 junior gold mining companies around the world, most of which are in exploratory or early development phases. I like GDXJ because it gives me diversified access to "up and coming" gold mining companies.

~ *Global X Silver Miners ETF (Ticker: SIL)* For investors seeking a pure play on the silver mining industry, SIL may be the right fit. SIL is currently invested in 31 global companies who are engaged in silver mining, refining, or exploration. SIL makes a nice addition to one's physical silver holdings.

- **Options and futures**. For those with experience in the futures markets, or with trading options, this can be a lucrative way to trade precious metals. However, this is purely a speculative investment and should be viewed as such.

Gold, Silver, and Palladium Investing 101

Due to my belief that the purchasing power of the U.S. dollar will continue to decline, resulting in widespread inflation, I personally prefer to take physical possession of my precious metals investments.

In order to decide which type of gold investment is right for you, begin by examining your own investment goals and available resources. If you are seeking a hedge against inflation, a store of wealth, or insurance against future financial calamity, owning the physical metal is often the best choice. Those interested only in speculating through short-term trading, however, would be better off buying ETFs or gold mining shares.

Before making a purchase, I recommend seeking out a reputable precious metals dealer. When choosing a precious metals dealer, be sure to select someone that functions as an advisor in addition to being a dealer. My personal precious metals advisor has been in the industry for over 36 years and has the heart of a teacher. Find someone with a passion for precious metals who can advise you on which forms of gold, silver, or palladium are best suited for your specific financial situation.

Where to Store Your Precious Metals?

I would encourage you to take physical possession of your precious metals if at all possible. Of course, by choosing to take physical possession, you must deal with storing the metals and you take on the risk of potential loss. Keep your metals in a safe and secure place somewhere within your home. Many investors store their metals in a home safe, which protects them from both theft and fire. Do not brag about your precious metals to neighbors or co-workers, as it will serve no good purpose and could potentially cause you problems. If the thought of holding thousands of dollars worth of precious metals in your home concerns you, there are plenty of legitimate companies that will store your gold for a small fee. Most reputable precious metals dealers can help you find a storage option for your precious metals.

How Much of my Portfolio Should Be Invested in Precious Metals?

As a strong believer in investment diversification, I would not put more than 25 percent of my money into any single asset class. For most people, 15–20 percent will provide their investment portfolio with ample exposure to precious metals. More conservative investors will want their investment exposure to be more heavily weighted toward gold. Those investors who are more aggressive should consider weighting their holdings more heavily toward silver and palladium.

Our organization has produced a free, 90-minute educational webinar on the basics of getting started in precious metals investing. You can watch it at www.ftmdaily.com/gold.

A = Agriculture, C = Commodities

Agriculture, and its related commodities, is another area that has historically performed well in times of inflation. Agriculture investments like farmland, livestock, and grains are considered pure investment plays on agriculture. Another profitable agricultural investment opportunity is found in agribusiness, which is composed of a wide and growing variety of businesses that provide goods and services to the global farming community. The trends driving the increase in agricultural commodities are easy to understand.

- *The human population is increasing at an exponential rate.* The world population is currently growing by nearly 80 million net each year. In 1960, the global population was three billion. In 2011, it reached seven billion, and the United Nations (UN) forecasts that the population will explode to over nine billion by the year 2050.

- *The quantity of arable farmland is decreasing.* As the global population grows, more people are moving to urban areas. The urban sprawl is replacing farmland with shopping centers and housing developments. Food shortages are expected to rise while the amount of arable farmland is decreasing.

- *Demand for grains and meat is rapidly increasing.* As millions of people join the ranks of the middle class around the globe every year, they are upgrading from grain-based diets to meat-based diets. It takes roughly seven pounds of grain to produce one pound of beef. Therefore, both are experiencing a spike in demand.

Add to this an alarming depletion in topsoil and we have the makings of a real global food crisis. It may not be today or tomorrow, but it will occur at some point in the future.

A few years ago, while watching a documentary on the global food crisis, a camera crew was conducting random man-on-the-street interviews in a large U.S. city. When asked where food came from, one woman responded, "The grocery store." Sadly, this seems to be the extent of much of the West's knowledge regarding where the food supply comes from.

Four Ways to Invest In Agriculture

- **Farmland**. Investing in farmland has become popular over the last few years, as yield-starved investors have begun turning to alternative investments for income. Historically, farmland has been a low risk investment that has provided returns of 3–5 percent. Farmland investors who are not interested in becoming farmers have options. Some investors buy the land and hire a professional farm manager to handle all of the day-today details. Others rent out the land to farmers who cannot afford to purchase their own land.

- **Agricultural companies**. For investors who want to profit from rising food prices without buying a farm, there is always the stock market. There are several companies that offer both excellent long-term growth prospects and dividend income. Two companies that I personally like include:

  ~ *CF Industries Holdings (Ticker: CF)* This company specializes in making nitrogen and phosphate fertilizer products for agricultural and industrial customers. A growing demand for food will create a growing demand for fertilizers. I believe that CF Industries is poised to benefit from this rising demand.

  ~ *Cresud Inc. ADRS (Ticker: CRESY)* Cresud is an Argentina-based company that produces basic agricultural commodities and owns over 500,000 acres of farmland. This stock offers investors exposure to farmland without having to own any.

- **Futures**. From cocoa to coffee and from soybeans to sugar, investors can trade virtually any agricultural commodity through the futures market. For those who understand the futures market, there are few more powerful ways to trade agricultural commodities.

- **Exchange-traded funds**. Agricultural ETFs can offer the average investor easy access to futures or to a basket of agricultural companies. Here are two of my favorite agricultural ETFs:

  ~ *Powershares /DB Agricultural ETF (Ticker: DBA)* This ETF, which was established in 2007, provides investors with exposure to agricultural futures including corn, soybeans, sugar, live cattle, coffee, and cocoa.

  ~ *Market Vectors Agribusiness ETF (Ticker: MOO)* For some time, MOO has been my favorite ETF for gaining broad exposure to the booming agribusiness market. MOO is composed of nearly 50 global companies involved in the business side of agriculture: from seed producers to fertilizer manufacturers and equipment manufacturers to biofuel companies.

I believe that investors who are well positioned within the agriculture and commodities sectors will continue to enjoy large returns over the next 5–7 years. This does not mean, however, that every single quarter will be good for these investment sectors. That is why investment diversification is so important.

Water: The Ultimate Commodity

In addition to investing in agriculture, I am also positioning my investments for exposure to global water supplies. Without major technological advancements within the next decade or two, we could be facing a global water crisis in addition to a food crisis. You would think that water would be the least of the world's concerns considering that it covers 70 percent of our planet. However, 99 percent of global water supplies are either saltwater, which is unfit for human consumption, or are locked up in glaciers or polar caps. That leaves just 1 percent of the global water supplies available for human use. The United Nations estimates that over the last century, human water use has grown twice as fast as the population. This is not hard to believe, considering that the world is using freshwater supplies at 100 times the natural replacement rate and over 80 countries are currently struggling with water shortages. By 2025, the United Nations forecasts that two-thirds of the world population will be facing serious water shortages.

Interestingly, over 70 percent of global freshwater supplies are used in agriculture. So as the demand for food continues to increase, so will the demand for freshwater supplies.

Because water is not a commodity that is traded on major markets, there are limited investment options for an investor seeking a pure play on the growing demand for clean, potable water. However, I expect that within a few years this will change.

In the meantime, one of the best ways to invest in water is to go straight to the source: water utility companies. Some of these companies pay sizeable dividends and are well positioned to provide investors with excellent long-term capital appreciation. If you prefer a more diversified approach, consider the PowerShares Global Water Portfolio ETF (Ticker: PIO).

E= Energy

The discovery of oil changed the world. Few other substances can carry so much energy per unit volume or per unit weight as oil. Today, the entire global infrastructure has become completely dependent upon growing sources of cheap oil. The problem is that oil is a non-renewable energy source and, therefore, its supplies are finite. There are just over 1.2 trillion barrels of oil left in the world, based upon current estimates. Yet, as the global economy continues to grow, credible sources are telling us that global oil supplies are rapidly dwindling. Limited oil supplies are bumping up against increasing global oil demand. This means one thing for oil prices: they will continue to climb higher. In Saudi Arabia there is a saying: "My father rode a camel. I drive a car. My son flies a jet airplane. His son will ride a camel." If our modern oil-dependent world wants to avoid a similar self-imposed energy calamity, it is vital that we invest in alternative energy sources. However, relatively little investment has occurred. This lack of foresight is providing oil-producing nations, such as OPEC, with a tremendous economic advantage as we march forward into the uncertain future.

While I believe that this crisis can be averted through aggressive development and investment into alternative energy sources, this shift will require an overhaul of the entire global infrastructure. The conversion costs will be immense and helps to explain why the globe is dragging its feet on making the switch. As an investor, I have no control over energy policy. I can only profit from the existing policies. I believe that the current global energy crisis presents investors with a lucrative opportunity if they are well-positioned.

Six Ways to Invest in Energy

- **Oil companies**. There are hundreds of publicly traded oil companies that can give you exposure to all aspects of the oil business including exploration and production, oil services, etc. While this is a broad category, I believe that every investor should consider having exposure to energy within their portfolio.

  ~ *Chevron Corp. (Ticker: CVX)* This oil behemoth has long been a favorite oil stock of mine for several reasons, including consistently increasing dividend payouts and global exposure to both the oil and natural gas markets. In fact, CVX has paid a dividend to its shareholders every year since 1912, and it has been increasing its annual dividends for 23 years. It is hard not to like a well-run company like CVX.

- **Exchange-traded funds**. For investors seeking broad diversification within a specific area of the energy sector, there is an abundance of ETFs to consider

  - *United States Oil Fund LP (Ticker: USO)* This ETF is designed to track the movements of light, sweet crude oil ("West Texas Intermediate"). While this fund offers an excellent way to speculate on short-term movements in oil prices, I would not use this fund as a long-term hold due to its complications with contango. ("Contango" is the market condition wherein the price of a forward or futures contract is trading above the expected spot price at contract maturity. The futures or forward curve would typically be upward sloping (i.e. "normal"), since contracts for further dates would typically trade at even higher prices.)

  - *Market Vectors Oil Services ETF (Ticker: OIH)* This ETF tracks 25 of the largest U.S.-listed, publicly traded oil service companies. Some of its top holdings include Schlumberger, Halliburton, Baker Hughes, and Transocean. This is one of my personal favorite ways for profiting from the long-term growth of these large oil service stocks.

- **Futures**. Unless you are familiar with the futures market, I would advise that you stay away from it. It is filled with expert traders who live and breathe oil prices. It can be a sure way to lose your shirt due to the highly volatile nature of oil prices.

- **Buy an oil well**. This has become an increasingly difficult investment option over the last several years. Very few producing wells are available for purchase, and the ones that are have outrageous asking prices. Of course, you could always drill your own well, but the upfront costs and risks are high enough to deter most investors. I would avoid this option unless you have a serious amount of speculative capital that you can afford to lose.

- **Royalty trusts**. Investors who are seeking a more direct form of ownership of oil, but who lack the capital or risk tolerance for buying an oil well, should consider buying shares in an oil royalty trust. Oil royalty trusts are a special kind of corporation that acquire producing oil and gas wells and are legally required to pay out 90 percent of their profits to their shareholders. These trusts make it easy to share in the profits on oil royalties without the need to buy an oil well. However, the income that is paid out (called dividends) can vary along with the price of oil. When oil prices are high, so are your dividends. Oil royalty trusts are worth considering if your goals are inflation protection and dividend income. And most of them are IRA-friendly.

- **Master Limited Partnerships**. MLPs, as they are known, are publicly traded stocks with all of the tax benefits of a partnership. Because they are not taxed as corporations, they provide investors with pass-through income. Like royalty trusts, MLPs pass through their income to owners, known as unit holders, making them attractive to income seekers. As of this writing, the current average yield on MLPs is 5 percent. Here are two MLPs worth considering:

  - Enterprise Products Partners (Ticker: EPD) This MLP is the largest in the country. As of this writing, it yields 5 percent.

  - Linn Energy, LLC (Ticker: LINE) This MLP has a good energy portfolio and they are well positioned to double their production through 2015. As of this writing, it yields 7 percent.

What About Alternative Energy Sources?

While both sectors have seen their prices collapse in recent years, I am a firm believer that both nuclear energy and natural gas are going to perform well over the next decade. This is primarily because they are both cheaper and cleaner alternatives to oil.

Nuclear (Uranium)

I expect uranium prices to increase over the next 18–36 months as demand is expected to outstrip supply. According to the World Nuclear Organization, there are currently 435 operable reactors worldwide. There are 61 reactors under construction globally, with 26 of these are China and 10 in Russia. Another 162 reactors are in the planning stages or have already been ordered. Of these, 51 are in China, 17 in Russia, and 16 in India. New production of uranium is badly needed, but given the current low prices in uranium and the tight financial environment, it is unlikely that a plethora of new uranium mining activity will occur before prices rise significantly. I expect the price of uranium to reach $68 per pound by December 2014. My favorite way to play this market would be a mixture of the *Global X Uranium ETF (ticker: URA)* and top uranium mining company *Cameco Corporation (ticker: CCJ)*.

Natural Gas

Over the last decade, America has witnessed an explosion in natural gas discoveries as new technologies have revolutionized the industry. These discoveries demonstrate that the United States is the "Saudi Arabia" of natural gas. Due to the current rock bottom prices on natural gas, I expect a shift to occur as the nation struggles with rising oil prices. As new uses for natural gas are developed, the overall demand will grow. This increasing demand will cause natural gas prices to climb steadily over the next decade. Also, keep an eye on several U.S. energy companies who are now seeking government permission to liquefy and export the abundant supply of natural gas to foreign countries. This will also cause demand for natural gas to soar in the coming years.

Endnotes
1. http://www.wpp.com/wpp/marketing/media/all-at-sea.
2. http://proteinwisdom.com/?p=16470.
3. Tony Allison, *The Year of Living Dangerously: Printing Our Economy Back to Prosperity?* http://www.financialsense.com/contributors/tony-allison/the-year-of-living-dangerously-printing-our-economy-back-to-prosperity.

Chapter 14

21 Income Streams
You Can Create Now
... and in Retirement

Knowing is not enough, we must apply. Willing is
not enough; we must do.[1]
— Bruce Lee

With money in your pocket you are wise, you are
handsome, and you sing well too.
— Yiddish Proverb

OVERVIEW: In this chapter, I will detail three different types of income: earned, portfolio, and passive. In addition, I will explain the importance of diversifying your income and provide a list of 21 potential income streams that you can create now and in retirement.

In my travels across the country, I have discovered that most people who are seeking to improve their personal financial situations have at least one of two goals: 1) to become a better investor or 2) to earn more income. While our organization is committed to helping people achieve both of these objectives, this chapter will focus on specific ways to increase the income flowing into your life. We are often told that diversification is an important financial strategy. But we are rarely told to apply this powerful financial principle to our source of income. That is what makes this book unique. My goal is to educate, equip, and empower you to develop a diversified portfolio of income streams that will protect you and your family's financial future. In this chapter, I have compiled a list of 21 income streams that nearly anyone can create now and in retirement. Before we dive into a brief summary of each of these 21 income ideas, I would like to share with you why I am so passionate about helping people create multiple streams of income. Let's begin by examining how the evolving concept of retirement has greatly increased the need for multiple income streams for our golden years.

Retirement: Then and Now

In ancient times, retirement was a virtually unknown concept. History has no record of any ancient citizen putting in 40 years at the vineyard only then to enjoy his golden years by touring the countryside in his horse-drawn "airstream." This is not to say that the ancients did not plan for old age. In early Greek and Roman societies, workers who wanted to protect their current income into the future could purchase an "annua," the earliest version of an annuity. Of course, longevity was not a concern in ancient times, and it certainly did not pose the same risk that it does today. However, our ancient elders had an asset class that could sustain them in the unlikely event they were to live long past their ability to work.

What was this unique asset?

Children.

Yes, believe it or not in times past, children were not considered liabilities, but assets. Today, many of our nation's elderly do all they can to "scrimp and save" to leave an inheritance to their families whom they may not have seen for years. But in former times, children were expected to take care of their parents in old age. That's why a father was considered blessed when he had many children.

Of course, I refer to children today as being liabilities mostly in jest. However, no one can deny that our modern approach to retirement is flashing danger signs to the nearly 10,000 Americans who will be retiring every single day over the next two decades.

Trouble Ahead for the "Golden" Years

An analysis of the six common methods for funding the cost of retirement in America shows that retirement as we have known it is in grave financial danger.

Social Security is in crisis — Without massive intervention, the Social Security program will be insolvent no later than 2033, based upon current projections.

Medicare is running out of funding — By 2024, the Medicare system is projected to go belly up due to skyrocketing medical costs and fiscal mismanagement.

Pension systems are underfunded . . . and failing — Under the weight of major market losses, years of low yields, and poor financial management, many large government and corporate pension plans are woefully underfunded. In a 2012 report released by the pension consulting firm Milliman, the 100 largest pension funds run by public U.S. companies had a record funding shortfall of $326.8 billion at the end of 2011. To make matters worse, the Pension Benefit Guaranty Corporation (PBGC) — the government agency charged with covering retiree benefits when companies go bankrupt and their pensions fail — is bankrupt. For millions of American workers, this spells disaster. What seemed like a good idea at the time is turning out to be unsustainable.

The personal savings rate is dismally low — In early 2012, the U.S. personal savings rate stood at 3.7 percent. Over 25 percent of American workers admit to having no personal savings whatsoever. It seems that the Consumption Trap has been effective in indoctrinating Americans to spend all they earn.

Employer-Sponsored and Individual Retirement Savings Plans (401ks, 403bs, IRAs) are underutilized — Today, only 40 percent of workers who have access to employer-sponsored retirement plans actually use them. Furthermore, due to a severe lack of personal savings, many Americans who actually have a retirement plan have used it as a piggy bank during difficult financial times. As of this writing, less than four in ten Americans have an Individual Retirement Account (IRA) of any kind.

Consumer debt levels are interfering with retirement savings — Increasing amounts of consumer debt has caused many Americans to decrease their retirement savings in order to service their debt obligations. In addition, reports of Americans carrying massive debt loads into retirement are sadly becoming more common.

Advances in medical technology have increased the risk of outliving your money — Who could have imagined that long life could be a curse? Numerous surveys show that the greatest fear shared by most Baby Boomers is outliving their money. Unfortunately, this is a legitimate fear, given our nation's low savings rates and overconsumption, coupled with ongoing medical advancements that are increasing the average lifespan. (I don't know about you, but I would rather be in the ground than live to 150 years old in a cardboard box on the side of the road.)

Put simply, Americans are *broke*. We have too much debt, we are not saving enough, and what we have saved is in jeopardy.

The Importance of Creating Multiple Income Streams

One of the primary reasons I wrote this book was to help individuals achieve financial liberty. Since 2006, I have been on a mission to help people from all walks of life understand the importance of wise financial stewardship. At the core of my financial teaching are three very basic principles:

1) **Savings diversification**
2) **Investment diversification**
3) **Income diversification**

In today's difficult economy, the need to develop multiple streams of income from different sources is more important than ever, as millions of Americans are literally one paycheck away from bankruptcy or foreclosure on their homes.

If you lost your job today, would you still have an income one month from now? How about six months from now? Who would sign your paycheck if you were in an accident and were laid up on the couch for an extended period of time?

If you cannot answer these questions, this chapter is for you. It is time to begin diversifying your income by adding another income stream. Just as spreading out your investments across various asset classes is wise, I also believe you should diversify your income. Like the old saying goes, "Don't put all of your eggs in one basket."

By diversifying your income through the creation of multiple streams of income, you will be placing a safety net under you and your family in the event of unforeseen circumstances. People who have diversified sources of income experience the peace of not feeling trapped in their jobs and are no longer at the mercy of their employers. As you begin developing multiple income streams, the financial stress of life will become easier to manage because you will know that if one income stream suddenly dries up, other steady sources continue to come in to your bank account.

Today, the average American working household has *three* income streams. Typically, this includes two incomes (husband and wife) and interest from a savings account or a bank CD. Interestingly, the average number of income streams does not change into retirement as the average retired American household has three income streams. Meanwhile, the average single American retiree has just two income streams.

Personally, I do not want to imagine the financial stress associated with only two or three income streams, especially in this very difficult economic climate. And besides, why should any household have just two or three income streams when financial advisors tell us that it is possible to have 11 income streams in retirement? In my own research, I have discovered several more potential income streams that virtually anyone can create. I have listed many of them below. Why work so hard your entire life to end up with just two or three income streams when so many are available for those who will just put forth a little effort?

One question that I am often asked is: "How many income streams should a person have?" It is my personal belief that every individual should have an *absolute minimum* of two streams of income in addition to their regular job during their working years, and a *minimum* of five streams at retirement. Obviously, the more income streams that you can create, the better.

Another question that I often get is, "Don't you need to have a lot of money to create multiple income streams?" The short answer is no. You *don't* need a lot of money to create multiple streams of income. What you will need is some creativity and a willingness to work hard. Over the years, my wife and I have created several passive income streams, which come into our bank account month after month, regardless of whether we work or not. The income streams that we have created do not require us to live in any particular city or area. We are free to travel as we wish. These income streams were *not easy* to create and they did not just magically appear in our lives. (Too many people today want to make money without working for it. If that describes you, I am sorry to admit that I cannot help you.)

In order for my wife and I to create these income streams, we had to develop a long-term mindset. There have been times when I have worked for several weeks or months, *and in a few cases even years*, for little or no money in order to properly develop an income stream. However, once I finally built the income stream, it began cash flowing on a regular basis with just a little bit of maintenance. This is the key: work really hard upfront . . . and then get paid for your efforts for the rest of your life.

On your pathway to success, you will inevitably go through a trial and error process just as I did. But this is a vital filtering process which will help you discover your true strengths and weaknesses. It took me years to discover my strengths. (My weaknesses, on the other hand, were easy to determine!) I remember kids in middle school and high school who had their whole life planned out. That was not me. And this cluelessness did not just plague my childhood — I virtually stumbled through my twenties without knowing exactly where I was going. Fortunately, over time, my strengths slowly began to emerge. For example, my creativity and leadership abilities helped me launch new income streams. And it was the actual launch and development of a new business or income stream that excited me the most. However, once the business moved out of start-up phase, or once the income stream had been developed, I got bored with the idea of managing it. Fortunately, my wife has an excellent gift of organizational management. So we work together as a team in all of our businesses. My gift of creativity and vision helps me dream up and build the income streams, and my wife helps me manage them.

But going back to my original point: Because I was a late bloomer, it took me a while to discover my own gifts and talents. Let that encourage those of you who feel like you are too old to start something new. Don't use your age, or any other factor, as an excuse. All things are possible. You have been blessed with unique gifts and special talents. You are one of a kind and you were placed on this earth for a very specific reason. You have a unique purpose. You just have to put one foot in front of the other. Don't expect anyone to do it for you. Breaking free financially will take time and effort, but it will be worth every second of your time. Will every new idea or concept be a success? Of course not. So don't set yourself up for failure by expecting too much too quickly. For example, with every new income stream I build, I set reasonable goals that I know can be achieved. With some of my very first income streams, I would celebrate when they began creating $100 per month! Then a few months later, when the income stream would start creating $200 per month, I would celebrate again. If you walk into this thinking that you are going to hit a homerun on your first turn up to bat, you are going to fail, period. Be humble and work hard. If you will spend your time working proven systems, you will succeed with time.

Before moving on to the 21 potential income streams, we need to understand the different types of income that you can create.

Three Types of Income

According to the Internal Revenue Service, all forms of income fall under one of three categories: active, portfolio, and passive.

Active (Earned) Income

Earned income, also known as linear or active income, is compensation earned from your labor, employment, or material involvement in a business. Small business income, salaries (W-2 income), commissioned sales income, tips, and consulting income are all various types of active income. Active income is the highest taxed form of income.

Portfolio Income

Portfolio income is composed of capital gains, royalties earned from books or patents, interest, and dividend income. This type of income is not created through normal business activity. Portfolio income is often taxed at a lower rate than active income, depending on how long you hold the investment prior to selling it.

Passive Income

Passive income is derived from business investments, such as a rental property or limited partnerships, in which you are *not* actively involved. According to the IRS, there are only two possible sources of passive income: net rental income (real estate or equipment) and business income from a business in which you do not materially participate. Basically, passive income is not "earned" by your time and effort. Passive income is usually taxed at the lowest rates and offers the highest number of potential tax deductions.

Sometimes it can be hard to determine the difference between portfolio income and passive income. Just remember the only real difference is their tax treatment. In reality, recurring income from dividends, royalties, or interest (portfolio income) is a form of passive income which does not require your ongoing presence and time.

In addition, there are two more hybrid forms of income that I want to share with you which are a blend of active and passive income. Therefore, they are not automatically taxed at the lower passive income tax rate. However, these two are among my favorite forms of income.

> *Residual Income:* This is recurring income. Residual income is an ongoing income stream that you receive for work that you did in the past. Insurance commissions are a great example of the power of residual income. For example, when a health insurance agent sells an insurance policy, he receives a recurring, or residual, commission every time the individual pays his monthly premium. The insurance agent worked hard up front to secure the client and is then rewarded with an ongoing income stream that continues as long as the client renews his policy! With residual income, you work hard upfront and then enjoy an ongoing stream of income month after month, often with little maintenance.

> *Leveraged Income:* This is another extremely powerful form of income that comes from leveraging someone else's labor. For example, several of my businesses rely exclusively upon the labor of sub-contractors. My role is to market effectively and to send business to the sub-contractors. I will share some specific ideas on creating leveraged income later in this chapter.

Active Income vs. Passive Income

Most Americans have been told from a young age that the key to financial success is to go to school and then to get a "good" job. As we have learned, those who have a regular "job" receive active, or earned, income. Ironically, active income is *the riskiest form of income*, as it is completely dependent upon your ability to work. It requires your continual presence and your constant labor. If you get fired, the income stops. If you become disabled, the income stops.

Active income is also *the most heavily taxed form of income*, as there are few current tax loopholes for employees. The Federal government does not provide tax incentives to people who have jobs. It provides tax incentives to the producers who create jobs.

Active income is a short-term solution to a long term problem. Our modern economy penalizes those who rely exclusively on active income. And while there is nothing inherently wrong with active income, there are better forms of income to consider if you desire financial freedom. Getting ahead financially today requires multiple streams of passive income. Of course, nearly everyone begins their working life with a single active income stream. Your goal, however, is to begin shifting from active income to multiple streams of passive income as early in your life as possible.

The Three Sources of All Passive Income Streams

All portfolio and passive income streams come from one of three sources:

- real estate
- paper assets
- your own business

To properly diversify your income streams, it is important to develop income from all three of these sources. For those of you who are serious about creating multiple streams of income, here's the secret that the wealthy have used for centuries:

1. Develop a sizeable cash flow from several passive income streams.
2. Use the cash flow as investment capital for investing into appreciating assets, like real estate, that will provide even more cash flow and tax benefits.
3. Repeat.

It sounds easy, doesn't it? Well, it's not.

Simple, yes. Easy, no. There's a big difference. This will take a lot of hard work, dedication, and commitment on your part. It will mean sacrificing some television time and other leisure activities. But I can promise that after you work hard to create your very first passive income stream that pumps money into your bank account with very little ongoing work on your part, you will be hooked.

Below, I have provided a list of 21 income streams that are available to almost anyone who wants to begin building them. It's time to get busy.

Income Stream #1 — Social Security Income

The primary source of income for many retirees today is the monthly check they receive from Social Security. Of course, Social Security income was never designed to be a vital component of the average retirement, but instead only as a supplement. Today, however, it is the *only* income stream for 26 percent of American retirees. That's one out of every four retirees! As of this writing, the average monthly Social Security benefit for a retired worker is about $1,230 and the highest possible benefit amount paid out is currently $2,513.

Who qualifies to receive Social Security income? U.S. taxpayers who have paid FICA taxes for a total of at least 10 years (40 quarters) throughout their working life are entitled to receive a monthly benefit check from the Social Security Administration upon reaching a specific age as determined by the federal government. As of this writing, the minimum age to qualify for benefits is 62. However, the formula that is used to determine your monthly benefit is based upon your best 35 working years. So if you worked for 40 years, your five lowest-paying years will be removed from the calculation. Because most people see their earnings rise over the course of their life, one common strategy for increasing Social Security income is to ensure that you have 35 high-paying years that can be used for calculation. For some, this will mean working longer than they had expected. Another common strategy that can increase your monthly benefits dramatically is to delay applying for Social Security as long as possible. Although retirees can apply for benefits as early as age 62, taking early benefits will reduce your monthly check by a whopping 30 percent! Those who can wait longer, until age 70, will get a 32 percent increase in their monthly check.

While I expect sweeping reforms to Social Security in the coming years, it still makes sense to maximize your monthly benefits. For more strategies for increasing your Social Security income, please visit http://www.ftmdaily.com/ssi.

Income Stream #2 — Defined Benefit Plan Income/Pension Income

Corporate pension plans have become a novelty in today's business environment. In 1983, 62 percent of all retirement plans offered were defined benefit retirement (pension) plans, but that dropped to just 17 percent in 2007, according to a study conducted by the Boston College Center for Retirement Research. Today, only 1 out of 10 companies offer a defined benefit retirement plan to their employees. If you are one of the 21 percent of Americans who have access to a pension plan today, consider yourself fortunate. You should also know that you have options when it comes to maximizing your pension income in retirement. For more information, go to http://www.ftmdaily.com/pensionmax.

Income Stream #3 — Defined Contribution Plan Income (401k, 403b)

Due to the increasing costs of managing a pension plan, many corporations have shifted to offering defined contribution plans, often known as 401(k) or 403(b) plans. To incentivize retirement savings, some employers offer a matching contribution for every dollar that you save, up to a certain amount. If your company offers a matching contribution, I would heartily urge you to consider contributing up to the matching amount. If your employer happens to offer a "Roth" version of your 401(k), I would strongly encourage you to see if it is a good fit for your financial situation. Similar to a Roth IRA, a Roth 401(k) allows you to put after-tax dollars back for retirement and then take income tax-free withdrawals at retirement. This could be enormously beneficial to you when taxes increase. Finally, selecting the right investments for your 401(k) and managing them can be time-consuming and frustrating. Due to the growing demand for investment help, there are a number of great 401(k) advisory services available today. Many of them provide one-on-one advice with investment selection, monitoring, buy/sell signals by email, and all for an extremely low cost. For more 401(k) investment tips and strategies, please visit http://www.ftmdaily.com/401k.

Income Stream #4 — Individual Retirement Account (IRA) Income

IRAs come in several flavors including: Traditional, Roth, SEP (Simplified Employee Pension), SIMPLE (Savings Incentive Match Plans for Employees), and Self-Directed. Here's a quick breakdown:

- *Traditional IRA:* Your savings dollars go in before being taxed (pre-tax) and all earnings and transactions are tax-deferred. Penalty-free distributions can begin at age 59-1/2 and become required at age 70-1/2. All withdrawals are taxed as ordinary income.

- *Roth IRA:* Your savings dollars go in after being taxed (after-tax) and all earnings and transactions are tax-exempt. Penalty-free distributions can begin at age 59-1/2 and all withdrawals are tax-free.

- *SEP IRA:* This is basically a profit-sharing plan set up by the self-employed or small business. If you have employees who qualify, they must all receive the same benefits. Your savings dollars go in before being taxed (pre-tax) and all earnings and transactions are tax-deferred. Penalty-free distributions can begin at age 59-1/2 and become required at age 70-1/2. All withdrawals are taxed as ordinary income. Many small business owners use these for their tax advantages as they allow higher annual contributions than Traditional or Roth IRAs.

- *SIMPLE IRA:* This is an employer-sponsored plan with similar rules to other IRAs with a few differences.

- *Self-Directed IRA:* Want to hold farmland, rental real estate, precious metals, commodities, or tax liens in your existing IRA? By opening or converting your existing IRA to a Self-Directed IRA, you can gain more control over your investments. This option is worthy of consideration by individuals who are overexposed to paper assets in their retirement accounts.

Today, there are a growing number of strategies that you can implement to maximize the benefits offered by IRAs. These include many powerful estate planning and tax strategies. For a list of these strategies, please visit http://www.ftmdaily.com/ira.

Income Stream #5 — Interest Income

When I was ten years old, I remember meeting a friend of the family named George. George was a little different from most people I knew at that time because he did not have a traditional job, but he did not appear to be broke either. When I finally gathered enough courage to ask him what he did for a living, he grinned and said, "I am living off of interest." At the time, my young brain did not fully comprehend what it meant to "live off of interest." Later, of course, I understood. (I seriously doubt that George is still "living off of interest" in today's ultra-low interest rate environment.)

Interest income is earned when money that you have invested accumulates interest. Developing a decent interest income stream requires one of two things: a sizeable amount of upfront investment capital or extremely high interest rates. While most interest income is taxed at ordinary income levels, there are a few exceptions. Interest earned on U.S. Treasury bonds and savings bonds are taxed at the federal level, but are tax-free at the state level. Many savvy investors have relied on municipal bonds as interest-bearing tax havens as they are tax-free at the federal level and often at the state level *if the bond is issued in your state of residence.* Recently, however, some investors have avoided municipal bonds due to financial solvency concerns at the local level. Most investors who successfully create a solid interest income stream use an approach called laddering. This approach diversifies interest rate risk and helps maintain liquidity by spreading out the investments into several savings vehicles over a period of time. You can learn our laddering approach at http://www.ftmdaily.com/interestladder.

Income Stream #6 — Dividend Income

Let's face it . . . dividends are boring. And the stocks that pay them are not the high-flying stocks that you would want to brag about at the next dinner party you attend. But I must admit that dividends, which are the portion of corporate profits paid out to shareholders, are one of my personal favorite income streams. Why? Because I do not view the stock market as the ultimate source of wealth creation. Instead, I view it as a place to steadily grow my wealth through smart diversification that creates a stream of reliable income. People that are broke look to the markets as a source of wealth creation. They invest in the markets because they want to hit a "home run." When they think about creating wealth, they think of winning the lottery, striking it rich in a penny stock, or some other nonsense. The rich view wealth differently. They know that wealth is not about a pile of cash, but instead, a steady passive stream of cash flow. If you give a lump sum of money to a person living paycheck to paycheck, they would likely turn around and spend it all on "stuff." In essence, they would give it right back to corporations run by the wealthy. This is because money always flows away from consumers and toward producers. However, if you gave that same lump sum of cash to a wealthy person, they would likely turn it in to a stream of *cash flow*. If you want to become wealthy, you must remember that *it is all about cash flow*. And that is why I like dividend-paying stocks. They provide not only potential capital gains, but *also* cash flow. With non-dividend-paying stocks, you have to sell in order to make money. But with dividend-paying stocks, you get paid an income just for owning them.

Here are a few of my own personal rules when it comes to investing in dividend-paying stocks:

- I invest in *well-managed*, dividend-paying companies that have solid cash flow and prospects of long-term capital appreciation.

- High dividends do not impress me. A long track record of consistent dividend growth impresses me.

- Except in unusual circumstances, I will choose to automatically re-invest the dividends. (If you want the income, however, you can simply choose to have the dividends paid out to you in cash.)

- If a stock cuts its dividend, it is usually time to sell.

In addition to regular dividend paying stocks, many other types of stocks pay their owners an income including: REITs (Real Estate

Investment Trusts), MLPs (Master Limited Partnerships), and Royalty Trusts. For more information on each of these types of income producing stocks, please visit http://www.ftmdaily.com/dividends.

Income Stream #7 — Real Estate Rental Income

Having been a landlord, I always get a kick out of the late-night television infomercials featuring real estate "gurus" sitting on the beach sipping on mai-tais as they sell the benefits of real estate investing. (I guess after you unclog a few overflowing toilets in the middle of the night, the reality sets in.) Without a doubt, investing in rental real estate is hard work. It takes time, energy, and effort. But as long as you understand that beforehand, then you will be all right. And while real estate investing is no "easy street," the benefits are difficult to ignore:

- Cash flow every month that increases with inflation
- Generous tax deductions (mortgage interest, depreciation, repair and maintenance costs, local and long distance travel, home office expense, and insurance costs, just to name a few)
- Renters pay off your mortgage and increase your equity in the property
- Real estate offers investors financial leverage through the use of OPM (Other People's Money) which can dramatically increase your returns on every dollar invested
- Capital appreciation of the property's value can increase your net worth
- Real estate investing offers an easy way to diversify your investments, especially for those currently overweighted in paper assets

I could literally write an entire book just on the benefits of real estate investing alone. I am a believer that owning property is one of the most surefire ways to become wealthy in America. Here are a few simple suggestions I have used personally in real estate investing:

- Stay liquid. I always maintain a six-month liquid savings reserve for emergencies and opportunities.

- Location, location, location. To minimize your risks, stick to areas that have growing populations, desirable school districts, low unemployment, and nearby shopping centers. If a local college or university is nearby, consider that a plus.

- Stick to three bedroom, two bathroom homes and larger. NEVER buy a two bedroom home. Your turnover rate will be higher as growing families will eventually run out of room. And if you decide to sell your property, a three bedroom home will typically sell much quicker than a two bedroom.

- When it comes to financing, only consider fixed rate mortgages. Do not be enticed by the low upfront interest rates offered by adjustable rate mortgages. When interest rates inevitably rise, you will regret it.

- Hire a property management company as soon as possible. In exchange for a portion of your monthly profits, they will take care of most of the headaches. This will allow you to focus on higher income activities, including finding more properties and/or developing more streams of income.

- Consider using an LLC (Limited Liability Corporation) for holding your investment properties to protect your personal assets.

For more tips on investing in rental real estate, please visit http://www.ftmdaily.com/rei.

Income Stream #8 — Wholesaling Real Estate

Have you ever seen those signs on the side of the road that say "We Buy Houses" or "We Pay Cash for Houses — Quick Close"? Those signs are all over America for one reason: they work. Many of these signs are placed by individuals who have no intention of buying your house. Instead, they are hard-working entrepreneurs, known as real estate wholesalers, who have developed a network of private real estate investors who have cash and are ready to buy properties. Interestingly, the real estate wholesaler does not care what the investor's purpose is for buying the house. Whether the investor decides to turn the property into a rental or simply wants to fix it up and sell it for a profit is not the concern of the wholesaler. Instead, think of the wholesaler as a *match-maker*. His job is to locate and connect the seller of a property with his list of cash-flush investors. The most successful wholesalers spend time developing a solid relationship with their group of investors, learning their tastes and preferences. The more knowledge that he has of his investors, the more success he will have in locating properties that meet their requirements. As the middleman between the seller and investor, the wholesaler is able to earn a handsome profit, often referred to as an *assignment fee*. In our current economic environment, real estate whole-salers are thriving. This small business requires a phone, a marketing plan, a solid list of private investors, and hardly any upfront capital. You don't even need a real estate license! There are many real estate wholesal-ers today earning well over $10,000 per month, while others earn much more. To see an example of a real estate wholesaling transaction and how it works, please visit http://www.ftmdaily.com/rei.

Income Stream #9 — Charitable Remainder Trust Income (CRT)

Would you believe me if I were to say that it is possible to pass along an asset to your favorite charity, receive the benefit of a tax deduc-tion, and on top of it all receive an income stream for the rest of your life? Does this scenario seem too good to be true? It is possible with an estate-planning tool called a Charitable Remainder Trust (CRT), and it is a powerful one indeed.

A CRT allows you to provide an additional income stream for you and your family today and to donate to your favorite charities later. Using a CRT, you (the donor) can reserve an income stream for a specified term of years, or *for the rest of your life*. Once your income stream ceases, the remaining principal of the trust and the accumulated income is distributed to your specified charity. During the donor's life-time, he will receive at least 5 percent of the initial amount placed in the trust annually (this percentage can vary, depending on the type of CRT and the percentage the donor specifies). One or more charities can be named in the trust, and the donor retains the right to change the charitable beneficiaries.

The tax benefits are two-fold. First, you will receive an immediate income tax deduction for the estimated amount that will be donated to the charity. Second, the trust itself is exempt from income tax.

Therefore, the trust can sell highly appreciated assets without being subject to pay any tax at the time of the sale. For those who are charitably minded, these powerful estate-planning tools can provide a lifetime stream of income that keeps on giving even after you pass. For more information how to set up a charitable remainder trust, please visit http://www.ftmdaily.com/crt.

Income Stream #10 — Annuity Income

An annuity is a contract between an investor and an insurance company. In exchange for your invested principal, the insurance company promises to make periodic payments to you. Immediate annuities begin payouts to you . . . *immediately*. Deferred annuities grow tax deferred and delay payments until a future date. Like IRAs, annuities are tax-deferred savings vehicles and are not accessible before age 59-1/2.

There are three types of deferred annuities:

- Fixed Annuity: Both the interest rate and the payout rate are predetermined. Payments can last for a set period or for life.

- Variable Annuity: You are permitted to choose how your funds are invested among an array of investment options.

- Equity-Indexed Annuity: These are a hybrid of fixed and variable annuities. The insurance company credits you with an annual return based upon an index, often the S&P 500 Stock Index.

Personally, I like fixed and equity-indexed annuities as they can offer principal protection, income for life, inflation protection riders, and often a death benefit in the event that you die prematurely. Those who complain about the costs and fees associated with annuities would do well to find a financial product that has similar features and benefits at a more reasonable cost. As a former financial advisor, I can think of no other financial product that offers principal and inflation protection *and* a lifetime income stream. Who would expect a product like that to be free? Remember, most of the noise that goes on around annuities is generated by those who sell them and those who sell competing financial products. Regardless, annuities are *not* for everyone — just those who do not want to place their retirement dollars at risk in the stock market and those who want a contractual guarantee that they will not outlive their money. If your goal is to convert your investment dollars into a stable lifetime stream of income in retirement, then an annuity may be right for a portion of your retirement savings. For strategies on maximizing your retirement income and to download a free report entitled "The Truth About Annuities," please visit http://www.ftmdaily.com/annuities.

Income Stream #11 — Tax-free Distributions from Cash-Value Life Insurance

One of the more unique and lesser-known income streams that you can create is through tax-free distributions from a cash value life insurance policy. Long despised by the mainstream financial media as a competitor for investment dollars, cash value life insurance provides an interesting vehicle for those in search of tax-deferred savings and tax-free distributions. Often called a "rich man's Roth" due to its ability to provide tax-free income to high wage earners, this strategy of using cash-value life insurance is most heavily used by the wealthiest Americans. According to Federal Reserve survey data, 22 percent of assets accumulated tax-free in whole-life and universal-life policies were held by the wealthiest 1 percent of U.S. families in 2007 — those with more than $8.4 million in net worth, and 55 percent of the assets in such policies were held by the wealthiest 10 percent of families. The bottom half by net worth held 6.5 percent of these assets.[2] Life insurance is one of the most unique and flexible financial and estate planning tools available today. To learn more about how this creative income strategy works, please visit http://www.ftmdaily.com/li.

Income Stream #12 — Reverse Mortgage Income (tax-free)

A reverse mortgage is a loan that allows older homeowners to access the equity in their home. To qualify for a reverse mortgage, you must meet these three requirements:

- Be at least 62 years old
- Own your home and have substantial equity
- Live in the home as your primary residence

There are no income or credit qualifications to being approved for a reverse mortgage loan. The bank or financial institution will determine the payment that you will receive each month through a calculation that includes your age, the current appraised value of your home, and current interest rates. The payment that you receive can come as a lump sum, an equity line of credit to be used as needed, or a regular monthly income stream for life.

In essence, a reverse mortgage creates a lien on your home but the title remains in your name. This lien does not have to be paid back until 1) all borrowers move out of the home, 2) all borrowers pass away, or 3) when the home is sold.

And like all loans, reverse mortgages have costs such as the interest charged on the borrowed money, application and origination fees, and ongoing service fees, to name a few. These costs are deferred and added to the balance due upon the repayment of the loan. While reverse mortgages are not for everyone, they can be a perfect fit for some individuals. For more information on reverse mortgages, including a unique reverse mortgage income strategy, go to http://www.ftmdaily.com/reversemortgage.

Income Stream #13 — Part-time Employment Income

For many people, the option of getting a side gig presents the quickest way to earn a new income stream immediately. And sometimes, a part-time job provides more than just another stream of income. One of our FTMDaily.com readers named Bill wrote in recently to tell us he had secured a part-time position with a Fortune 500 delivery carrier in addition to his regular full-time job. But it wasn't just for the money.

In his email, Bill said: "While I like my full time job, the company is too small to offer any meaningful employee benefits. Instead of leaving the security of my job, I decided to pick up a side job with benefits. I work three evenings a week at this new company, and now I have cheaper health insurance, a 401(k), and even tuition assistance if I decide to go back to school. And I have decided to save all of the money that I make from this new job to build my DSL savings" (Diversified Six Month Liquid Savings Reserve).

In addition, many retirees who become bored in retirement often benefit from taking on a part-time job. For our list of the ten highest paying part-time jobs, go to http://www.ftmdaily.com/secondjob.

Income Stream #14 — Covered Call Option Income

Everyone knows that landlords earn rental income from rental real estate. But did you know that thousands of people rent out their *stocks* every month to generate an additional stream of income? This income strategy is known as writing covered calls and it is a great way to generate income for those with existing stock holdings. By using the options market, you have the ability to write (sell) an option to purchase your shares of stock at a specified price to another investor. In addition, the options market offers financial leverage to those who are starting off with little investment capital. To learn more about the powerful option trading strategies that I personally use, go to http://www.ftmdaily.com/optiontrading.

Income Stream #15 — Tax-Lien Investing Income

One of the more interesting, yet little known, investing strategies is to purchase real estate tax liens. If you have never heard of investing in tax liens, you are not alone. So what exactly is a tax lien? Every state and locality requires real estate owners to pay taxes on their property. Property taxes are vital to every community as they serve as the primary funding vehicle for local services such as police, firefighters, libraries, public schools, roads, etc. Typically, all property taxes are collected by each county on an annual basis. However, not every property owner is able, or willing, to pay their annual property taxes by the due date set by the county. Each year, tens of thousands of homeowners from every state fail to pay their property taxes in a timely manner. When a property owner does not pay his property taxes within a set period of time, the county typically charges a late fee. This late fee usually takes the form of an interest charge and/or a penalty charge. But because most counties are dependent upon a predictable and stable income to fund their activities, they cannot wait for every property owner to pay their property tax bill in full. Therefore, when a property owner fails to pay their taxes by the effective due date, the county will turn to private investors. In essence, the county will place a lien on the property and then attempt to sell the tax lien to private investors through a public auction. (While many states sell "liens," others sell the actual "deeds" to the properties at these auctions.) At the auction, an investor will have the opportunity to purchase the tax lien. So why would an investor be interested in buying a tax lien on a property from a local county auction? There are several reasons, including the following.

- Rate of Return — When the property owner finally agrees to pay the county his outstanding property taxes, he will be required to pay a late charge that often takes the form of an interest or penalty charge. These late charges, which are often anywhere from 5 to 25 percent per year (every state is different), are paid directly to the tax lien investor!

- Collateral — Tax lien investors are in a unique position. Their investment is not only secured by the underlying real estate, but they are also placed as a first position lien holder on the property. This means that the tax lien investor is ahead of the mortgage company when it comes to repayment.

- No Volatility — Tax lien investors do not have to worry about a fluctuation in the value of their investment. Instead, they receive a fixed interest rate on their investment.

There are many other benefits, as well as potential pitfalls, to investing in tax liens. For more information on the basics of tax-lien investing, please visit http://www.ftmdaily.com/taxliens.

Income Stream #16 — Referral Business Income

In the age of Internet marketing, the barriers for small business owners have been shattered. Several years ago, small business marketing costs were prohibitively high with expensive yellow page ads, costly direct mail campaigns, and more. Today, everything is different. If you want to succeed with a local business, your goal is to be on the first page of Google for your related keywords. For example, I own a successful appliance repair business located in a major city in Texas. Through my knowledge of keyword research and search engine optimization techniques, our appliance repair business is consistently on the first page of Google's search results for hundreds of related phrases to my business. Interestingly, I do not live in Texas. Instead, I found an appliance repair company in the area that was interested in receiving more business. Our role is to advertise and send them business. They run the service calls and we split the profits. In this Internet age, this is an extremely powerful wealth-building income stream that anyone with a little bit of Internet marketing knowledge can start right now. Begin by thinking of small business owners that you know that could benefit from your services.

I have personally used this income strategy to develop over seven income streams in the last few years alone, and have personally taught hundreds of people just like you how to do the same! For my personal step-by-step strategies for setting up a referral business, go to http://www.ftmdaily.com/referralbusiness.

Income Stream #17 — Internet/Affiliate Marketing

How would you like to make money for sharing your favorite products and services on the Internet? If you think about it, isn't this exactly what many websites and bloggers do? Most online companies today offer an affiliate marketing program for anyone to join absolutely free. Some of the more popular ones include Amazon.com, Walmart.com, and Ebay.com. As an affiliate, you will be given a unique web address that you can share with others. Because this unique web address is tracked, you will be paid if someone clicks to their website through your unique link. There is a lot of hype surrounding affiliate marketing because it seems like a dream business. Just put a few links on the web and sit back and collect the checks. Nothing could be further from the truth. While it is true that affiliate marketers can make good money, don't believe the hype of easy profits. I have personally made a lot of money with affiliate marketing online, and it is one of my favorite income streams. But it is without a doubt very difficult. To succeed you will need to leverage many online platforms to deliver your unique content including your own website and blog, email marketing, Youtube, and social media outlets like Facebook, Twitter, and Google+. To learn more about the work that is involved in becoming a successful affiliate marketer and to download a list of my favorite affiliate programs, including many that pay recurring commissions, please visit http://www.ftmdaily.com/affiliatemarketing.

Income Stream #18 — Network Marketing/Direct Selling

J. Paul Getty once said, "I'd rather have 1 percent of the efforts of 100 people than 100 percent of my own efforts." This is a perfect description of how people in network and direct marketing earn money. It's all about leverage and teamwork. While I am not a fan of multi-level marketing in general, I do believe that there are some excellent and well-run companies to consider if you are interested in developing this income stream. I have found the best companies are the ones that most resemble an affiliate marketing set-up. Personally, I would never partner with a company that did not pay lifetime residual income. The best companies have excellent and reasonably priced products and services with a high customer retention rate. Look for opportunities that require no large upfront investment, no high pressure sales pitches, and no inventory. For more tips on selecting the best direct marketing opportunities, please visit http://www.ftmdaily.com/lifetimeincome.

Income Stream #19 — Trade Stocks and ETFs for Income

The business of trading stocks has come a long way since the early days. Today, you can instantly place a trade on virtually any publicly traded stock or exchange-traded fund with the click of a mouse. In many ways, trading is the ultimate work-from-home business. Trading stocks and ETFs has long been a passion of mine. I traded my first stock in 1996. I have been trading stocks and ETFs ever since. I began as a day trader. During the dot-com bubble, there was a lot of money to be made in day trading. Today, however, instead of day trading, I focus on a special type of trading technique known as swing trading. Unlike the rapid buy and sell action of day trading, swing trading involves buying a position within a stock or ETF and holding it anywhere from three days to three months. Swing trading is better suited to my schedule and can be a perfect complementary income stream for those with a regular full-time job. To successfully trade stocks and ETFs, you will need specialized knowledge, a pool of investment capital, and enough time to conduct adequate research. And trading is not for the faint of heart. This is a highly speculative venture. However, there are several methods that traders can use to hedge their risks and limit their losses. Nevertheless, you should never use money that you cannot afford to lose. If you think that you are an exception, the sharks of Wall Street would love to meet you. Successful traders know that trading is a numbers game. They will lose money at times. The goal is to limit their losses and let their winners run. I have taught hundreds of people just like you the basics of successful trading. For more information on trading stocks, and a free online trading video tutorial, please visit http://www.ftmdaily.com/stocktrading.

Income Stream #20 — Venture Capital

Venture capital is a sophisticated way of saying that you are a lender to a new fledgling start-up business. For those seeking new opportunities with their investment capital, this can be a great source of income. For example, I recently met a young man who was seeking to start his own used car lot. I provided him with some seed capital to buy used cars that he would flip and we would split the profits. The investment provides me with double digit returns on my capital every month and it provides him the means to earn a nice income. Never loan out money without doing your own due diligence and ALWAYS use a contract. (If you don't have an attorney, get one. Surrounding yourself with a wealth of wise advice is critical to your success.) Keep your eyes open for opportunities. They are all around you.

Income Stream #21 — Royalties/Patents

Patents, mineral rights, music and book royalties, and copyrights are among the many pieces of intangible personal property that can create a sizeable income stream for you. It has been said that everyone has at least one book in them. Today, with the advent of self-publishing and the growing popularity of e-books and e-readers, it is easier than ever to put your thoughts into a book and sell them to a global audience. As a published author, I receive royalties from the sales of this book. Musicians and artists can earn royalties on their creative work. Those who own mineral rights on their land can earn royalties. Software developers earn royalties. Inventors can earn money from a patent. Licensing is a common way to earn a recurring stream of income from a patent. Develop an idea and rent it to a business and earn income on every item that is sold. Others may secure a patent only to sell it later.

Conclusion

I hope this list has helped ignite your thinking about the many possibilities that exist for creating income. Take heart! You don't have to remain hostage to one single income stream for the rest of your life.

By creating multiple streams of income, you do not have to worry if one income stream dries up or slows down because you have others flowing in that will pick up the slack. But best of all, with multiple income streams you will be able to enjoy something that few people have today: time freedom. (What is time freedom? It means being able to spend your time pursuing the things that you desire without having to trade your time for money.) While this will definitely not be the case in the beginning, it will be the end result. After you commit to working hard for a period of time, you will no longer have to trade your time for money. Instead, you will be building many passive streams of cash flow that will continue without having to sacrifice time away from your family. For my wife and me, having multiple streams of income means that we can be more involved in our Christian ministry work. I believe that every person has been placed on this earth for a very specific purpose. Our culture has taught us that to survive we need to work for a business owner. That is false. *You* can be the business owner. My wife and I did it. And you can too.

Is this concept of multiple income streams a new idea? No, the Bible tells us that Abraham was rich in gold, silver, livestock, and slaves (employees).

> The LORD has blessed my master greatly, and he has become great; and He has given him flocks and herds, silver and gold, male and female servants, and camels and donkeys (Genesis 24:35).

The Bible also teaches the importance of diversification:

> Cast your bread upon the waters, for you will find it after many days. Give a serving to seven, and also to eight, for you do not know what evil will be on the earth (Eccles. 11:1–2).

While the benefits of diversifying your income are numerous, I should also add that it isn't the right path for everyone. The skills required and the demands on your time grow with each stream you add. Each stream of income requires its own skills and expertise. Each stream of income makes demands on the most precious and limited resource in your life — time. That's right. To reap the benefits of "time freedom" will require you to sow large amounts of time up front. In short, there is a price to pay for each stream of income, and only you can decide if multiple streams of income are really worth that price.

While I have listed 21 potential income streams in this chapter, I truly believe that the list of possible ways to earn money is endless. We are only limited by our imaginations. But I have found that the best types of income streams are the ones that we enjoy. Take inventory of your passions and hobbies and determine if there is a way to turn them into a steady stream of income. Remember, the whole point of diversifying your income is to generate a number of different paychecks. As the U.S. economy continues to weaken, you will be glad you did.

You can find more details about each of the income streams listed above by visiting http://www.ftmdaily.com/incomebook.

Endnotes

1. Bruce Lee, *The Art of Expressing the Human Body* (Boston, MA: C.E. Tuttle Publishing, 1998), p. 16.
2. "Shift to Wealthier Clientele Puts Life Insurers in a Bind," *Wall Street Journal*, October 3, 2010; http://online.wsj.com/article/SB10001424052748703435104575421411449555240.html.

Chapter 15

Eight Key Strategies to Protect Your Finances

The wise have wealth and luxury,
but fools spend whatever they get.
— Proverbs 21:20; NLT

The time to repair the roof is when the sun is shining.[1]
— John F. Kennedy

OVERVIEW: In this chapter, you will learn eight wise financial strategies that you can begin using in your journey toward financial liberty.

Every day, my online financial education company is helping inform Americans on how to properly diversify their savings, their investments, and their income. I urge you to take advantage of the many free resources available at our website: www.FTMDaily.com. We also host a weekly radio program called "Follow the Money Weekly," conduct free monthly educational webinars, and publish a quarterly investment newsletter called *Follow the Money Quarterly*. Because our content directly confronts the current economic challenges facing Americans, we receive many questions. The most common one I receive after lecturing on the topic of America's economic crisis is: "What should I be doing with my money right now?" Since I do not believe in a one-size-fits-all approach to personal finances, I am always hesitant to hand out specific advice to someone I have just met. However, I do believe that nearly everyone can benefit from considering a handful of common-sense financial strategies. Of course, you should always consult with a professional financial advisor prior to making financial decisions.

In this chapter, I am going to share seven powerful financial strategies that we use every day here at our organization. I believe these will help you weather the current financial storm — and especially the greater one to come. These strategies are certainly not all you will need for the days ahead, but they provide a good start in the right direction.

Strategies for Overcoming Economic Adversity

Today, many people have no financial game plan and, if they do have one, it is often backward. Some may have a few investments, but little in liquid savings. Others may have some savings and investments, but they are woefully underinsured in the event of a personal crisis. Still others have investments that are poorly diversified. Furthermore, most people are dependent upon only one stream of income and are, therefore, financially vulnerable in the event of a sudden job loss.

If any of the above describes you, take heart. It is not too late to make a positive change for your financial future. Regardless of your age or economic situation, you still have time to set financial goals. In fact, setting financial goals is one of the most important steps you can take to wisely steward the money that has been entrusted to you. This brings us to our first financial strategy.

Financial Strategy #1: Commit Yourself to Financial Education

"My people are destroyed for lack of knowledge" (Hosea 4:6).

For far too long, Americans have been economically illiterate. This is not acceptable if we desire to be wise stewards of the finances and resources that have been placed into our lives. The Bible says that those to whom much is given, much is required (see Luke 12:48). The journey toward becoming good overseers of our God-given resources begins with information. There is much you can do to inform yourself and others.

First, dedicate yourself to economic awareness. With the unfolding of the U.S. financial crisis, the importance of understanding basic economics has been forced upon average Americans. Every day, we hear words like "interest rates," "the Fed," and "the euro," just to mention a few. The truth is that the basic laws of economics are important to every American because they affect every American. By choosing to buy and read this book, you have demonstrated concern about the direction of this nation's economy. You have also shown that you are dedicated to good financial stewardship. But don't stop here. Commit yourself to becoming financially aware, and then do all you can to safeguard your financial future. Remember, very few people are really looking out for you in this world. No one cares about your financial future as much as you do.

Second, keep current with financial news both here and abroad. Life in the information age is interesting. On one hand, it means we have information literally at our fingertips 24 hours a day. But it also means we must be careful in deciding to whom we choose to listen and what we believe. The more you read about money, the more you will discover that a substantial amount of economic news is not worth the paper it is printed on. Much of the financial press contains contradictory advice on money and investing and can confuse more than it helps. However, I do recommend a few news sources. The *Wall Street Journal* is still one of the best sources for getting solid reporting on financial news and global economic issues. Another U.S. publication I recommend is *Investor's Business Daily*. As far as international news sources, I highly endorse the *Financial Times*. It is based in London and provides a European perspective of the global economy. I also suggest visiting our website, www.FTMDaily.com, which is committed to publishing important economic trends and forecasts you and your family can use to make wise decisions.

Third, take an economics or money management course. Check with your local community college for a beginner's course on economics or money management. This is such an important step because most of us have never learned how money really works. I believe every high school student should have to pass an economic and money-management test before obtaining a diploma. It is simply amazing how little real-world training goes on in most of our public schools. Many high school graduates don't even know how to make a basic budget or how to write a check! You can also find helpful financial and investing articles for beginners online at www.investopedia.com.

Fourth, study personal finance books. An abundance of books have been written to help individuals become better money managers. Many offer great insights and are worth reading. Visit your local library and pick up some titles that interest you. While this may sound strange, the best recommendation I can make is to study what the Bible says about money management. Before you say that the Bible is an irrelevant guide to financial matters, consider that the Bible has more than 2,350 verses directly dealing with money, wealth, and possessions. That's around twice the number of verses the Bible contains on faith, prayer, and love combined! Many people mistakenly believe that the Bible is a religious book filled with moral stories irrelevant to modern-day life. Nothing could be further from the truth! In my own studies, I have found the Bible to be highly practical on matters related to finance and economics. I urge you to find out what the Bible has to say about money. It will revolutionize your views and anchor you with wisdom in times of volatility.

Fifth, share what you have learned with others. One of the most important things you can do for others is share the truth about what is really happening in our economy so they can make wise financial decisions, too. If your eyes have been opened to the truth about America's financial system, tell those you love and care about what you have learned. Pass this book on to them. In fact, the very worst place for this book is on your bookshelf. Lend it out to others. Underline and highlight the parts that you found to be important. Gather a small group together and download our free study guide. (For the free study guide, please visit http://www.ftmdaily.com/studyguide.) Don't let the thoughts that have been provoked within you end when you finish this book.

Action Step #1 — The first action step in creating your financial game plan is to commit to educating yourself about money, economics, and personal finance. Consider starting a small group of like-minded people to discuss this book and others like it.

Financial Strategy #2: Create a Charitable Giving Plan

But this I say: He who sows sparingly will also reap sparingly, and he who sows bountifully will also reap bountifully. So let each one give as he purposes in his heart, not grudgingly or of necessity; for God loves a cheerful giver (2 Cor. 9:6–7).

The first financial strategy mentioned above involves the mind. But this second financial strategy relates to the heart. Money is a curious thing. While it is completely morally neutral in and of itself, it has the unusual power of being able to destroy an individual like few other things can. As highlighted throughout the preceding chapters, the love of money is strongly warned against in Scripture, particularly in 1 Timothy 6:10, which makes the profound statement that the root of all evil is "the love of money." Money can make our lives very comfortable, but it can also darken our hearts and cause us to rely less on our faith and more on our own abilities. For this reason, the second strategy in creating your financial game plan must be to determine how much money you are going to give away. If that sounds backward, it is because our culture has infiltrated and poisoned our minds to the point that we have forgotten that the money we earn, save, and invest is not ours in the first place. It has been said that "Christians show who they are by what they do with what they have." That is true because "where your treasure is, there your heart will be also" (Matt. 6:21). All of us have been entrusted with what we have. Our first priority is to properly recognize this truth by taking time to decide how we will go about the joyful task of giving. Unfortunately, many people skip this most important step. They justify it by promising themselves that they will come back to it later when they actually have some money to give. But this logic is usually flawed, for if they won't give a small gift, why would they ever give a large one? This is a crucial step, one that will determine the direction you will head, and the blessings that will await you in the future.

What exactly do I mean by creating a charitable giving plan? If you are an investor, you know that before purchasing an investment it is wise to do your own due diligence. That is, you want to investigate before you act to determine whether the investment is a wise idea for your particular situation. I have personally spent days, and even weeks, sizing up an opportunity before investing. Why? Because I wanted to maximize my returns and limit my risk. I believe it is wise to approach our charitable giving in a similar manner. As you build and create a financial plan, you will inevitably set financial goals for the future. These goals will require you to dream about the future and what you want it to look like. So why not spend some time "dreaming" about your *future giving* as well?

It's easy to think, *Wouldn't it be nice if I made $250,000 per year?* or *I can't wait until I finally save $1 million and then live off the interest.* But what if our dreams also included things like: *I hope I can make a difference with the money I am going to make through my wise investments,* or *My goal is to give more this year than I gave last year — for the rest of my life.*

Can you imagine how much richer our lives would be if, instead of seeking to consume all of our future wealth, we would look for ways to help others with it!

I know what you are thinking right now because I have had the same thoughts myself: if you give away all of your money, how can you enjoy any of it? Rest assured, I am not talking about giving away all of your money — just a percentage. This percentage can, and should, be defined in advance. Perhaps it is 10–15 percent, or possibly even more. Regardless, the specific percentage is between you and God, and no one else.

One of the greatest hallmarks of true Christianity is generosity. The Bible tells us that genuine happiness is found when we give. When we give, we are simply imitating God, the biggest giver of them all. As the Scripture says, "For God so loved the world that He gave His only begotten Son" (John 3:16).

It can be very tempting to ease up on giving to the work of the gospel during a time of personal financial crisis. However, slowing giving is a dangerous practice because the Bible tells us that God watches how we use the money He places in our lives as a way to examine our hearts. The money that has entered your life is a test, pure and simple. If we believe that God owns everything, then we must admit that He owns the money sitting in our bank account. He is not a tyrant who demands all of your money. On the contrary, He is a loving Father who knows what's best for His children. He knows that the greatest joy in the world is found in giving of ourselves and our resources for His divine purposes.

Action Step #2 — Before moving on to the next strategy, take some time to "dream" up a charitable giving plan and then take steps to put it into action.

Financial Strategy #3: Begin a Systematic Savings Plan

> Go to the ant, you sluggard! Consider her ways and be wise, which, having no captain, overseer or ruler, provides her supplies in the summer, and gathers her food in the harvest (Prov. 6:6–8).

Let's face it: Americans are not good savers. Apparently, we think we don't need to worry about having a "rainy day" fund because we assume the sun will always shine. Nothing could be further from the truth. Saving money is a biblical principle that helps insulate us from peril during times of economic uncertainty.

When we talk about saving money, we are really talking about planning. In order to plan, you have to get serious about your money. You have to take control of what you have, and you must *want* to save. But planning to save money is just the first step. Someone once accurately said, "You can be on the right track, but if you just sit there, you may get run over." Being on the right track by planning to save money is good, but if it just remains a plan that never gets put into action, it will never bear fruit.

However, once we do begin to *work our plan* by saving money, we often find distractions along the way. The road to success is marked with many tempting parking spaces. Something will always come up to compete with your plan to save. This is why I recommend automating your savings plan. This is easily accomplished now with direct deposit and automatic debiting of specified percentages of your paycheck into your savings account.

Perhaps some of you already have a systematic savings program. For others, saving money on a regular basis may be a difficult habit to form. This is especially true if it seems that you are barely getting by right now without saving any money. If this describes you, then creating a systematic savings program is one of the most important financial steps for you to take right now.

Several years ago, when I first started trying to save a percentage of my income, I became very easily discouraged. Something would come up every month to prevent me from putting money back in reserve. It was not until I learned about something I call the Profit Principle that I realized the importance of saving money. What is the Profit Principle? Let me explain. Several years ago, while reading through the Book of Proverbs, a verse literally jumped off the page. Has that ever happened to you? The verse that caught my eye was Proverbs 14:23. It says: "In all labor there is profit: but the talk of the lips tendeth only to penury" (ASV).

In particular, the phrase "In all labor there is profit" kept rolling around in my mind. I was aware that the definition of the word *profit* was essentially the amount of income left over after expenses. It was at that moment that I discovered the Profit Principle.

The Profit Principle simply says this: An individual's profit from his labor or work is equal to the amount of money saved. In mathematical terms, it's PROFIT = SAVINGS.

The Profit Principle literally blew my mind because I realized that each month that I did not save money from my paycheck was a month when I did not earn a profit! Suddenly, I recognized that I was going to work at my job every single day for zero profit! Who in their right mind would do that? Apparently I did. Today, large corporations operate their businesses for maximum profit. Additionally, small business owners are dependent upon their profits to survive and thrive. So why should you view your job any differently? Would you ever agree to work at a job without earning a profit? Of course, not! Yet, millions of Americans work for *no profit* because they save nothing. I should know, because I used to be one of them!

To make matters worse, many Americans not only earn zero profit from their labor because they do not save, but they actually agree *to give away all of their profits* to credit card companies and other corporations. How is this not a form of voluntary financial slavery?

This financial strategy will help you take back the most basic of your fundamental financial rights — your right to earn a profit from your labor. It is biblical, and it makes common sense that you should have control of the profits that are created as a result of your hard work.

After I discovered the Profit Principle, my view of money was drastically changed. Suddenly, the distinction between my "wants" and my "needs" came sharply into focus. I began to prioritize and cut the "fat" from my monthly budget. Things that used to be important to me, such as maintaining a particular image or keeping up with the Joneses, began to fade. (After all, in case no one has told you, the Joneses are broke. So why try to keep up with them anyway?)

I urge you to really think about the Profit Principle in your own financial life. Are you making a profit from your labor? Or are you giving it all away to the corporations who have deceived you into believing that you cannot survive without all of their "stuff"?

The next step, after deciding it is time to start earning a profit from your labor, is to determine your desired monthly profit rate. Unless you live in your parents' basement rent-free, then your profit rate cannot be 100 percent (although, wouldn't that be nice?). So how much money should you save each month? Personally, I believe the minimum amount that anyone should save is 15 percent of monthly income. Why 15 percent and not 10 percent, as most financial advisors recommend? I suggest 15 percent because of the various eroding factors that affect our money. For example, the combined impact of inflation and taxes alone are a good enough reason to save more than 10 percent. These two factors have a tremendous wealth-destroying effect and must be fought aggressively. Those who recommend a 10 percent savings rate may have good intentions, but that percentage will barely keep your financial head above water over the long run when inflation drifts even higher and when, not if, tax rates increase.

I would recommend that you begin by setting your profit (savings) rate at 10 percent and then slowly raise it to 15 percent. Others can set their profit rate higher at 15–20 percent. Many people living in Asian countries, especially in China, have savings rates of over 40 percent!

But what if you are just barely getting by right now with very little money to spare? Try setting your profit rate at 1 percent right now. Then, every month thereafter, you can attempt to raise your profit rate by another percentage point. This will allow you to ease into this strategy without throwing your entire monthly budget into chaos. With this approach, you could realistically have a 10 percent profit rate from your labor by the end of the year. The important thing is to begin saving money now and saving it regularly. It's time for you to finally earn a profit from your labor!

Action Step #3 — Determine what you want your profit rate to be and then begin withholding it from your paycheck systematically. Do not settle for less than a 15 percent profit (savings) rate from your labor!

Financial Strategy #4: Build and Maintain Six Months of Emergency Liquid Savings

> A prudent man foresees evil and hides himself: but the simple pass on, and are punished (Prov. 22:3).

After you decide on your monthly profit (savings) rate, you will have the satisfaction of seeing your savings grow each month. The next step in your financial strategy is to build this savings into an emergency pool of liquid savings that is equivalent to six months of your gross income. For example, if you earn $3,000 per month, your goal will be to save $18,000 ($3,000/month x 6 months).

Without an adequate emergency fund, you will have to rely upon credit, family members, friends, or current investments every single time a crisis arises. But this will no longer be necessary (except in rare cases) when you have accumulated a six-month supply of cash.

Additionally, having extra money in the bank will provide you with a peace of mind that is simply priceless. This is especially true in our current environment of creeping inflation, corporate layoffs, and high unemployment.

And as you begin to save, you will actually set yourself up to become a savvy investor. This is because good savers make even better investors. Why? Due to something I call the "Risk Relation Principle." That is, *the amount of risk someone is willing to take is inversely related to the amount of liquid savings he or she holds.* This principle explains why many investors who have little or nothing in savings seek to "hit a home run" with virtually every investment. Because people who do this have no liquid savings, they take excessive —

and often unnecessary — risks with capital in the hopes of parlaying the little money they do have into something bigger. In essence, they want to make up for their lack of disciplined savings through gambling with investments. This investing approach is usually a sure ticket to the poorhouse!

Furthermore, those who have no liquid savings are often required to tap whatever little money they do have in investments when a calamity arises. This truth became abundantly clear in our most recent financial crisis. Sadly, many financially unprepared and/or unemployed Americans were forced to cash in their 401(k)'s and IRAs in order to pay their mortgages or monthly bills. Others were even forced to sell their homes or other investments in order to cover payments that a well-planned emergency fund would have easily covered. And not only did some Americans have to cash in their long-term investments just to cover short-term expenses, many of them did so as the financial markets were at a major low.

Despite their lack of financial planning, it is hard to direct the blame entirely upon them. After all, these underprepared Americans were simply following the financial advice of Wall Street — or even worse, of their human resources department at work. The bad advice they consistently receive goes something like this: "Max out your 401(k), open a traditional IRA, and buy a house, because real estate always goes up in value." Unfortunately, all three of these investment vehicles are designed to be illiquid; they will do little good when you need cold, hard cash quickly.

There is one final rule regarding your six-month pool of emergency savings. You *must* keep it liquid at all times. This means that it should never be "locked up" in any way. You will not be investing this money. You must always have immediate access to these liquid funds, or else it does you no good.

Action Step #4 — Flow your profits (savings) into a savings or money market account until it reaches an amount that is equivalent to six months of your gross income, and keep it accessible and liquid at all times.

Quick note: The first four strategies we've suggested are designed to get your financial house in order. The final four strategies relate exclusively to diversification — namely, diversifying your six-month pool of liquid savings, your investment portfolio, and finally, your income. Let's now consider the importance of diversifying your savings.

Financial Strategy #5: Diversify Your Savings

"The silver is Mine, and the gold is Mine," says the LORD of hosts (Hag. 2:8).

One of the most popular financial concepts today is the need for diversification. Unfortunately, most financial advisors only apply this notion to your investments and not to your savings or income. In this financial strategy, I will explain how you can diversify your six-month liquid pool of savings.

Once you commit to a 15-percent savings plan, it won't be long before you begin to accumulate a nice sum of money. As we discussed in the last strategy, your initial goal will be to save 50 percent of your annual gross income (or six months of income) through your monthly contributions. Building that reserve of liquid cash will help shield you from the uncertain times that lie ahead. This means that if you earn $30,000 per year, you should build and maintain a minimum of $15,000 in liquid savings, at all times.

As your savings continue to grow, you will want to begin diversifying the funds in safe places. These funds will need to remain in highly liquid accounts, in case you need to access them quickly. The diversification model I personally like is the following:

- One-third U.S. dollar denominated assets (interest-bearing accounts, CDs, properly structured cash-value life insurance, etc.)

- One-third hard assets (precious metals, real commodities)

- One-third select, stable foreign currencies (hard currency, CDs, etc.)

By spreading your liquid savings across a variety of savings vehicles, you will help ensure that your money is not too highly exposed to risk in any one area. And by keeping only one-third of your money in

Sample Liquid Cash Savings Allocation

33% - Precious Metals

34% - U.S. Dollars

33% - Stable Foreign Currencies

U.S. dollar-denominated assets, you will protect yourself from further declines in the dollar's purchasing power.

Just as diversifying your money is important, so too is keeping it in a safe place. Just ask anyone who lived during the Great Depression when more than 10,000 banks closed their doors. Many of these institutions did not allow their customers to withdraw their funds. Why was that? Well, it's a little-known fact that the banks do not actually have all of your money. This is due to the legal practice of fractional-reserve banking, covered earlier in this book.

I recommend periodically investigating the bank or financial institution that is holding your money. Make sure it is FDIC (Federal Deposit Insurance Corporation)-insured. The FDIC is a government entity that insures the majority of the nation's banks. If your money is on deposit in a FDIC-insured bank, then it is insured up to an amount regulated by the federal government. Currently, this maximum is set at $250,000.

Recently, however, there have been many concerns about the FDIC's ability to handle a major banking crisis. According to the latest reports, the FDIC is responsible for covering $5.4 trillion of qualified bank deposits. How much money does the FDIC have to cover those deposits? Zero. It is actually running an $8 billion deficit. While this may be good cause for concern, in reality, the FDIC will never run out of money because they have a line of credit with the Federal Reserve. If the FDIC needs more cash, the Fed will simply print more money. Washington learned its lesson during the Great Depression. They would rather create massive amounts of inflation than to allow the public's faith in the FDIC to falter. It is still imperative, however, to keep no more than the government-determined amount insured by the FDIC in any one bank. Also, take note that items placed in your bank's safe-deposit box are not FDIC insured.

In addition, it is a very good idea to investigate the banks where you are currently, or are considering, conducting business. To check your bank's health, visit www.veribanc.com or www.bankrate.com.

To learn more about foreign currencies, visit www.everbank.com. This site has a large amount of information about all of the popular foreign currencies available to U.S. citizens. To learn more about precious metals like gold and silver, check out our free 90-minute webinar on precious metals at www.ftmdaily.com/gold.

Action Step #5 — Protect the purchasing power of your six-month pool of liquid savings by diversifying it among a few select areas.

Financial Strategy #6: Begin a Diversified Investment Portfolio

> Cast your bread upon the waters, for you will find it after many days. Give a serving to seven, and also to eight, for you do not know what evil will be on the earth (Eccles. 11:1–2).

Once you have built up your six-month savings reserve, then, and only then, it is time to think about "investing." The difference between saving and investing has been lost in today's financial world, which has become dominated by Wall Street banks that need your capital to survive. Therefore, they de-emphasize your need for liquidity and emphasize investing your money with them for as long as possible.

You will want a portion of your investments to be liquid. However, because you have built up your six-month savings reserve, you can more easily invest for the long term without constantly needing to tap your investment funds in times of an emergency.

When it comes to diversifying your investments, you should seek to spread your funds among various asset classes. Today, the most common retirement plan in America consists of owning a house and having a 401(k) retirement plan. The major problem with these assets, besides being very illiquid, is that *they are both completely government-controlled.* Does this mean that these are poor investments? Not at all! Instead, they should simply be considered as a good addition to your overall financial game plan.

Some people will say that diversification is only important for those who do not know how to invest. This is false. The truth is that diversification is the ultimate protection against an out-of-control government and federal tax code.

Earning, saving, and investing in America today have become a game. And the rules of the game are found in America's tax code. Those who learn the rules, and play accordingly, can prosper financially in this country. Those who fail to learn the rules, and play by them, will be punished.

Who makes the rules? The federal government.

Since the federal government can change the rules at any time, your only real defense is to diversify across a wide variety of asset classes with different tax treatments. This way, if the rules change suddenly, you will not be wiped out. For example, the tax code currently favors investing in real estate and tax-deferred retirement accounts. However, if the tax code were to change, which it could at any time, then those who have all of their investments in these vehicles could be in for a big surprise. For this reason, smart investors and astute business owners seek out the best tax advisors money can buy.

When I approach investing, I look for investments that have favorable tax treatment and provide inflation protection. The best hedges against inflation are hard assets. These include precious metals, commodities, energy, fine art, and more. Basically, hard assets are tangible assets that you can physically touch and handle. Two of the more exciting areas of hard assets right now are precious metals and agricultural commodities. Here at our organization, we have created an inflation-proof investment philosophy called P.A.C.E. investing. This is an acronym: P= Precious Metals, A= Agriculture, C=Commodities, E= Energy.

We have been focusing on these areas for several years, and the benefits have been immense. Since 2007, I have been urging individuals just like you to consider diversifying their investments into these areas. In 2012, we even launched our own actively managed P.A.C.E. investment portfolio. You can get all the details at our website at www. ftmdaily.com/pace.

I consider precious metals to be one of the most exciting areas of investment right now. What I find interesting about precious metals

Breakdown of Global Liquid Wealth

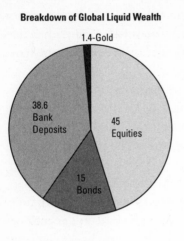

is their current lack of ownership in America. For example, consider the chart detailing the breakdown of global liquid wealth.

Across the globe, investors now own the largest amount of liquid "paper" wealth in recorded history. Out of all of the liquid assets owned worldwide, gold only makes up a fractional 1.4 percent. According to Anthony Allison from the PFS Group, "If just one or two percent of the world's liquid wealth moved into gold in future years, the price rise would be explosive."[2]

Precious metals are typically scorned by governments that churn out paper (fiat) currencies. Their disdain for precious metals is obvious, as precious metals have historically constrained the overproduction of paper currencies. In today's economy, U.S. dollars are printed at will and devalued as needed. Regardless of the government's opinion, precious metals such as gold and silver easily outperform in the midst of economic uncertainty. And if anything is certain, it is that the outlook for the global economy in the coming years is uncertain. Precious metals have always been the beneficiary of poor monetary policies. As America's economy continues to worsen over the coming months and years, I expect more investment dollars to pour into the safe haven of precious metals, thus driving their prices up to very high levels.

Before you invest in gold or silver, or any investment for that matter, always seek advice from a financial professional. Our organization has produced a free, 90-minute educational webinar on the history and future of precious metals. You can watch it at www.ftmdaily.com/gold.

While I am on the topic of investing, allow me to issue a cautionary note about stock investing in general. Many good men and women who want to get ahead financially come to the stock market with dollar signs in their eyes. They simply want to provide a better future for themselves and their families. Be warned up front: no one

— not even the professionals who manage money for a living — knows what the stock market will do. Wall Street is a well-oiled machine in which a novice investor can lose his shirt overnight. Like many, I have made money in the stock market — and I have also lost money. Investing should be approached only after due diligence. Maintain realistic expectations, and don't fall for the hype. Before investing in anything, consult a trusted financial advisor.

Like never before, it has become vital to read between the lines of the news coming daily from the American media machine, especially in the business world. The American media is largely economically illiterate and pushes "doctored" government numbers for a living. I cannot even begin to tell you how many contradictions I see in the business news on a monthly basis.

If you desire to invest in the markets, do so carefully and after much research. You owe it to yourself and your family to distinguish between fact and fiction in the stock market. Not only will a keen awareness of the economy allow you to protect your current assets, but your future wealth depends on it.

Action Step #6 — Protect your growing investment portfolio by keeping it diversified among a variety of asset classes, and commit to learning the "rules of the game."

Strategy #7: Be Cautious of Government-Controlled, Tax-Deferred Savings Plans — IRAs and 401(k)s

> Render to Caesar the things that are Caesar's, and to God the things that are God's (Mark 12:17).

In the past, American companies took responsibility for their employees' retirement by paying for, managing, and placing a guarantee on their retirement benefits. Not so in today's fast-paced and cutthroat business world. Gone are the days of company-paid pension plans and other defined benefit plans. Today, the responsibility for retirement savings has been placed squarely upon the American worker. Instead of the company-funded pension plans of yesteryear, many employees are turning to a variety of other retirement savings vehicles to save for their golden years. Two of the most popular financial products used for retirement are IRA's (Individual Retirement Accounts) and employer-matching 401(k) plans.

What you should know about these two retirement savings vehicles is that they are both government-created and, therefore, government-controlled plans. Under these government-controlled plans, the federal government makes all of the rules, both on the money going in and on the money coming out.

Today, many financial advisors are advising their clients to "max out" their contributions to their company 401(k) plan and to traditional IRA plans. Their motive in advising their clients to contribute to these tax-deferred plans is likely rooted in the desire to help them accumulate enough money to retire comfortably. This is a good goal, but I believe that this method may have more risks than meet the eye.

To understand why I am cautious about aggressively funding these plans, you must first understand what it means that these two products are "tax-deferred." When a financial product offers tax-deferred savings, this means that taxes owed on the future growth of the savings are allowed to be "deferred," or delayed, until the person begins receiving distributions at retirement. So far, so good.

Many financial advisors consider the tax-deferred savings provided by the 401(k) and the IRA to be a huge benefit to their clients. The logic goes something like this: since the client will be spending his entire working lifetime in a higher tax bracket and will retire in a lower tax bracket, doesn't it make sense to delay the payment of taxes until he retires and is in a lower tax bracket? Because Americans will be in a lower tax bracket at retirement than in their working years, many consider the tax-deferral provided by the 401(k) and the traditional IRA to be the greatest retirement savings vehicles ever invented.

Sounds good, right? Then let me ask you a question: Based upon what you know so far about the economic challenges facing America, *do you think taxes are going to be higher or lower in the future?* (If you said lower, then proceed to page 1 of this book and begin reading this book again, a little more slowly this time.) If you said that taxes will likely be higher in the future, then you now realize one of my main concerns about these popular retirement savings plans. The logic behind stuffing them full of money breaks down once you think about it longer than five minutes.

In addition, why start with the premise that you are going to be in a lower tax bracket upon retirement? Shouldn't your trusted financial advisor be creating a pool of money for you so that you will be in an even higher tax bracket when you reach the retirement finish line? The whole logic behind these plans seems a bit counterintuitive.

These plans also lack cash flow and provide you with little liquidity. If you have to access this cash, or to begin a cash flow stream, at any point prior to the government-mandated distribution age (currently 59-1/2), you will be hit with a penalty, with few exceptions. These tax-deferred plans are also huge targets of estate taxes, which means that if you pass any of this qualified money on to your heirs at death, the government will take a nice chunk for themselves, again with few exceptions. If you desire to have more control over your own finances, these plans are poor choices.

And don't forget, since they are government-controlled plans, guess who makes all of the rules? What if the federal government decides to help solve the Social Security crisis by placing a 40 percent surcharge on all withdrawals from 401(k)s and IRAs beginning in the year 2020? Could they do that? Sure, they could. Always remember, he who makes the rules, wins.

And your government makes every rule and controls every aspect of the 401(k) and IRA savings vehicles. And while no one can predict future tax law, placing your trust in politicians to keep their hands off your money is a bold wager. Putting your money into a tax-deferred plan is like placing your retirement savings into a lockbox and giving the key to the government. How much of your money do you think they will give back to you? I personally do not want to gamble with the government. I would rather pay the hungry beast their tax money now and walk away than defer the taxes owed only to pay them when the government is even more desperate.

Therefore, I suggest that you consider all of your options before simply placing all of your retirement money into a government-controlled tax-deferred plan. Those who wish to pay taxes up front on a portion of their retirement savings can consider funding a Roth IRA, (or a Roth 401(k) if your company offers one.) A Roth IRA differs from a traditional IRA in that you pay the taxes up front and withdraw your money and earnings tax-free at retirement. Of course, the government knows that this is a sweet deal so they have strict income guidelines on who can participate in these types of plans. There are other creative strategies for those who do not qualify for a Roth IRA.

Finally, understand that your retirement savings plans are not a part of your six-month savings reserve that I have recommended you maintain at all times. Retirement is a long-term need and should not be 100 percent liquid, as a rule. Your six-month savings reserve is for short-term needs and should remain liquid at all times. Because our nation has such poor savings habits, many people only save for retirement but have no liquid savings for emergencies. Confusion over this matter has been the reason that many Americans have had to begin borrowing from their 401(k) or their IRA (long-term savings) just to cover short-term needs. You can avoid falling into this trap by choosing to save for both short-term needs and long-term needs.

Action Step #7 — Use tax-deferred savings accounts like IRAs and 401(k)s with caution. If you work for a company that offers a matching 401(k), take advantage of the match. If you are still more than 15 years away from retirement, consider a Roth IRA.

Strategy #8: Diversify Your Income

> The LORD has blessed my master greatly, and he has become great; and He has given him flocks and herds, silver and gold, male and female servants, and camels and donkeys (Genesis 24:35).

Today, millions of Americans are one paycheck away from bankruptcy or foreclosure on their homes. If you were to lose your job today, would you still have an income one month from now? If not, I would definitely urge you to consider diversifying your income by adding another income stream. Just as you should spread out your savings and investments, I also believe you should diversify your income. It is my personal belief that everyone should have a minimum of two streams of regular income during their working years, and a minimum of five streams at retirement. Abraham exhibited this quality in that the Bible tells us he was rich in cattle, slaves, gold, and silver (see Genesis 13:2, 24:35).

The nice thing is that you do not need a lot of money to create multiple streams of income. But you do need some creativity and a willingness to work hard. Over the years, my wife and I have created several passive income streams, which means they come in month after month regardless of whether we work or not. By diversifying your income through the creation of multiple streams of income, you will be placing a safety net under you and your family in the event of unforeseen circumstances. People who have diversified income also experience the peace of not feeling trapped in their jobs and of not constantly being at the mercy of their employers. When you have multiple streams of income, you can breathe a lot easier knowing that if one stream dries up, other steady sources continue to come in.

We have a new e-book on this topic available on our website at www.ftmdaily.com. It contains details on how to create over 20 different streams of income both now and in retirement. You can get your copy online at ftmdaily.com/incomebook.

While we have compiled a list of over 20 potential streams of income, I truly believe that the list is endless. We are only limited by our imaginations. I have found that the best types of income streams can be found by examining your own hobbies and passions. Determine if there is a way to turn them into a steady stream of income. The whole point of diversifying your income is to generate a number of different paychecks. As the U.S. economy continues to weaken, you will be glad you did.

Action Step #8 — Commit to adding another stream of income to your financial life in the next 12 months.

Conclusion

I want to leave you with one final thought. As you have gathered from this book, the economic system of the United States of America is flawed in a number of ways. The reason the system is so imperfect is the nation's faulty financial foundation. Once you truly grasp the fatal flaws within the system, you may be tempted to become angry. This is especially true if you have a great patriotic love for America. Some may react to this new-found awareness by engaging in activism in the political and economic arenas. While I certainly do not want to discourage anyone from informing the public regarding the impending collapse of our nation's economy, I urge you to protect your own interests first — those of yourself and your family. If you have your entire house in order and have made adequate preparations, then I say debate to your heart's content. But for those who have not, now is *not* the time for debate. It is time to take action!

Thank you for taking time to read this book on the growing American economic crisis. As a Bible-believing Christian, and a businessman, I am genuinely concerned about the economic, cultural, and social path that America is currently on. If you feel the same, I want to urge you to become a part of our growing online community. We need your help to warn the nation about the crisis that is facing all of us. You can contact us with any questions, comments, or speaking requests by visiting our website at www.ftmdaily.com.

Endnotes
1. Craig Copeland, *Finish What You Start* (Santa Monica, CA: Reach Now Institute, Inc., 2010), p. 133.
2. Tony Allison, "The Year of Living Dangerously: Printing Our Economy Back to Prosperity," March 17, 2008, http://financialsense.com/Market/allison/2008/0317.html.

Appendix A

The DSL Savings: A Strategy to Combat Inflation

For the last several years, I have been explaining the importance of diversification when it comes to your finances. I believe diversification should apply to at least three separate areas of your financial life.

1. **Savings diversification** (diversifying your liquidity)
2. **Investment diversification** (diversifying your investment dollars across a wide variety of asset classes)
3. **Income diversification** (creating multiple streams of income into your financial life)

In Level Three of our Five Levels of Financial Freedom, we teach the need to have six months of liquid savings at all times. (That is, six months of your gross income. If you earn $2,000 per month, you should have $12,000 in extreme liquidity at all times.) However, simply having the savings is not enough. Inflation is a constant threat to your financial plan in any modern fiat monetary system. Since the U.S. government can order the Federal Reserve to print money at any time, you better believe that inflation will continue to pose a hazard to your finances. So if you want to dampen the ravaging effects of inflation that cause a loss of purchasing power on your money, diversifying your savings should be a priority. I call this strategy the *Diversified Six-Month Liquid Savings* strategy, in short, *DSL Savings*.

The following describes a sample DS strategy. Let's assume that you earn $30,000 per year. In order to create your DSL Savings, you would need to start saving until you have a total pool of $15,000. The DSL allocation looks like this:

- One-third ($5,000) in U.S. dollars (i.e., savings account or money market)

- One-third ($5,000) in a stable foreign currency or a stable basket of currencies

- One-third ($5,000) in precious metals (i.e., gold and silver)

While this is only one possible diversification strategy for your DSL Savings reserve, I have personally found it to be particularly effective in protecting purchasing power. In fact, my organization has commissioned a study to back-test the performance of this strategy using historical data from the past 20 years.

The analysts who performed the test used the sample allocation strategy described above on the following time periods:

- A 5-year back-test (2007–2011)
- A 10-year back-test (2002–2011)
- A 20-year back-test (1992–2011)

The analysts also had a control test for each time period that compared our DSL Saving strategy to a typical savings account. In this control test, the savings were not diversified, but rather all savings dollars were placed into U.S. treasury bills receiving the 3-month T-bill rate. The purpose of the control test was to determine whether a person using DSL Savings would have accumulated more money over each time period than a person keeping all their savings in a U.S. dollar-denominated savings account. Our findings were completely stunning. The first results you will see in figure A.1 represent the control group, which used only 3-month Treasury bills. The relevant measure used in our study was the total return on savings after inflation. Also, all interest earned during a particular year was assumed to be reinvested back into the Treasury bills. The results are shown in the table below.

Figure A.1 Return on Non-Diversified Savings

Time Period	Percent Return on T-Bills after Inflation
2007–2011	-5.1
2002–2011	-6.7
1992–2011	10.0

Notice that the only positive return (10.0 percent) in the non-diversified savings strategy occurred in the 20-year time period, from 1992 to 2011. But the total return for the other two periods was negative. How can this be if the rate of return for a T-bill was never negative? Simply put . . . inflation. Inflation is a major eroding factor on money, and although the savings dollars in the non-diversified strategy were earning interest, the interest earned was counteracted by the effects of inflation, which actually caused the purchasing power of the savings account to fall below the original principal amount in real terms.

So how did our DSL Savings strategy hold up under these same back-testing methods? Let's take a look. This next section of results in figure A.2 represents the DSL Savings allocation model. Remember, the money is allocated three ways according to the following model:

- One-third in 3-month T-bills (constantly being reinvested each time they matured)

- One-third in stable foreign currencies (equally divided among Swiss Francs, Canadian Dollars, and Australian Dollars)

- One-third in precious metals (equally divided among gold and silver). If you are wondering whether physical bullion is liquid, it is, especially when you use a dealer like we do who does not charge a sell-back fee.

As in the first test, all returns of this separate test were calculated on an after-inflation basis. Additionally, the same time periods used in the control group were used in this test.

Figure A.2 Return on DSL Savings

Time Period	Percent Return on DSL Savings
2007–2011	54.7
2002–2011	205.2
1992–2011	201.6

As you can imagine, we were stunned by the results. We found that the return on DSL Savings was well above the return on non-diversified savings in every single time period. For example, if we look at the time period of 2007–2011, the return on undiversified savings is -5.1 percent, whereas the return on DSL Savings strategy is 54.7 percent!

To further visualize the difference diversification makes in your savings dollars, we have summarized the results in the graph labeled figure A.3.

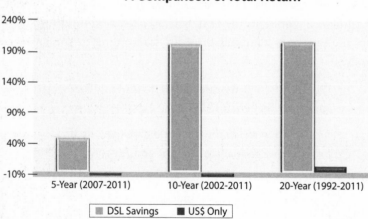

Figure A.3. 'DSL' Savings vs. Regular Savings:
A Comparison of Total Return

As you can see, the return on DSL Savings far exceeds the return for the non-diversified savings in each of the time period studies. In two of the time periods, the non-diversified savings actually loses money (after inflation). Finally, let's consider the results of the study from one more angle: the total dollar amount accumulated in savings. Check out the charts on the following page.

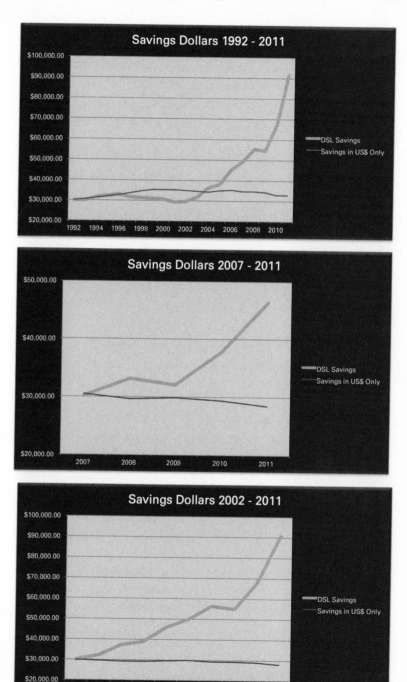

The charts show the total dollar amount in both savings strategies each year over the given time period. The amount in the non-diversified savings remains flat or even drops below the initial amount. Meanwhile, the DSL Savings strategy increases overall, not only helping to hedge against inflation, but also earning money on an after-inflation basis! (And isn't inflation protection what every wise investor is seeking right now?)

Finally, it is important to remember what the DSL Savings strategy is, and what it is not. It is a savings strategy. It is not an investing strategy. Thanks to decades of brainwashing from Wall Street and the mainstream financial media, most Americans do not understand the important difference between investing and saving. They are entirely different topics and should be treated as such.

The bottom line: Based on historical data, diversifying can protect your savings from the eroding power of inflation and can even help grow your savings on an after-inflation basis.

I will admit that I was completely shocked by the results. In fact, when I first saw them, I remember demanding that they be re-checked for accuracy. But sure enough, the returns were real. And while I expected my DSL Savings strategy system to outperform a typical savings account, I did not expect it to even outperform many investments during the same period! All it took was a little bit of diversification. We held the money in three separate areas: stable foreign currencies, precious metals, and U.S. dollar-denominated assets, which are all very liquid.

And that's it. No secrets, no magic tricks, and no late-night infomercial gimmicks (although that last one would have been fun). Just plain vanilla diversification. Isn't it amazing how just a little bit of diversification can make such a big difference!

It is important to remember that the primary goal when choosing a holding place for your DSL Savings reserve dollars is liquidity, since your DSL Savings serves at least two purposes:

- **Emergency fund** (When you have six months of liquid savings, you won't need to rely on your credit cards as much when a need for cash arises.)

- **Opportunity capital** (Those who have a ready pool of liquid cash are able to take advantage of opportunities that those without cash cannot.)

Here's what your DSL Savings reserve is not:

- **Retirement savings** (Retirement savings is often not very liquid because you are not going to use it until retirement; think IRA or 401k.)

- **Education saving**s (That is separate from your DSL Savings reserve.)

- **An investment** (Unlike an investment, DSL Savings is a powerful liquidity system that is designed to give you a cushion in times of emergency, as well as to take advantage of special opportunities when they come your way.)

Over the years, I have run into many people who think saving money is a waste of time or that it is unnecessary. These are usually the same people who rely on credit cards when they get a flat tire and who have to pull money out of their IRA or 401(k) when an emergency arises. Usually, these are also the same people who feel that they need to hit a home run with every single investment. In my opinion, this is a poor lifestyle choice. I prefer to have diversified liquid cash on hand that I can quickly access in case of an emergency or if a great opportunity arises.

Let me make this clear: A lack of liquidity is not an option for the days ahead. You must have access to liquid cash if you are going to create a successful financial game plan.

Appendix B

The Five Levels of Financial Freedom

THE **FIVE** LEVELS OF **FINANCIAL** FREEDOM

1	2	3	4	5
BUILD AN EMERGENCY RESERVE	ASSET, INCOME & LIFE PROTECTION	BUILD & DIVERSIFY FINACIAL RESERVES	BUILD & DIVERSIFY INVESTMENTS	ADVANCED INVESTING SPECULATIVE

Level One — PREPARE — Build An Emergency Reserve

In Level One, your goals are to:

Create a Charitable Giving Plan — (Similar to a financial plan, but here you are estimating a goal of how much money you want to give away over your lifetime.)

Create a "Go" Bag — (A 72-hour emergency kit containing all of life's essentials for at least three full days in case of a home fire, wicked weather, or other disaster.)

Create 3 Months of Food and Water Supplies

Begin a Systematic Savings Plan — (Your ultimate goal is to save at least 15 percent of your income each month, but begin where you can, even if it is only 1 percent.)

Build Two Months of Liquid Savings — (Base this upon your current gross monthly income. If you earn $3,000 every month, you would build up $6,000.)

Level Two — PROTECT — Asset, Income, and Life Protection

In Level Two, your goals are to obtain adequate:

Asset Protection — Auto, home, and liability insurance

Income Protection — Disability, health, and long-term care insurance

Life Protection — Life insurance, wills, and trusts

Level Three — SAVE — Build and Diversify Financial Reserves

In Level Three, your goals are to:

Build a Total of 6 Months Food and Water Supply

Build a Total of 6 Months Gross Income Saved — (Base this upon your current gross monthly income. If you earn $3,000 every month, you would build up $18,000.)

Diversify Six Months Liquid Savings — (Example: 1/3 in U.S. dollars, 1/3 in stable foreign currencies, 1/3 in precious metals)

Level Four — INVEST — Build and Diversify Investments

In Level Four, your goals are to:

Invest Broadly Across Various Asset Classes

Remember P.A.C.E. for Inflation Protection — (P = Precious Metals, AC = Agricultural Commodities, E = Energy)

Avoid Overweighting in One Area — (Because the "rules of the game" can change at any time)

Trade Cash for Cash Flow When Possible

Create Multiple Streams of Income — (In order to achieve financial freedom, income diversification is vital)

Level Five — FREEDOM — Advanced Investing and Speculation

In Level Five, your goals are to advance into:

Opening or Expanding Your Own Business

Stock/Option Trading Strategies

Venture Capital

Real Estate Investment Strategies

For free articles and videos on how to begin implementing our Five Levels of Financial Freedom in your own life, please visit www. ftmdaily.com/5levels.

Frequently Asked Questions from Our Readers

Q: If gold prices are going to go higher, why not put all of my money into gold?

A: I teach the importance of diversifying your investments across various asset classes: some paper assets, some hard assets, some real estate, etc. While it may seem smart to put all of your investment funds into something that you feel will perform well in the future, it is not. The key to safeguarding your future wealth is positioning your investments in such a way that they can withstand any change in the "rules of the game." The federal government makes the "rules" and the rules are found in the Federal Tax Code. In order to stay in the game, you have to play by the rules. To avoid being punished, it is vital to not have all your "eggs in one basket."

Q: Where is the best place to buy gold?

A: Over the years, I have purchased gold and silver from various sources. Today, however, I purchase all of my gold, silver, palladium, and investment-grade diamonds from one company that I have come to trust. They provide me with the best rates, free shipping and insurance, and great customer service. If you have a similar relationship with a precious metals dealer, I recommend that you buy from them. However, if you don't have a trusted precious metals advisor, then feel free to contact mine. His name is Tom Cloud and he has been in the precious metals business since 1977. He not only has the best prices but he also takes the time to discuss my goals and my overall portfolio. The best part is that he personally answers the phone, and you do not have to listen to any recordings, like "Press 1 for Gold."

Since the price of gold has been in a decade-long bull run, you may have noticed the TV commercials, billboards, radio ads, and magazine spreads with many of the major gold companies touting the reasons you should buy gold from them. Although I am sure there are many great dealers out there, I personally do not buy my gold through a call center, where I will likely be talking to a new hire trying to get as much commission as he or she can.

Tom buys and sells more than just gold. He also deals in silver, palladium, platinum, and diamonds. I would encourage you to visit www.ftmdaily.com/gold to learn more about precious metals investing. I have conducted several video and audio interviews with Tom about the fundamentals of precious metals investing.

Q: I have heard some experts say that you should hold your physical gold and silver forever. Do you think there's ever a time to sell?

A: I believe that there will come a time in the next 4–6 years when I will begin selling at the peaks to the late-comers. For now, I am buying more on the dips. Nothing goes up in a straight line forever. It's that type of thinking that created the dot-com crash, the real estate crisis, and every other bubble throughout history. I do not believe that precious metals are in a bubble yet. But when I believe that a bubble is forming, I will begin slowly exiting the market. I will alert our FTM Insiders when I begin selling.

Q: I used to watch CNBC quite often (not so much anymore because I listen to your show and check your website daily). They hardly ever talked about the benefits of gold and silver as an investment? Why is this?

A: The mainstream media likes its advertisers . . . pure and simple. For the last couple of decades, mutual funds have ruled Wall Street. They are major advertisers with the mainstream media. It is a fact that they practically own many of today's most prolific financial commentators. Suze Orman and Dave Ramsey are two great examples of commentators who are sponsored by mutual funds. If you have ever listened to Dave Ramsey's program, he thinks everyone needs to put their money in "good growth mutual funds." By the way, Mr. Ramsey hates gold. Coincidentally, so do mutual fund companies.

That's why I am huge proponent of independent news sources and the independent media. Those who don't know how Wall Street works should read a great book entitled *The Pirates of Manhattan* by Barry James Dyke.

Q: Jerry, I am 32 years old and I want to open an IRA to begin saving for retirement. Should I open a traditional IRA or a Roth IRA?

A: The key to answering this question is to ask yourself, "What kind of tax benefit do I need and/or prefer?" The first type of tax benefit you can receive from an IRA is the tax deduction now. When you deposit money into a Traditional IRA, assuming you meet all other requirements, you receive a 100 percent tax deduction up to the max (currently $5,000) for the current tax year. This benefit is useful in two ways. First, for those who need a tax break now, you get to keep your money in a savings account and get the tax deduction up front. Second, the money grows tax-deferred until you begin taking withdrawals at age 59-1/2 or later. Withdrawals are taxed as ordinary income at the rate you pay at the time of withdrawal. In essence, you will end up paying taxes on your capital gains, dividends, and interest once you begin taking the money out.

The second type of tax benefit you can receive from an IRA is the "tax-free growth" benefit. You can take advantage of tax-free growth through a Roth IRA. Basically, when you contribute to a Roth, you do not get the tax deduction in the current year. Instead, you pay your ordinary income tax rate on all contributions in the current year (up to the contribution limit). However, the withdrawals you take from a

Roth, beginning at age 59-1/2 or later, are tax-free income. Therefore, all capitals gains, dividends, and interest earned on the money are able to grow completely tax-free. One caveat is that you cannot contribute to a Roth IRA if your adjusted gross income is over $110,000 (single) or $173,000 (married filing jointly) in tax-year 2012. Please see the IRS website or speak to your tax advisor for up-to-date data on IRA limits and income ranges.

One factor that I believe everyone should at least consider when deciding between Roth and traditional is whether you believe tax rates are going to increase in the future. This is very important because, if you are like me and believe taxes will increase, it may be smart to go ahead and pay Uncle Sam now (as much as you don't want to!) instead of 20–30 years from now. A quick look at the history of tax rates demonstrates that the highest marginal tax rate has averaged 59 percent since 1913 when the income tax was introduced. Currently, people in the top tax bracket only pay about 35 percent, which is well below the historical average. Furthermore, during the entire period between 1940 and 1963, the top marginal tax rate was above 80 percent. If you have read the rest of this book, I don't have to tell you that our government "needs" more money, and increased tax revenues is one way to get it! I believe the tax rates will increase dramatically in the future, making a Roth a better choice personally.

But you should always speak with a trusted financial advisor before making any financial decisions. If you need help finding a financial advisor, please visit www.cfanetwork.org.

Q: My company offers a Roth 401(k) option for employees. Should I roll over my 401(k) to the Roth?

A: Without knowing your age and your current tax situation, this is difficult to answer. Due to my belief that tax rates have nowhere to go but up, I would personally prefer the Roth 401(k). While you forgo the benefit of an upfront tax deduction, the advantage of tax-free withdrawals at retirement is hard to ignore. I would meet with a trusted financial advisor who can advise you based upon your specific financial situation.

Q: I have read in numerous financial publications that annuities are very expensive. However, in your quarterly newsletter and on your radio show, I often hear you speak positively about annuities. Why should I buy an annuity if I will be charged such large fees?

A: Annuities are not good . . . and they are not bad. As a financial product, they are simply a tool that can be used for a specific financial purpose. Your financial goals should dictate your financial strategy. And your financial strategy should then dictate the kinds of financial products that you use to achieve your goals. If your goals include not outliving your money, then why would an annuity be ignored as a potential financial product? An annuity is just a tool that you can use to construct your financial house. Who would say that a hammer is a bad tool? That would be absurd, especially if you needed to drive a nail into the wall. An annuity is a unique financial product, or tool, that is specifically designed to convert a pile of cash into a lifetime stream of cash flow. What other product does that?

You will never hear me say, "Everyone should invest in this, or no one should buy that." The people who make such remarks are those who are controlled by their sponsors (think Dave Ramsey, Suze Orman).

So what kinds of people should think about purchasing an annuity? Those who desire protection of their principal, tax-deferred growth, and a guaranteed lifetime stream of income. Some annuities even offer inflation protection. What product can compete with this? And who expects these benefits to be free? Of course these benefits will cost you money. But I have seen many mutual funds that cost way more than the fixed annuities that I like. So the question is not why should you buy an annuity. It is more accurate to ask: "Do my financial goals include not outliving my income?" And if so, "What is the best financial product for achieving that goal?" If there is a better financial product offered at a lower cost for achieving a lifetime income stream than a fixed or fixed indexed annuity, by all means go with it. Personally, I know of none.

Q: You talk about the "wealth effect" on your radio show a lot. What exactly is this?

A: I have talked about the "wealth effect" frequently over the years. Basically, the wealth effect is defined as a phenomenon when you raise your consumption level in response to a rise in the value of your personal assets — such as real estate holdings, 401(k) plan, or stocks.

It's a basic economic principle that when we feel richer, we feel more confident and therefore, we tend to spend more. Think about how your own lifestyle has changed over the years along with your income. The wealth effect is rooted in the same basic principle. In essence:

> More perceived wealth = more confidence.
>
> And more confidence = more consumption.

Why is this important? Because Washington and the Federal Reserve are currently working overtime to create a wealth effect among consumers in order to drive consumption higher. In fact, one of the primary reasons that the Federal Reserve is pumping so much money into the economy right now is to cause asset prices to rise, which in turn, creates the wealth effect.

Consider this statement, from Federal Reserve Chairman Ben Bernanke, which was published in the Washington Post on November 5, 2010, right after the Fed announced that they were going to begin their QE2 program:

> Higher stock prices will boost consumer wealth and help increase confidence, which can also spur spending. Increased spending will lead to higher incomes and profits that, in a virtuous circle, will further support economic expansion.

Unfortunately for Mr. Bernanke, QE2 did not lead to increased real estate prices or meaningful employment levels.

Q: Do you do seminars or conferences at churches? If so, how can I book you at my church?

A: Yes. Jerry Robinson and the FTMDaily team can bring the "Building True Wealth" financial seminar to your church or organization.

Attendees of our seminars learn vitally important information through a series of sessions tailored to meet your audience's needs. Sessions include topics such as multiple streams of income, precious metals investing, coping with debt, charitable giving, business creation ideas, economic crisis updates, and FTMDaily's exclusive Five Levels of Financial Freedom.

Attendees are also given the rare opportunity to ask Jerry Robinson all their questions about money, business, investing, and where the economy is headed. Each Building True Wealth seminar includes Q&A sessions all throughout the seminar, as well as unique opportunities to speak with Jerry one-on-one.

If you are interested in bringing Jerry Robinson and the Building True Wealth seminar to your church or organization, please visit www.ftmdaily.com/seminar to find out more.

Q: Jerry, you talk about the collapse of the dollar like it will definitely happen, but I want to know when it will happen. What are the signs that a dollar-collapse is near?

A: The question of timing is interesting and yet very difficult. We live in a very different economic era than we experienced just a few decades ago. From the 1940s–1990s, the U.S. dollar was the international reserve currency held by virtually all nations for the settlement of global trade. Those of us who were not alive to witness any other economic system can barely fathom the thought of the dollar losing its supremacy in global affairs. The same problem affected Great Britain in the early 20th century. Throughout the 18th and 19th century, the British pound currency was the international reserve currency. Because of the immense economic power of the British Empire, the pound was widely held and used for transactions all over the world. But early in the 20th century, the United States of America began rising to global prominence — first economically, then politically. (Remember, economic power typically precedes political power . . . think China.)

As the nimble United States grew, it gradually displaced the debt-burdened and militarily overextended British Empire. As nations began to depend more on the U.S., they began to rely less and less on Great Britain. The loss, and subsequent transfer of global empire status to

America, was bruising to the British psyche and to their national pride.

Today we are witnessing something remarkably similar to the transference of global economic and political power that occurred at the beginning of the 20th century. This time, the mantle of global empire is falling from the shoulders of a debt-burdened and militarily overextended United States, and into the hands of a growing crop of new competitors. Europe and China both immediately come to mind. Of course, there are others. But these two regions stand out as real contenders as we head further into the 21st century.

With this background, I expect to see the United States continue to suffer consistent and devastating blows to its international credibility and to its economic supremacy.

The events that I will be monitoring are 1) the U.S. government bond market, 2) the continual rise of China and Europe, 3) the continued destruction of the U.S. dollar through more monetary stimulus via the Federal Reserve, 4) the inability of the United States to gain military victories in places that should be easily obtained, and finally, 5) the complete breakdown of the petrodollar system.

Q: I have heard you say over and over on your show that people should sit down with a trusted financial advisor. I am a very organized and educated person when it comes to my finances. Is a financial advisor a good idea for everyone?

A: A good financial advisor has the benefit of being able to look at your entire financial picture prior to making a recommendation. Giving out recommendations without knowing a person's entire financial picture is akin to malpractice in my mind. There is no "one size fits all" approach when it comes to your financial game plan. While there are certainly some good guidelines, there is no silver bullet that will work for everyone every time. It is vital that you know your entire financial picture, including your financial goals, prior to making any investment decisions. This is why meeting with a trusted financial advisor is so vital. You may, in fact, never conduct any business with an advisor. But just the act of meeting with one and gathering all of your financial information will be an educational experience that will help you better understand your finances.

Q: I am a Christian believer, and I have heard my pastor say that if you are storing food and water supplies, you are not trusting God to provide for your needs. Do you advocate the "Go Bag" and the 6-months' food and water supply for *Christians*?

A: I have a very wise and experienced Christian friend named Rob, who wrote the following in a recent issue of our quarterly newsletter. I am in full agreement with what he says about the wisdom of preparing for emergency situations.

There is wisdom in preparing you and your family but I must tell you before we get started that I believe this action is but ONE part in a larger and more comprehensive approach. As a follower of Christ, this so-called "survival" mindset is terribly handicapped if we cannot translate it into serving something greater than ourselves. We can be a tremendous service to our community if we are prepared with just the basic emergency supplies that are outlined by the American Red Cross and Federal Emergency Management Agency (FEMA). In doing so, we would be able to weather the first critical 78 hours of a disaster and not be a drain on the scarce food and water supplies coming in from the government relief mechanisms and first responders. Those scarce resources could then go to the people who really need the assistance. The more people who prepare with basic food and water, the easier it will be on the community as a whole to recover from the emergency. Instead of trying to find food and water for your family, you'll have your own ready supply. It increases your chances of being a part of the solution rather than being on the other side needing assistance.

On a practical level, imagine the following scenario. A modest 100-member church could work wonders in its community by developing and implementing a food storage plan

---

FREE STOCKPILE LIST!

Pre-planning is key to an effective emergency supplies list. Need help in preparing your list? Get a free comprehensive stockpile list today by visiting www.ftmdaily.com.

to be able to feed themselves and hundreds of other people in their community in an emergency. The church leaders would encourage each member to build a one-year food supply. This would enable church members to be self-sufficient in food with at least two meals a day per person for six months. They would have the remaining four months of food to help out the needy in their community. If all 100 members did this, the church combined would have 12,000 days of food with two meals per day or 24,000 meals. This one church could feed 500 people one meal a day for 48 days. There is strength in numbers.

The Scriptures are full of examples like Joseph who implemented a countrywide master plan for the Egyptian pharaoh. Joseph collected grain over the seven years of plenty in preparation for seven years of famine. Joseph's plan was comprehensive in that he built the necessary grain storage facilities, collected the grain and had in place a grain distribution system during the years of famine. Egypt was saved and so was Jacob's house. Prepare your plan before a crisis happens and do not wait until it is upon you. Remember too that it was not raining when Noah built the ark.

Q: In October 2007, you stated, "We (America) are about to enter the greatest financial crisis in world history." How did you see this crisis coming when it seemed like such a shock to the media?

A: I recall the internal difficulty I had with making such a statement, as I am extremely proud of the entrepreneurial strength of our nation. It has been America's ingenuity and strong work ethic coupled with our attempt at a free-market system that has allowed us to rise to the top of the world's heap. Unfortunately, along the way there were a number of negative influences upon our nation, including central banking schemes. The Federal Reserve System is nothing more than a leach upon our government and upon the American people. The government has knowingly allowed the Fed to bring untold damage to this nation. The central bank's destructive policies, along with its foreign entanglements, make it enemy number one on my list.

Additionally, our monetary system is fraudulent because it is faith-based. No paper currency on this planet can offer any true store of value, because the only thing backing it up is the "full faith and credit" of the underlying government. Today, people around the world are losing "faith" in their governments and in their governments' ability to maintain financial order. The world is waking up and smelling the coffee regarding the global fiat paper money system.

In addition to being "faith-based," our monetary system is also debt-based. It is absurd to even say this, but today's paper currency is debt. Hold a dollar bill in your hand and you are holding one dollar worth of debt. Every dollar in existence has been loaned to the federal government at interest by the Federal Reserve. It's all debt. And it's not just America that is this way. Every nation is the same because the global central banking interests have wrapped their tentacles around this world. They are intent upon maintaining their stranglehold as long as possible.

To me, it is simple economics:

1. Central banks have a history of exploiting nations

2. Paper currencies have a 100 percent failure rate

3. We have a population that has trained its leaders through the ballot box that it expects low taxes, more benefits, global wars, low gas prices, and low interest rates

4. You cannot spend more than you earn

5. You cannot fight a debt problem with more debt

The greatest financial crisis in world history that I referred to in 2007 is still coming. We have only witnessed the warm-up.

Q: I have a 12-year-old son and a 5-year-old daughter. I know they will not receive a proper education on money in the public (or even private) school system. What is a good way to start teaching my children some of the principles you advocate?

A: All of the financial and business principles that have made me successful came from real-world experience. None of them were taught to me in the public school system. Even as an economics student at the university level, many of the principles I learned turned out to be highly impractical. My wife, who has a master's degree in finance, has expressed on numerous occasions that she did not learn the true essentials of money until after she graduated college. So we as parents must take on the responsibility of training our children properly when it comes to making money and using money wisely.

I believe there are two basic principles you can teach your children from a very early age:

1. **Don't expect handouts**. Now, this may seem a bit harsh, but children need to learn this or else they will grow up thinking they are entitled to a job, entitled to a house, entitled to a car, entitled to a new flat-screen TV, etc. Of course, parents should always provide for the basic needs of their children no matter what. I am talking about the extras here.

   My wife and I have a baby boy, and although he is not even out of diapers yet, we have already discussed a plan to help him learn about money. Part of this plan includes alternatives to the customary big-ticket items that parents dole out to their children (for which they often go into massive debt). For example, we do not see the need to buy our child a brand new car at age 16, pay for a $50,000 wedding at age 22, or even pay for college (gasp!). We do not hold these beliefs because we want to make our child suffer, but because we care too much about him to pass on an entitlement mentality.

2. **Saving money is a good thing**. Children are bombarded with just as many marketing ploys as adults. If they are not taught properly, they will be convinced that they need to spend all the money they receive on the newest toy or gadget. Trust me, they will not automatically want to save their money. We must teach them this by speech and by example. And since my wife and I are not planning to buy the big- ticket items that are unnecessary, our children will need to have some savings if they want to buy a car, go to college, or take a big vacation when they graduate.

Some practical ways to teach these concepts to your children include:

- *Commission, not allowance.* Post several jobs your children can do during the month in addition to their regular chores. Let them know that completing these tasks goes above and beyond, so they will receive a commission based on their effort.

- *Start a business.* Children can learn entrepreneurship at a very young age. They can scrap metal, bake cookies, mow lawns, make crafts, tutor younger children, and the list could go on.

- *Make gifts instead of purchasing gifts.* Instead of spending hundreds, if not thousands, of dollars on birthdays and Christmas gifts, teach children that meaningful gifts come from the heart. Do you feel like you have to out-do last year's birthday for your children? Or get them a bigger Christmas gift than last year? Why? Because you may have taught them to expect these gifts, and they will be disappointed if they don't receive them. Making gifts lowers the expectation and also gets rid of the entitlement mentality that children often possess on those special days of the year. As a bonus, making gifts instills creativity, too.

- *Create a simple budget.* Teach children to allocate their money properly at an early age. For example, 10 percent goes to charity or church, 50 percent goes to long-term savings (he won't touch until age 18), 20 percent goes to short-term savings (new bike, cell phone, weekend trip, etc), and 20 percent is spending money.

Q: Should I buy term life insurance or whole life insurance? Dave Ramsey says term is the only way to go, but you say whole life insurance is also worth considering. What should I do?

A: It depends on your purposes and financial goals. Term life insurance is a good option for those who want to rent their insurance. Whole life insurance is best for those who want to own their insurance.

Q: If I retire and move out of the country, do I still get (USA) Social Security?

A: Yes! If you are an American citizen or are a legal immigrant and move to another country then you can receive your Social Security in just about any country in the world. You can either receive it in form of a check sent to you overseas, or you can open a bank account in a legitimate and credible bank overseas and then request your Social Security checks to come in the form of direct deposit. Usually, if you are in a country where there is a U.S. embassy, they have a Social Security office inside the embassy. The U.S. consulate can also assist you as far as accrediting who you are and helping with the filing of the transfer of your Social Security checks to either a physical address in that country or by way of direct deposit to a bank of your choosing in the country where you want to live.

Q: Do you have an investment fund for those of us who wish to invest the way you do?

A: While I am not an investment advisor, I have teamed up with a faith-based investment professional and certified financial planner to create my very own P.A.C.E. investment portfolio. It is composed of stocks and ETFs in companies involved in precious metals, agriculture, commodities, and energy. It also contains many world-dominating dividend-paying companies. To learn more about our investing approach, please visit http://www.ftmdaily.com/pace.

Glossary

2036 crisis. The crisis that is forecast to take place in the year 2036 due to entitlement spending at the federal government level; the entire federal budget is expected to be consumed by Social Security and Medicare payments alone by 2036.

bank failure. Occurs when a bank is unable to meet its obligations to its depositors or other creditors because it has become insolvent or too illiquid to meet its liabilities.

bank run. Occurs when a large number of customers withdraw their deposits because they believe the bank is, or might become, insolvent.

bear market. A condition of the stock market in which stock prices are generally declining and most of the participants expect this decline to continue for months or even years; investors see a sluggish, stagnant economy with few signs of robust growth.

Bretton Woods Agreement. A post-World War II agreement among 40 allied nations that called for the United States to link its currency to gold at a pre-determined fixed rate of $35.00 per ounce. This agreement also instituted the World Bank, the International Monetary Fund (IMF), and the General Agreement on Trades and Tariffs (GATT).

bull market. A condition of the stock market in which stock prices are generally rising and the trend is expected to continue.

"buy now, pay later." The mentality that has infiltrated the government and the citizens of the United States that has created the massive debt burden in the nation; the mentality that one does not need to possess adequate funds to obtain goods and services.

capitalism. An economic system characterized by private or corporate ownership of capital goods, by investments that are determined by private decision, and by prices, production, and the distribution of goods that are determined primarily by competition in a free market.

central bank. The entity responsible for overseeing the monetary system of a nation or group of nations; responsibilities include issuing the national currency, regulating money supply, and controlling interest rates.

Certificate of Deposit (CD). A type of savings account, commonly termed a CD, maintained by banks and other depository institutions that pays higher interest rates than normal savings accounts, but requires that the funds not be withdrawn for a specified time period.

commodity. A basic good used in commerce that can be exchanged for other goods of the same type.

commodity money. A form of money that has an intrinsic value. Commodity money can be used for trade or can be consumed by the owner.

communism. A theory advocating elimination of private property; all goods are owned in common and available to all as needed.

compound interest. Interest that accrues on both the principal and the accrued interest.

consumption trap. Three powerful financial forces (corporations, media/advertisers, and financial institutions) that work in a unified way to slowly erode your wealth on a consistent basis.

debt slavery. The sabotaging of one's own financial future in order to obey the commands of corporate masters through overconsumption with borrowed money.

debt stacking. A method of paying off debt that involves paying down the debt with the highest interest rate first, while making only minimum payments on other debt. Once highest rate debt is paid off, use the payment you were making to pay down the next highest interest rate, and so on.

debt-based wealth. An illusion of wealth that is created by an ever-increasing amount of debt; there is no equity in the assets owned, only liabilities.

deficit spending. The amount by which a government, private company, or individual's spending exceeds income over a particular period of time.

deflation. An extended decline in the average level of prices.

demand. An economic principle that describes a consumer's desire and willingness to pay a price for a specific good or service. Holding all other factors constant, the price of a good or service increases as its demand increases, and vice versa.

"dollars for gold." The arrangement under the Bretton Woods Agreement under which any person holding U.S. dollars was able to exchange those dollars for a fixed amount of gold; this arrangement ended with President Richard Nixon in 1971.

"dollars for oil." The arrangement under the petrodollar system under which any person holding U.S. dollars is able to purchase oil from OPEC nations; this system is currently breaking down as many Middle East nations are accepting other forms of currency.

DSL Savings. A diversification strategy for savings dollars that is intended to protect savings from the eroding factors on money: D = Diversified, S = Six Month, L = Liquid.

empire. An extensive group of states or countries under a single supreme authority.

"faith-based" currency. See fiat currency.

Federal Reserve Note: Paper currency issued by each of the 12 Federal Reserve District Banks in denominations of $1, $5, $10, $20, $50, and $100. Unlike paper currency of the past that was issued by the U.S. Treasury, these notes are backed by the Federal Reserve System.

FDIC. An independent agency of the United States (U.S.) federal government that preserves public confidence in the banking system by insuring deposits.

fiat currency. A currency that is backed up only by government decree; a fiat currency has no intrinsic value.

financial literacy. The ability to understand finance, and more importantly, to possess skills and knowledge that allow you to make informed decisions about your personal financial situation.

First Bank of the United States. A central bank, chartered for a term of 20 years, by the United States Congress on February 25, 1791.

fiscal policy. A governmental policy that attempts to influence the direction of the economy through either an increase or decrease in government spending and taxes.

Five Levels of Financial Freedom. Developed by Jerry Robinson, these are the five levels of economic and financial planning that are designed to help an individual achieve true financial freedom (see appendix for more).

fractional-reserve banking. A banking system in which only a fraction of bank deposits are backed by actual cash on-hand and are available for withdrawal.

global reserve currency. A currency that is held in significant quantities by many governments and institutions as part of their foreign exchange reserves. It also tends to be the international pricing currency for products traded on a global market, and commodities such as oil, gold, etc.

go bag. An emergency kit that contains everything necessary for survival for a period of up to 72 hours.

gold standard. A monetary standard under which the basic unit of currency is equal in value to and exchangeable for a specified amount of gold.

goldsmith banking. A system under which an individual deposits gold with a goldsmith in exchange for a paper receipt stating the amount on deposit.

government-controlled savings plan. Savings plans, such as IRAs and 401(k)s, for which the Congress makes all the rules, including tax consequences and early withdrawal penalties.

"Greenspan Doctrine." The consistent reduction of interest rate targets in response to financial turmoil (originated by former Federal Reserve Chairman Alan Greenspan).

gross domestic product (GDP). The monetary value of all the finished goods and services produced within a country's borders in a specific time period, though GDP is usually calculated on an annual basis. It includes all of private and public consumption, government outlays, investments, and exports less imports that occur within a defined territory.

hyperinflation. An inflation that is very high or out of control. See also inflation.

hyperinflationary depression. An extreme increase in inflation and an extreme deflation in debt.

illusion of prosperity. The financial state of a debt-based monetary system in which citizens seem to be prospering financial, but the intrinsic value of the money is zero.

income diversification. Creating streams of income that originate from multiple sources, not simply relying on one job or one business for total income.

inflation. An increase in the quantity of money that is not offset by a corresponding increase in the need for money, so that a fall in the objective exchange-value of money must occur.[1]

interest. Money that is paid to a lender on money that is borrowed; the cost of borrowing money.

International Monetary Fund (IMF). An organization of 188 countries founded in 1944, working to foster global monetary cooperation, secure financial stability, facilitate international trade, promote high employment and sustainable economic growth, and reduce poverty around the world.

intrinsic value. The actual value of an asset based on an underlying perception of its true value.

Medicaid. A joint federal and state program that helps low-income individuals or families pay for the costs associated with long-term medical and custodial care, provided they qualify. Although largely funded by the federal government, Medicaid is run by the state, where coverage may vary.

Medicare. A federal system of health insurance for people over 65 years of age and for certain younger people with disabilities.

medium of exchange. Something that is universally accepted as a payment for goods and services and repayment of debts.

mercantilism. The main economic system used during the 16th to the 18th centuries; it was believed that a nation's strength could be maximized by limiting imports via tariffs and maximizing exports.

monetary policy. Attempt made by the Federal Reserve to influence the economy through either an increase or decrease of interest rates, reserve requirements, and/or securities purchases.

money. Something generally accepted as a medium of exchange, store of value, or a unit of account.

money supply. The total amount of money available in the economy at a specific time.

National Banking Act. Passed in 1863 in the United States, this act made provisions for the federal government to control a number of national banks, who were responsible for purchasing the federal government bonds with their own created bank notes.

National Monetary Commission. A team of experts commissioned in 1908 by President Theodore Roosevelt to learn how to create a central bank in America; their findings became the basis for the Federal Reserve System.

national debt. The total amount of debt a country's government has on its accounting records.

Organization of Petroleum Exporting Countries (OPEC). A group of countries founded in 1960 that choose to collaborate in order to manage the exportation of their crude oil to the rest of the world; due to their ability to adjust production levels, this group possesses a great deal of influence over the price of oil.

outsource. Obtain goods or a service from an outside supplier in place of an internal source.

overconsumption. A situation where resource-use has outpaced the sustainable capacity of the ecosystem. A prolonged pattern of over-consumption leads to inevitable environmental degradation and the eventual loss of resource bases.

P.A.C.E. An investing philosophy originally developed by Jerry Robinson in order to protect assets from inflation and/or hyperinflation: P = Precious metals, A = Agriculture, C = Commodities, E = Energy.

petrodollar system. A system developed in the 1970s whereby Middle East oil sales would be denominated in U.S. dollars in exchange for political, economic, and military benefits.

principal. Amount of money borrowed, or the amount borrowed that remains unpaid (excluding interest).

purchasing power. The amount or number of goods and services that can be purchased with a unit of currency.

receipt money. A form of money in which paper receipts are acceptable payment for financial transactions. Paper receipts are issued to an individual, stating the amount of commodity on deposit.

recession. A general period of declining economic activity that can last anywhere from 6 to 18 months, with one year being common.

recovery. An early expansionary phase of the business cycle shortly after a contraction has ended, but before a full-blown expansion begins; unemployment remains relatively high but starts to fall.

reserve requirement. Amount of money and liquid assets that Federal Reserve System member banks must hold in cash or on deposit with the Federal Reserve System, usually a specified percentage of their demand deposits and time deposits.

Roth IRA. An individual retirement account that allows an individual to set aside after-tax income up to a specified yearly amount set by the federal tax code.

"rules of the game." The "rules of the game" refers to the U.S. Tax Code. Knowing these rules will help an individual make wiser financial decisions.

S & P 500. An index of 500 stocks chosen for market size, liquidity and industry grouping, among other factors. The S&P 500 is designed to be a leading indicator of U.S. equities and is meant to reflect the risk/return characteristics of the large cap universe.

Second Bank of the United States. Chartered in 1816, five years after the First Bank of the United States lost its own charter.

silver certificate. Paper currency issued by the U.S. Treasury from 1878 until the 1960s that could be exchanged for an equal value of silver. An occasional silver certificate will pop up in circulation, but for the most part they have been relegated to the storage vaults of collectors and have been replaced by Federal Reserve Notes as the nation's paper currency.

Silver Tsunami. The wave of elderly people expected in the near future due to the massive population growth in the post-World War II era and modern medical advances that increase life expectancy.

Social Security. A federal insurance program in the United States that provides benefits to retired persons, the unemployed, and the disabled. Social Security is funded through dedicated payroll taxes called Federal Insurance Contributions Act tax (FICA).

stagflation. Persistent high inflation combined with high unemployment and stagnant demand in a country's economy.

standard of living. The financial health of a population, based on the amount of consumption by the members of that population.

store of value. Any form of commodity, asset, or money that can be stored and retrieved over time.

supply. A fundamental economic concept that describes the total amount of a specific good or service that is available to consumers.

Treasury bill (T-bill). A short-term debt obligation backed by the U.S. government with a maturity of less than one year.

Treasury bond (T-bond). A marketable, fixed-interest U.S. government debt security with a maturity of more than ten years.

Treasury note (T-note). A marketable U.S. government debt security with a fixed interest rate and a maturity between one and ten years.

unit of account. A standard monetary unit of measurement of value or cost of goods, services, or assets.

United States Treasury Department. An executive department and the treasury of the U.S. federal government, established by an Act of Congress in 1789 to manage government revenue, and administered by the secretary of the treasury, who is a member of the Cabinet.

unjust weights and balances. In biblical times, unscrupulous businessmen would readjust their scales and easily cheat and deceive customers. The Bible consistently condemns the use of unjust weights and balances.

World Bank. An agency of the United Nations that was established in 1945 to promote the economic development of the poorer nations in the world by providing low-interest loans to less developed countries and offering technical assistance on the best ways to use these loans.

World Trade Organization (WTO). An international organization, consisting of about 150 member countries, which oversees multilateral trade among nations. Established in 1995, the WTO administers multilateral trade agreements, provides a forum for trade negotiations, handles trade disputes, monitors national trade policies, and provides technical assistance and training for developing countries.

Endnotes

1. Ludwig von Mises, *The Theory of Money and Credit* (Orlando, FL: Signalman Pub., 2009).

About
Jerry Robinson

Jerry Robinson is an entrepreneur, Austrian economist, published author, and conference speaker. In addition, Robinson hosts a weekly radio program entitled *Follow the Money Weekly*, an hourlong radio show dedicated to deciphering the week's top economic and financial news. The weekly show is available online at http://www.ftmdaily.com.

Robinson has appeared on numerous TV and radio programs, including FoxNews, to discuss global economic topics. Recently, Robinson has been quoted by *USA Today* and other news agencies on the topic of the economy, and his columns have appeared regularly in numerous print and web publications, including *WorldNetDaily*, *Townhall*, and *FinancialSense*.

Robinson has spoken on the topics of money and economics around the globe, including the United States, Israel, Turkey, and Greece. He holds a bachelor's degree in economics with honors from the University of Tulsa. He has taught a course in macroeconomics at the college level. In addition, Robinson is also the editor-in-chief of the popular economic and investment newsletter *Follow the Money Quarterly*. He owns and operates his businesses with his beautiful wife and business partner, Jennifer Robinson.

To contact Jerry Robinson, visit his website at http://www.ftmdaily.com or call (800) 609-5530.

Become an FTM Insider
and get even MORE from Jerry Robinson

Only $9.95 per month!

As an FTM Insider, you will receive:

- **Jerry Robinson's** popular *FTM Quarterly Newsletter* (online edition)
- Exclusive access to Jerry Robinson's **P.A.C.E. Investment Portfolio**
- Real-time buy and sell alerts for P.A.C.E. delivered to your email inbox
- **Access to Jerry Robinson's Weekly Conference Call** containing the latest economic updates as well as investment and income strategies
- Exclusive access to the membership area of our website, FTMDaily.com
- **A free copy of Jerry Robinson's upcoming e-book,** *The Perpetual Money Machine: 22 Streams of Income You Can Create Both Now and in Retirement*

You get all of this for only $9.95/month or $99/year!

Visit us online or call us to become an FTM Insider today:
www.ftmdaily.com
(800) 609-5530

What are you doing to protect
your golden years?
Do you have a "Plan B"?

Whether you are looking to supplement your current income, embark on a new career, or create a consistent stream of reliable income, we have a solution that can work for you. Jerry and Jennifer Robinson have partnered with a Wellness company that specializes in helping people like you create lifetime residual income. The marketplace for this company is recession-proof, universal, and will experience strong global demand for generations.

This business model is ideal for the 21st century.

- NO inventory
- NO selling products
- NO taking orders or making deliveries
- NO risk
- NOT Multi-Level Marketing (MLM)
- Part-time/Full-time
- Unlimited income possibility
- Work home-based from anywhere in the world
- Team up with Jerry and Jennifer Robinson who will both personally teach you how to succeed in building a business to last a lifetime.

If you are coachable and are ready to be mentored
step-by-step on how to build a residual income today, call us at:

(800) 609-5530